"As 'News Dissector' on Boston radio, Danny Schechter literally educated a generation . . . "
—Noam Chomsky

"Danny Schechter, a kind of journalist without borders, has shaken up public broadcasting, among many other media institutions, in the course of his career as a self-styled 'News Dissector' and human rights advocate . . . "
—*The Nation*

"We need 50, 100, 1000 Danny Schechters. And we need everyone to take his words to heart . . . "
—Professor Robert McChesney, Media Historian

"By using the media to give insight into decisions that a powerful elite prefers to make behind closed doors, Schechter helps prove time and time again that once we know, we can become players in the events that define much of our lives."
—*National News Reporter*

"Few can match Schechter's work as an investigative reporter . . . (His) keen sense makes him a falcon among hummingbirds."
—*Our Town*, Portland, Oregon

"It's no overstatement to suggest that Schechter's resume alone makes better reading than a thousand slaved-over manuscripts."
—*Cleveland Plain Dealer*

"In the era of the incredibly shrinking sound bite, producer Danny Schechter stands apart."
—Associated Press

FALUN GONG'S CHALLENGE TO CHINA

SPIRITUAL PRACTICE OR "EVIL CULT"?

A REPORT AND READER BY

DANNY SCHECHTER

AKASHIC BOOKS

NEW YORK

Published by Akashic Books
First hardcover printing ©2000 Danny Schechter
First paperback printing ©2001 Danny Schechter

Akashic Books
PO Box 1456
New York, NY 10009
Akashic7@aol.com
www.akashicbooks.com

ISBN: 1-888451-27-0
Library of Congress Control Number: 2001089856
Cover photo taken with hidden camera by anonymous Falun Gong practitioner in Tiananmen Square
Author photo by Li J. Chen
Design and layout by Sohrab Habibion

Printed in Canada
Grateful acknowledgment is made for permission to reprint the following:

"An American Practitioner's Story" by Gail Rachlin (©1999 Gail Rachlin)

Excerpt from Amnesty International Report, "The Crackdown on Falun Gong and Other So-Called 'Heretical Organizations' " (©2000 Amnesty International Publications, 1 Easton Street, London WC1X 0DW, United Kingdom, http://www.amnesty.org)

"The Wheel of Law and the Rule of Law" by James D. Seymour (©1999 *China Rights Forum*)

"Unprecedented Courage in the Face of Cultural Revolution–Style Persecution" by Liu Binyan (©2000 *China Rights Forum*)

"Falun Gong and the Internet" by Stephen D. O'Leary (©2000 *Online Journalism Review*)

"Falun Dafa—A Science of Body, Mind, and Spirit" by Jingduan Yang, M.D. (©2000 Jingduan Yang)

Statement by Human Rights in China, July 22, 1999 (©1999 Human Rights in China)

Excerpt from *Falun Gong* by Li Hongzhi, Chapter 3: Cultivation of Xinxing (©2000 The Universe Publishing NY Corp.)

Articles by Li Hongzhi: "Cultivation Practice Is Not Political," "Wealth with Virtue," "Realms," "What Is Mi Xin (Blind Belief, Superstition)?" and "Further Comments on Superstition (Mi Xin)." (©2000 The Universe Publishing NY Corp.)

For George Schechter, who as a soldier helped in the fight to topple Imperial Japan, and first introduced our household to Asian cultures.

For our muse, Ruth Schechter, whose spiritual essence opened me to the spiritual aspirations of others.

And for Sarah Debs Schechter, who will one day see the fusion of Asian wisdom and the culture of human rights.

TABLE OF CONTENTS

AUTHOR'S NOTE

Falun Gong's Challenge to China is a report and a reader about a controversial spiritual practice that in just nine years rocketed from the backwaters of China onto the front pages of newspapers around the world.

Falun Gong's Challenge to China is intended to encourage a deeper understanding of developments that few, both inside and outside China, know much about. It offers a collection of documents to help readers acquaint themselves with ideas driving one of the most rapidly spreading spiritual movements in the world, and discover why it has become so high-profile and controversial. Although an issue with Chinese origins, it has universal implications for the application of international human rights covenants, agreements, and protections for freedom of association and religious freedom. It is a story with many Cs: China, conflict, consciousness, courage, cruelty, compassion, and contradictions.

This volume is also offered in the hope that it will encourage more interest and support for Falun Gong's right to exist and to practice its beliefs freely. It is a response to a Chinese government crackdown that has resulted in deaths, detentions, tortures, and the burning of books. It seeks to contribute to the peaceful resolution of a tragic and unnecessary confrontation, not to more China-bashing. Sadly, China's Communist leaders, who propagated the concept of self-criticism, seem unwilling to undertake any themselves.

My special thanks to a number of Falun Gong practitioners who encouraged me to take on this project, including Gail Rachlin, Kaishin Yen, Yun Song, Erping Zhang, Feng Yuan, and my colleague Perro 5. They, of course, are not responsible for my interpretations of their experiences or beliefs. My appreciation goes out as well to my editor Sophie Beach and to Johnny Temple of Akashic Books, who saw the importance of this subject right away, when others failed to do so, and said: "Let's Go." Thanks also are due to Johanna Ingalls, Dann Baker, Amira Pierce, Alexis Sottille, and Spencer Sunshine for their help with various aspects of the book's production.

I first heard about Falun Gong months before it became a global news story from Gail Rachlin, who had worked with me on promoting an earlier book, *The More You Watch, The Less You Know* (Seven Stories Press). She told me how Falun Gong had transformed her life, but as a skeptical New Yorker, I at first considered it just another story of an infatuation with an obscure New Age–type movement. Yet Gail, a high-powered public relations professional and one-time corporate executive, persisted, both as a believer and a new friend who wanted to expose me to its benefits. Initially, I didn't have the time nor inclination to learn more, even though she seemed very sincere when telling me about experiences during a trip she took to China that had influenced her to become a committed practitioner.

When China started cracking down on Falun Gong, because of her PR background Gail and a few colleagues volunteered to serve as liaisons with the press. She looked me up as a "friendly" and internationally oriented media person, who could give her advice on how to deal with all the press requests that were deluging them. Innocently enough I said, "Sure, I'll try to help," and I did. As I learned more, I decided that this was a subject worth exploring and writing about as a journalist who has spent many years covering human rights stories. Only this story, I soon discovered, had many unfamiliar twists.

I first read press accounts about Falun Gong after the April 25, 1999, mass "appeal" when an estimated 10,000–15,000 Falun Gong practitioners gathered outside the central government offices in Beijing. This unprecedented mobilization caught the attention of the international press because it happened in the political center of Beijing. Also, because protesters were requesting governmental acceptance of their practice, many journalists portrayed it as a political act, comparable to the 1989 Tiananmen Square demonstrations. *Time* magazine, like most of the foreign press, put it in a familiar anti-regime context: "The silent sit-in was by far the boldest protest in Beijing since the butchering of the pro-democracy movement almost exactly a decade ago." There had been earlier Falun Gong vigils in other provincial cities, but they did not make news because they occurred out of media view. This one raised eyebrows, and later, in response to the press attention as much as to the practitioners, the hackles of the Chinese authorities. At first, the national leadership did nothing and said even less, but in some regions, local leaders began to harass practitioners, who reported having had their phones tapped and being followed. "Inscrutable," I joked to myself about the national leadership's initial silence, but hey, the Chinese government often functions in mysterious ways.

What was not inscrutable was the staggering size of this movement. The figure that kept coming up was 100 million practitioners, a number that is of course highly disputed and impossible to confirm. If anywhere near accurate, it amounts to almost one third of the population of the United States—and almost twice the membership of the Chinese Communist Party, which claims 56 million members. According to Falun Gong, this estimate originally came from the Chinese government itself. After the crackdown, the government officially and dramatically lowered its estimate to only two million, as part of an effort to downplay the extent of mass involvement with what they had branded an "evil cult."

I later realized that I had heard about Falun Gong the way most people find out about it, through the world's most effective communications system: word of mouth. Gail Rachlin introduced me to many Chinese friends, fellow practitioners, whose intelligence and dedication impressed me. She arranged for me to interview Li Hongzhi, the controversial founder of the practice. I then went to see his followers in action, doing their distinctive slow-motion exercises and discussing their beliefs. Later I began reading more about it, interviewing practitioners and attending "experience-sharing" conferences to investigate a phenomenon that I have come to believe has been terribly misrepresented and distorted in many news reports. I helped Gail produce a video so that Falun Gong's views could at least be presented in a debate in which they were rarely heard in any depth. Soon afterwards, as so many of the journalistic accounts seemed more and more incomplete, or even bizarre, I decided to examine it more deeply with a focus on the human rights dimensions.

This is not to say that the spiritual aspects of Falun Gong are not central. In my own experience, religion and spirituality can be powerful influences in historical transformation. The American civil rights movement that I took part in was energized by the passion of the black church and led in many communities by preachers, pastors, and their followers. Martin Luther King Jr., Jesse Jackson, and many others were driven by religious conviction. Ditto for Malcolm X, a Muslim Minister. Episcopal priests like Bishop Tutu helped lead the liberation struggle in South Africa, while Bishop Belo, a Catholic, did the same in East Timor. Many progressive Jews have turned towards "the politics of meaning" in an attempt to synthesize their traditions with their involvement in movements for social change. The point is that religion and spirituality are deeply involved in many aspects of contemporary life and politics. At the same time, I wholeheartedly support the separation of church and state.

I should add that I am not a Falun Gong practitioner, and I have tried to maintain a professional distance and objectivity in covering the subject, knowing full well that one rarely achieves true objectivity, if it exists at all. At first, I was not so open-minded. As a reporter with a progressive orientation, who is more political than religious, I was suspicious of what on first glance appeared to be a strange group of true believers. I wondered if Master Li, as they refer to him, was just a Chinese version of the Korean self-styled messiah, Reverend Sun Myung Moon, using his followers to amass wealth and power. Was all of this just some scam, I wondered, or even possibly a CIA plot to destabilize China?

I was also quickly unnerved by one of Falun Gong's symbols—a swastika—until I realized, upon closer examination, that it was not the same as the Nazi emblem. Hitler had actually expropriated his version from a Buddhist symbol, while various indigenous cultures have used other versions for centuries. The Nazis blackened their swastika and inverted it. Falun Gong displays the original image, in gold, which I learned is a Buddhist symbol of good fortune.

There are mystical and strange aspects to this story, but perhaps these are no more perplexing than the many supernatural belief systems and New Age–type practices in the United States whose ideas do not have, or do not yet have, mainstream acceptance. The drift of many Chinese into Falun Gong is mirrored in other cultures by an explosion in the popularity of alternative health regimens and a hunger for spirituality. A Gallup poll published in the United States in 1999 showed an overwhelming majority of Americans expressing a desire for a richer spiritual life. It is my view that this story ultimately belongs as much in the realm of politics as in science or pseudo-science. I can respect the strong beliefs of Falun Gong practitioners without subscribing to all of them; in the same way, I can recognize the skepticism of the Chinese government's "experts" without agreeing with their motives, and can still criticize the government's brutal tactics.

Falun Gong seems to fall outside conventional left-right political categories. The United States religious freedom crowd backed by the right, which is largely dependent on money from Christian organizations, supports Falun Gong as a way to criticize China's unwillingness to allow in foreign evangelists (even as one anti-Communist TV preacher from the United States recently attacked Falun Gong as a cult on a radio station beamed into China). The Communists, on the other hand, consider it radical in their context, and a threat, too. The few Western leftists who have written about it seem confused, either suspecting it as a CIA plot, or as a troubling fundamentalist group. Writing in *Tikkun*, voice of progressive Judaism, freelancer Rebecca Weiner, who has lived in China, says Master Li has "taken a leaf from the fundamentalist movement. He denounces drugs, modern music, funny hairdos, homosexuality, and 'sex out of marriage.'" She also complains of a lack of commitment to women's liberation. From what I saw of practitioners in the United States, however, women seem to play a leadership role, although I don't know what the situation is in China.

In writing about China, I am mindful of the need to avoid reducing developments there to a single, simplistic news frame. As James Mann of the *Los Angeles Times* explains in *Media Studies Journal*: "In the 1950s the 'frame' was of China as little blue ants or automatons. In the 1970s, the frame was of the virtuous (entertaining, cute) Chinese displaying their timeless qualities even under Communism. In the 1980s, the frame was that of China 'going capitalist,' and for most of the 1990s, the frame was of a repressive China." Mann's injunction to journalists certainly resonates with this story: "Above all," he concludes, "American media coverage of China needs to challenge existing assumptions and be ready for the unexpected."

The press is frequently more interested in what's happening in the higher circles of politics than what may be stirring down below. They cover the palaces of power, not the people in the parks. They focus on mainstream conventional thinking, not counter-cultural ideas. They are often suspicious of, and hostile to, spiritual and religious ideas. For eight years, as Falun Gong's spiritual practice was mushrooming in size and influence, it was barely acknowledged in the media or reported on outside of China. The Falun Gong story does indeed challenge many assumptions.

Yet from the perspective of China's 5,000-year history, Falun Gong is anchored in certain traditions, and some scholars see it as just the latest in a long lineage of popular folk-based spiritual movements, which have sprung up in times of social disorder and decaying leadership. True or not, this takes nothing away from its uniqueness or our need to understand it. As I write at the turn of a new century, in the Chinese Year of the Dragon, I am told that the unexpected is what is to be expected in the year ahead.

The Chinese Communists claim to base their ideology on Marxism, in part because they believe it is scientific in its analysis and materialist in orientation. They see Falun Gong as unscientific, promoting superstition, and by so doing harkening back to a feudal past of underdevelopment. The country is officially atheist although it does sanction some religious activity. No doubt, it is motivated in its crackdown on Falun Gong, in part, by Marx's view that religion is the "opium of the people." That perspective must resonate in a country that survived the opium wars. But China needs to be reminded that Marx himself was a dialectition and recognized the need for spirituality in the very paragraph leading up to his famous phrase. Here's the whole passage, including the parts that most commentators leave out:

> Religious suffering is the expression of real suffering, and at the same time the protest against real suffering. Religion is the sigh of the oppressed creature, the heart of a heartless world; it is the spirit of spiritless conditions; it is the opium of the people . . . The demand to abandon illusions about our conditions is a demand to abandon conditions which require illusions.

PART I

REPORT ON THE FALUN GONG CRISIS IN CHINA

INTRODUCTION 2001

Twelve months after this book was first published, Falun Gong's challenge to China grinds on, as does China's unyielding response. It has been a year of intensified repression and continuing resistance. It has also been year in which the Falun Gong story began to receive more media attention globally and, perhaps as a consequence, more attention from government bodies and human rights groups.

The Falun Gong practitioners living in the People's Republic continue to be battered, and yet, somehow, continue to fight back—while counterparts outside of China have sustained a passionate solidarity campaign. China's leaders meanwhile have escalated their war against the "evil cult," clinging to hostile rhetoric like dogs to a bone. By September 2001, Falun Gong claimed that the death toll of their practitioners in police custody had reached 270, with many occurring in the five-month period leading up to the 2001 meeting of the UN Commission on Human Rights in Geneva.

As an investigative journalist and media critic who complains in these pages about the quality of media coverage in the West, I've noticed recent trends toward better reporting on the crisis, as well as more ink and air-time devoted to explanation rather than defamation. At the same time, the story remains obscure to many for whom China is far away—out of sight and out of mind—unless, that is, there is a military incident or a dramatic US–China confrontation, as there was in April 2001, heating up the story and the issue. Without a larger "news peg," repression churns on systematically without too much attention being paid to it.

In an effort to update my reporting since the book was first published, I have tangled with some Chinese citizens who have condemned me as "anti-China," as if criticizing the Chinese government's actions is in itself a sign of prejudice. Since many of these reactions simply echoed a government line, I reminded them of Chairman Mao's axiom: "No investigation, no right to speak." That usually produced a smile. I was always surprised about how many of these Beijing boosters acknowledged the difficulty in finding objective information—with all sides represented—in China. The Falun Gong side is strictly *verboten* there.

Unfortunately, this book was not allowed into China, and some of the columns I have written about media coverage of the issue for the MEDIAchannel.org website I edit were filtered out by the country's powerful Internet-screening software (which I have been told was developed in part under contract with US firms). China's stance in favor of one-sided propaganda is unlikely to change. On March 30, 2001, *Beijing Youth Daily* quoted China's propaganda chief, Ding Guangen, as saying that media must "adhere to the Party's basic line, serve the people, socialism, and serve the work of the nation and Party." That's the task that Beijing assigns to journalists.

Seeking Out Chinese Officials

I have also tried to seek out Chinese officials for their side of the story. In June 2000, I was at a UN reception attended by Li Peng, the head of China's National People's Congress, which had rammed through a draconian anti-cult law. A day earlier Li Peng was reportedly furious after being served papers by Tiananmen Square survivors who are suing him in American courts for ordering human rights abuses in China—in the same way that accusations against Chile's General Pinochet were first brought in Spain and then England. Li Peng, referred to now by some activist students as the "Butcher of Beijing," was toasting other Parliamentarians when I moved in to question him. I was quickly spotted by his security cordon and prohibited from approaching the man.

I had more luck in mid-March 2001, when China's Vice Premier of the State Council, Qian Qichen, came to the United States to meet President George W. Bush to discuss trade and Taiwan. As the highest ranking official to visit the US since President Jiang Zemin's tour three years earlier, Qian was invited by New York's Asia Society to address a high-powered $125-a-plate luncheon at the Waldorf Astoria Hotel, which I infiltrated easily by simply buying a ticket.

Luncheon guests were encouraged to write out their questions, which I did, asking how he envisaged a peaceful resolution to the conflict with Falun Gong. To my surprise, the question was read to him aloud—at least part of it, with some of my critical language sanitized by his American host. Qian's unflappable response was perfunctory, with no follow-up permitted. The conflict will be resolved, he said, when "everyone obeys the law"; he then asserted, without evidence, that Falun Gong's teachings had led to the deaths of 1700 practitioners. That's 300 more than other Chinese leaders were claiming at the time.

Falun Gong practitioners at the luncheon read his response more positively than I did, simply because he did not voice a longer litany of abusive condemnations typical of Chinese officials. "It could have been much worse," I was told. Writing about this exchange in Hong Kong's *South China Morning Post*, Greg Torode noted: "Mr. Qian's brief performance under questioning after a speech to the Asia Society in Manhattan early yesterday appeared to win him few converts. 'If that was him pouring on the charm, I would hate to see him angry,' one banker said. 'He did not seem interested in serious answers to what to us Americans are some rather vexing questions.' "

Back to Geneva

In this same period, the UN Human Rights Commission was back in session in Geneva, where for the eleventh year in a row, the United States government was seeking a debate on China's human rights record. Hundreds of practitioners assembled in Switzerland for the annual ritual that China has successfully maneuvered through year after year. The new Bush administration vowed, as had the Clinton administration, to push the resolution. In an address to the American Jewish Committee, President Bush went on record with the following statement:

> We hear alarming reports of the detention of worshippers and religious leaders [in China]. These acts of persecution are acts of fear—and therefore of weakness . . . Churches and mosques have been vandalized or demolished. Traditional religious practices in Tibet have long been the target of especially harsh and unjust persecution. And most recently, adherents of the Falun Gong spiritual movement have been singled out for arrest and abuse . . . This persecution is unworthy of all that China has been—a civilization with a history of tolerance. And this persecution is unworthy of all that China should become—an open society that respects the spiritual dignity of its people.

Despite these remarks, by early June 2001—less than two months later—Bush was endorsing the renewal of normal trade relations with China. Like his predecessor, Bush did not match his words with any personal intervention or White House–led initiative.

To thwart attacks on its human rights record, China mounted a counterdemonstration of sorts, unveiling a state-sanctioned petition condemning Falun Gong signed by one million Chinese. Government-organized petition drives like this often generate lots of "support," but rarely have any credibility. Not long after this charade, UN human rights commissioner Mary Robinson, the articulate ex-president of the Republic of Ireland, announced her decision to leave the post, arguing that she could be more effective outside the UN system. This is not an encouraging sign for international human rights advancement.

As the hearings got underway, Falun Gong lobbied with press conferences by female practitioners describing how China's police had singled them out, subjecting them to sexual harassment and abuse. One practitioner offered the following testimony:

> Ms. Xu Aihua, sixty-five, described in vivid detail the torture she was subjected to during twenty days' detention in May 2000. She said she was electrocuted twice, and was in a coma for a day and a half following the second instance. Ms. Jiang Ying, now in Germany, told of a

personal friend whose wife had only a moment to identify the bruised and battered body of her husband before a hasty cremation in November 2000. Zou Songtao was detained, beaten, and died in Shandong #1 Labor Camp, known as "Hell on Earth." Only twenty-eight, Zou Songtao left behind a widow and eight-month-old baby daughter. The death was reported as a suicide by "jumping from a first floor balcony," an incredible assertion given the state of the body. All causes of deaths of Falun Gong practitioners in custody are officially listed as "natural causes" or "suicide."

News organizations had also reported many new cases of abuse. On March 17, for example, ABC's *Nightline* returned to the story after many months of silence, interviewing Sophie Xiao, a spokeswoman for Falun Gong in Hong Kong. *Nightline* reported that "thousands of Falun Gong followers have been sent to labor camps and mental hospitals, a campaign that reminds [Xiao] of the hysteria during Mao Zedong's Cultural Revolution. People fired from their jobs, publicly humiliated, forced to confess . . . Xiao says the relentless persecution is taking a toll, driving practitioners deeper underground."

On April 9 in Geneva, China responded to the UN with its own human rights report characterizing its crackdown on Falun Gong as "safeguarding social stability and the people's lives and property." Its "White Paper on Human Rights" read more like a white-wash, concluding that human rights in China "maintained positive forward momentum." The bulk of the report focused on rising economic standards. It said that China put "people's rights to subsistence and development on the top of its agenda." Yet it also included a frank admission that there is "still much room for further improvement" in China's human rights conditions.

Then, on April 18, for the eleventh straight year, China succeeded in squelching the debate. Human Rights in China condemned the outcome:

> Once again, China has prevented the fifty-three-member Commission from voting on a resolution concerning its human rights record by initiating a "no-action motion," which was adopted today by six votes—with twenty-three in favor, seventeen against, and twelve abstentions. This motion prevents any vote on the resolution itself. China has been the only country ever to resort to this motion in the Commission. It uses this procedural device as a form of veto power to shield itself from any criticism.

And so the games of diplomacy are played, with other human rights abusers supporting China's stance. A Falun Gong statement reminded the world of what had happened following the UN meeting in 2000: "After China's escape from censure last year at the Commission, the crackdown on Falun Gong escalated drastically, with killings increasing from 11 to

193. During this year's month-long Commission alone, at least fifteen practitioners have been murdered while in custody . . . It is a shame that some countries have turned a blind eye to China's horrible abuses."

But there was a big surprise still in store for the United States in Geneva. As the session ended, maneuvers by European countries annoyed by the US tendency to dominate the proceedings of the Human Rights Commission—while applying human rights standards selectively—resulted in a vote to oust the US from the Committee for the first time in its history. China couldn't have been more pleased, though this political payback was more related to other human rights issues, particularly in the Middle East, where the US has been less than evenhanded. The reaction among conservative American politicians was one of fury—as if Washington has a divine right to steer the Committee. Ironically, members of Congress who are often loudest in their support for democracy abroad wanted to sanction the UN when the US lost a majority vote. Officials in Beijing must have been chuckling at these contradictions in Western human-rights posturing.

China, however, is plagued with its own contradictions. Its denunciations of Falun Gong seemed to be falling on deaf ears. Two months earlier, in February 2001, the Chinese government had begun applying pressure on Party officials to step up a crackdown that appeared to have cracked, failing to contain continuing protests and international condemnation. As described in press accounts, an unusual gathering of 2,000 Party chiefs was assembled in which seven top leaders delivered sound-alike denunciations of Falun Gong. As members of the Communist Party inner circle that governs China, each official used similar Party-speak to lambast the "evil cult." For good measure, the cabal also justified anew its bloody 1989 massacre of pro-democracy protesters as part of an ongoing response to the publication of the *Tiananmen Papers,* a book containing the alleged secret minutes of high-level government meetings that ordered the crushing of those uprisings. The *Papers* suggest that China's current president, Jiang Zemin, who is leading the anti–Falun Gong campaign, was selected then because of his hardline approach to shutting down newspapers when he was mayor of Shanghai.

This orchestrated show of unity sought to obfuscate growing misgivings with the failed crackdown. Back in July 1999, when Jiang initially vowed to crush Falun Gong, most experts thought the campaign would face few obstacles. After all, the regime wiped out the student movement in days (even if it relied on tanks to do so). Why not this latest challenge?

A Stealth Repression

Since the banning of this spiritual movement, which synthesizes the traditional Chinese qigong exercise system with Buddhist and Taoist ideas (described in detail in Chapter 3, "What Does Falun Gong Believe?"), the Chinese government has hit hard while attempting to avoid any conspicuous show of force that might trigger international sanctions. The repression has remained a stealth campaign—low-key but systematic. There are secret trials on a daily basis with no due process permitted. Recently, there has been an escalation of brutal force and torture, as documented in a 2001 report by Amnesty International. (The report also noted that China executes around 40 people a week, recording at least 1,263 executions in 1999 and 2,088 death sentences; an excerpt from Amnesty International's 2000 report on China is reprinted in Chapter 15.)

As anti–Falun Gong rhetoric heightened, there was a new claim by Professor He Zuoxiu—the scientist who had launched the initial public attacks on Falun Gong (see Chaper 6, "Promoting Falun Gong in China")—that the spiritual practice is financed by the US Congress. Falun Gong dismissed this: "Falun Dafa (Falun Gong) has not and is not receiving funds from the US government, as every member of Congress and journalist knows and can independently confirm." What is most remarkable about this widely reported and preposterous charge by He Zuoxiu is that it did not discredit his previous allegations; in fact, he was emboldened by the turn of events, escalating his vituperative broadsides.

China has also tried to force the government of Hong Kong to accept a ban on Falun Gong—in clear violation of the "one country, two systems" policy. Such a ban is already effectively in place in Macau, the former Portuguese territory returned to China under the same terms as Hong Kong. In June 2001, some leaders in Hong Kong began escalating their anti–Falun Gong gestures in order to appease Beijing—taking solace from the passage in France of a broadly framed anti-sect law. On June 3, the Hong Kong–based *South China Morning Post* quoted a US cult expert to debunk Hong Kong Chief Executive Tung Chee-hwa, who had compared Falun Gong to the Jonestown cult of 1978:

> Author Deborah Layton, one of the few surviving members of the People's Temple cult, said the Chief Executive was guilty of misleading the public. The Chief Executive made his latest and most damning attack on Falun Gong two weeks ago to a press agency and a newspaper controlled by the controversial Unification Church—commonly known as the Moonies—a group often compared with a cult. The Moonies are banned in Singapore. Layton said: "The comparison is not valid, it does not even make sense. If anything, Jonestown was like the re-education camps of the Cultural Revolution. Jonestown was not a suicide, it was murder. How that can be compared with people doing breathing exercises? I don't know."

So, enter the Moonies—on the side of China! The Hong Kong controversy was still simmering at this writing, although officials in the former British colony were eventually able to nix a local ban.

Exiled Falun Gong founder Li Hongzhi remained in the background for most of the year following the crackdown, but early in 2001 became more assertive and proactive. He gave a few talks at "experience sharing" conferences organized by US practitioners and issued a statement titled "Coercion Cannot Change People's Hearts," posted in March on a Falun Gong website. In it, Li declared, "Never in history has someone who persecuted those with upright faiths ever succeeded." Li's support for the right of practitioners to stand up for their beliefs was then interpreted by some media outlets as pressure on followers to boost their sacrifices, putting them at risk. The implication is that they are being *ordered* to act, as opposed to acting on their own volition. Whatever their motives, many do persist in defying the government's ban.

"Besides exposing themselves in protests, they work clandestinely to provide information, housing, and moral support for the faithful through an informal but highly effective nationwide network with its hub in Beijing," reported *Wall Street Journal* correspondent Ian Johnson. "To do this, they must live on the run, forced to sever family ties, leave jobs, and break off friendships in order to survive while trying to stay a step ahead of the security forces and their unrelenting efforts to crush the group with arbitrary detentions, torture, and killings."

A statement by Li Hongzhi was presented in March 2001 at a ceremony in which Li and Falun Gong were honored by the conservative group Freedom House with an International Religious Freedom Award. The gathering took place at the hearing room of the Senate Foreign Relations Committee, which was at that time headed by the conservative Jesse Helms, who called on the world to reject China's bid to host the 2008 Olympic games. Li's statement, read by his translator and spokesperson, Erping Zhang, said, "For the past decades under one-party rule in China, the people have never enjoyed actual freedom of belief, nor have they been allowed to have faith in God, deities, or Buddha. They have been forced to believe in the Party." The statement argued that these prohibitions "promote violent revolution and conflict. What's more, this type of conflict is one that resorts to any means to achieve its goals, being a wicked collective in which people fight among themselves . . . [Falun Gong] has seriously threatened the wicked nature of the Party. This is the real reason why Falun Gong is persecuted in China. The goodness has challenged the evil's nature. That is why I hold that you who support us are certainly good and opposed to wicked dictatorship." It had been Li's first public statement in twenty months.

So now, in response to China's use of the term "evil," Falun Gong is countering with "wicked," giving the whole dispute an eerie doctrinal dimension with hyperbole and righteous language that harkens back to the Middle Ages. Still, Falun Gong's polemics were no match for the more practiced state propagandists. As Princeton professor Perry Link explained in the *Asian Wall Street Journal,* "A key problem here is that the regime's language sometimes has nothing to do with truth or falsehood. When necessary, even the nativist Falun Gong movement can be called a 'tool of the foreigners.' What matters in such rhetoric is only raw effect: Will it work? Can it stoke nationalism, that trump card of regimes that have none other to play?"

Sometimes the propaganda barrage led to absurdities, as when a regional TV station falsely implied that China's prime minister was a Falun Gong leader. "Chinese TV says PM 'is Falun Gong leader,' " the *Sing Tao Daily* reported on March 18, describing how a station in Guangzhou had run a video clip of Prime Minister Zhu Rongji during a news broadcast with the words "Falun Gong leader" superimposed on the screen. "Around thirty million people were watching. The government is investigating . . . The government says the mistake may have been masterminded by members of the movement who infiltrated the station."

Economic Issues in the Background

Leaving aside notions of good and evil, there are other factors at work here. China's rulers are clearly using this issue to divert attention from far more vital economic crises as well as an increase in corruption and an upsurge in unrest tied to unemployment. Throughout 2000 and 2001, there have been many incidents of labor unrest. Agence France-Presse, for example, reported: "Several hundred disgruntled workers in eastern China demonstrated in front of local government headquarters on Monday [April 2, 2001] in the latest report of discontent within the country's huge labor force as pressures mount from lay-offs and lagging pay."

In early June 2001, the Chinese government published an unprecedented 308-page report criticizing corruption and failed policies within its own ranks: "China Investigation Report 2000–2001: Studies of Contradictions Among the People Under New Conditions." According to the *New York Times,* the study addresses "mounting public anger over inequality, corrruption, and official aloofness and it paints a picture of seething unrest as bleak as any drawn by dissidents abroad." The Chinese government report cites incidents of violent protests involving tens of thousands of people—greater in scope than any actions mounted by Falun Gong—and states that relations between the government and the Chinese people are "tense, with conflicts on the rise."

In terms of actual government policy, however, China's official response has been to harden their line. Like religious zealots themselves, their ideology seems to preclude flexibility or even reason. The only pause in their repressive campaign came in the aftermath of the early April incident in which a Chinese pilot was killed after colliding in mid-air with the wing of a US intelligence plane flying surveillance missions off the China coast. In its response to the US, the Chinese government successfully played to nationalist sentiment to rally support. They had never been able to generate as much intense feeling for their anti–Falun Gong effort.

But absence of public support doesn't seem to stop the government from operating as if by rote. "The gerontocrats who run China find safety in their ability to impose their version of history on others," wrote Jim Hoagland, the veteran foreign correspondant of the *Washington Post,*

> Today's Falun Gong movement must be vilified with monstrous distortions of its aims and practices. All blame for problems in the US-China relationship must lie with Washington. And so on. Politburo politics have become extremely unstable as the true Leninist survivors of the 1948 revolution dwindle, and as the pace of economic and social change accelerates to bypass the dying Communist Party. A struggle for power within that body drives the excesses of the brutal crackdown on Falun Gong, just as it drove the massacres around Tiananmen Square nearly twelve years ago.

Nevertheless, China's leaders may see Falun Gong as a more insidious threat than the student protests of 1989 precisely because it is an internal phenomenon growing out of economic and political conditions. Falun Gong is not limited in its appeal to intellectuals or students, and it has attracted many indigenous leaders and Party members. *Nightline's* Mark Litke commented: "What angered the government in the first place was the enormous popularity of the spiritual group, especially among China's elite. Retired civil servants, even Communist Party members, were signing up in droves."

Here are some of the other reasons for Beijing's fears:

> • Falun Gong has won the hearts and minds of millions who have lost faith in a dated Communism that paradoxically boosts capitalism. As James North explained in *The Nation* in 1997, two years before Falun Gong erupted into world consciousness, "Jiang Zemin is the leader of a China that is becoming a bureaucratic capitalist state at a dizzying pace. He heads a new ruling class, composed mainly of Communist Party officials and their allies among the new entrepreneurs, an emerging elite that the Chinese people have started to call *dahu,* or 'big-money bugs.' " There is opposition to these "bugs" in the Party structures in which many Falun Gong practitioners have long participated, although there are also reportedly more Falun Gong practitioners than Communist Party members—even as many practitioners see no conflict between Party loyalty and their spiritual practice.

> • Millions in China feel a spiritual void as the country transitions from Marxism to the market. Falun Gong offers an individual-centered self-improvement philosophy, not a top-down collectivist approach.

• Falun Gong opposes the materialistic direction China has taken, suggesting that inner growth (or "cultivation," as they call it) is more important than the "progress" of consumerism promoted by Beijing. Clearly, the benefits of China's economic boom have not reached everyone. "As the new China takes shape," noted North, "profound doubt is rising about whether most Chinese people are still gaining from the economic expansion." China's economy has grown over seven percent in recent years with a GDP that exceeds one trillion dollars. According to Qian Qichen, the foreign exchange reserves stand at $160 billion, and growth is expected to double in the next decade.

This expansion of the Chinese economy is being driven in part through billons of dollars in foreign investment, which is partially being "diverted" by corrupt officials who justify privatization as enhancing competition and efficiency. In reality, privatization has often become a strategy by which the so-called big-money bugs consolidate control and profit by selling off illegally acquired gains to foreign investors.

US companies want to be part of this economic boom, especially as growth slows in the West. So far, no US corporations doing business in China—freed of most human-rights restraints thanks to the passage of the China trade bill—have spoken out against the persecution of Falun Gong. A Falun Gong press release carried allegations from a practitioner who had been detained in China that she and fellow detainees had been forced to make toys for McDonald's outlets.

Falun Gong fears that China may resort to even more violence than it did in 1989 unless there is more outside pressure. A third-party initiative to promote talks and a peaceful resolution to the crisis is urgently needed. "People outside China cannot cause real change there," concluded James North. "But they can contribute—just as a worldwide movement helped end apartheid in South Africa." Perhaps, but the anti-apartheid movement around the globe was greatly assisted by sympathetic press coverage. That has been much less the case with Falun Gong. Our media has to do more to explain this story better. A good starting point would be to refrain from using pejorative language to describe Falun Gong, such as "cult" and "sect." This terminology distances Americans who would care more if they knew more.

The Media Coverage

There are three developments in the media coverage of Falun Gong that best capture how the story has been reported in the year since this book's initial release. The strongest coverage, in my view, appeared in the *Wall Street Journal,* and was reported by Ian Johnson, offering lengthy accounts of the repression in detail, and descriptions of how Falun Gong has used cellphones, beepers, and the Internet to resist. But in early 2001, the *Journal* transferred Johnson to Europe.

A second notable media event was distressing, because it involved one of America's most credible news-magazine programs, *60 Minutes,* and its famous correspondent, Mike Wallace. CBS carried a rare two-segment interview with Jiang Zemin on the eve of his arrival in New York for the UN Millennial Summit. In advance of Jiang's trip, China, with advice from American PR agencies, mapped out a multimillion-dollar PR "charm" offensive. The Chinese offered an "exclusive" to *60 Minutes.* CBS hyped its program thusly: "The discussion between Wallace and Jiang ranges in tone from slightly tense to lighthearted and humorous. Wallace asks all the difficult questions." For his part, Jiang made clear that the interview was intended as a propaganda exercise to "win understanding" from the American public. He grinned, sang a song, and repeated aphorisms, but was never confronted by the kind of tough cross-examination for which Wallace is known. CBS appeared to be using Jiang to score a celebrity-style media coup; Jiang, meanwhile, was using CBS to score a political coup.

My eyebrows always rise when news organizations pat themselves on the back for asking "difficult questions." Difficult for whom—Wallace or Jiang? Did I miss something? Isn't asking difficult questions what journalists are supposed to do? Would news programs in an earlier era boast of "lighthearted and humorous" exchanges with a repressive leader? Although Wallace did ask some serious questions, and tried to follow up with dramatic finger-pointing and clichés about democracy, if it were a prizefight, I would judge it a TKO for Jiang. CBS managed to raise the issue of human rights violations against Falun Gong practitioners late in the second segment, but the network was probably unaware that some of the footage identified as showing Falun Gong exercises was, according to Falun Gong's spokesperson, actually from another group.

Wallace's interview never attempted to explain what Falun Gong is. That obviously pleased Jiang Zemin, because a few weeks later, while scolding local reporters in Hong Kong for being too critical, he allegedly called upon them to be "more like Mike Wallace of *60 Minutes.*" According to the *New York Times,* Jiang lectured the Hong Kong media, calling them "too simple" and "naïve" to question his political motives. The *Financial Times* reported that the Hong Kong papers reacted negatively. "Jiang Zemin Throws Tantrum, Loses Stature," headlined the widely circulated *Apple Daily.* Like the *Apple,* other newspapers gave front-page treatment to Jiang's tirade, and many ran scathing editorials. "[Jiang's] condescending manner . . . shows the hollow-heartedness and arrogance of Chinese leaders," commented the *Hong Kong Economic Journal.*

The papers did not explain Jiang's affinity for an American journalist once considered the toughest interviewer on the tube, but their conversation certainly caught the eye of one US leader. When Bill Clinton met

Jiang at the UN, the president praised the Chinese leader for outmaneuvering Wallace and getting him to "purr like a little child." "I am so jealous," Clinton said with an ingratiating smile.

The third and most significant media development over the past year revolved around an alleged immolation incident on January 23, 2001, in the heart of Beijing. What could be more dramatic than Falun Gong practitioners setting themselves on fire in Tiananmen Square? The Chinese police just happened to have fire extinguishers on hand, and the victims were rushed to a hospital after their agonies were thoroughly photographed for state television. While the government-controlled media uncharacteristically released the story at once, it took a week of production before video footage was aired.

The incident occurred just days after Jiang intensified his official nationwide anti-cult media campaign. CNN was in Tiananmen Square at the time of this incident and reported on the alleged suicides, but its videotapes were confiscated and never aired. Seven days later, China's official TV shocked the nation with footage of five people engulfed in flames, pictures said to be taken from nearby surveillance cameras. A tragically disfigured twelve-year-old, Liu Siying, was shown, explaining that her mother had told her to set herself on fire to reach the "heavenly golden kingdom." She has become a sympathetic symbol, even a poster child for supposed abuses by the "evil cult." Her image was circulated widely; her tragedy outraged many. Yet only state-approved media outlets in China have been permitted access to the girl. Western reporters have been barred from direct contact.

Was she a Falun Gong practitioner? That seems doubtful, especially after the *Washington Post's* Philip Pan located her home in Kaifeng, a town in a region that drew negative publicity after a recent fire in a disco killed hundreds and scarred many others. Pan discovered that the young girl's mother, who had died in the fire, was not known locally as a practitioner, but was depressed, mentally unstable, and accused of beating her daughter and mother.

One of the CNN producers at Tiananmen Square at the time of the incident, standing just fifty feet away, said she had not seen any children there. The government claims that doctors performed a tracheotomy on the victim, but a pediatric surgeon said that if that were true, the child wouldn't have been able to speak to the Chinese media so soon after the tragedy.

Falun Gong spokespeople in the US have vehemently denied that they ordered and participated in the incident. But in their official statement, which has not been carried in full anywhere, they go a step further and indict the Western press:

> It is troubling to us that the Party line from the PRC mouthpieces, Xinhua News Agency and CCTV, is being given so much air-time and so much credibility by the foreign press. Xinhua and other state-run

media outlets are generally never considered credible sources, as even they openly admit that their function is to disseminate propaganda for the Chinese regime. In fact, Xinhua is the Party line.

There is so much that remains unclear and unknown about the circumstances surrounding the incident. And no one knows what occurred in the week after the actual event and before the Chinese media outlets finally released their fully engineered news articles and television programs. We must remember that the Chinese regime is so tightly controlling every aspect of this case that none of Xinhua's claims have been corroborated by independent sources.

Why would Falun Gong deny its role in the incident if it was a protest? The Laogai Foundation, which monitors Chinese prisons, had similar questions in the *National Review:*

Was this event staged or allowed to happen by China's government in order to discredit Falun Gong? It is hardly a farfetched hypothesis. China's government has promised to extinguish all problems connected with Falun Gong in advance of the eightieth anniversary of Chinese Communism, which Beijing plans on celebrating this July . . . Justin Yu, a journalist for *World Journal,* the Chinese-language daily, reflected on the confusion faced by many Chinese over what to believe. The PRC's propaganda coup against Falun Gong relies upon people's understanding of events in recent Asian history, such as the seventy-three-year-old Buddhist monk in Saigon whose self-immolating was a form of protest to fulfill his beliefs, [like] Koreans cutting off their fingers and the Japanese ritual of hari-kari. But this situation is not clear. Who do we believe—the Communists? They have lied to us so many times, another lie for them is nothing.

I asked Beatrice Turpin, who covered Falun Gong inside China for Associated Press TV and wrote about her experiences for the Media Channel, for her analysis of these developments. She responded from her home in Thailand: "There was a big brouhaha with Falun Gong protests and footage of police beating practitioners last Chinese New Year and it would certainly fit in with typical China strategy to stage an event this year and make the show their own."

Falun Gong practitioners told me their suspicions about the Tiananmen Square incident were aroused for three additional reasons:

1. The people shown on video in the Square weren't conducting Falun Gong exercises correctly;

2. Authorities did not show any Falun Gong pictures, signs, or books (which prohibit suicide) that protesters usually bring with them into the Square; and

3. The school that one of the victims was said to have graduated from was, in fact, closed at the time.

These are perhaps small details, but they may be telling. In a press release, Falun Gong pointed to other inconsistencies:

> Xinhua News Agency claims that within a minute of the man setting himself ablaze, police had dashed over to him with four fire extinguishers and quickly put out the flames. A European journalist based in Beijing, however, told us: "I have never seen policemen patrolling on Tiananmen Square carrying fire extinguishers. How come they all showed up today? The location of the incident is at least twenty minutes roundtrip from the nearest building—the People's Great Hall. If they were to have dashed over there to get the equipment, it would have been too late." Is it even possible that the police could have responded with not one but four fire extinguishers within the space of a minute if they didn't have prior knowledge that this was going to occur?

> In terms of response time, another foreign journalist in Beijing expressed shock that Xinhua was able to release the first report on the incident almost immediately, and in English, no less. Every Chinese citizen knows that every report from Xinhua usually has to first go through several rounds of approval by higher-ups and is generally "old news" by the time it is published. Moreover, state-run media have never released any photos or videos of Falun Gong protests in the course of eighteen months of persecution to the foreign press, so why now and with so little hesitation? And why only in English and not in Chinese?

Soon, horrific images were rocketed around the world, seeming to confirm China's charges that an evil cult was ordering brainwashed members to commit suicide. Citing this new "evidence," the government insisted that what it had been saying all along about fanatical Falun Gongers was true, and these people must be prosecuted as a threat to themselves and the nation. Then on February 16, another suicide was attributed to Falun Gong. Alongside a charred body, an uncharred note was reportedly found claiming the victim took their own life to support Li Hongzhi's spiritual practice.

The *Wall Street Journal's* Ian Johnson was skeptical due to the speed with which this story was covered, observing that the state media

... reported [the victim's] death with unusual alacrity, implying that either the death took place earlier than reported or the usually cautious media had top-level approval to rush out electronic reports and a televised dispatch. The 7 p.m. local evening news, for example, had a filmed report from Mr. Tan's hometown of Changde, a small city in Hunan province. Most reports for the evening news are vetted by noon, so the daily broadcast rarely carries reports from the same day, let alone an event that happened at noon and involved satellite feeds from relatively remote parts of the country.

Associated Press writer Christopher Bodeen wrote that "China's government is seizing on the dramatic suicide attempt by purported members of the Falun Gong sect to try to sway a public that has stood on the sidelines during the eighteen-month-long crackdown on the banned group." He cited some of the inflammatory press acounts such as the headline blared by the Communist Party–controlled *People's Daily:* "Blood Debts Old and New Will be Thoroughly Reckoned."

On February 28, Chinese officials held a rare press conference to reiterate that recent events proved the depravity of Falun Gong. Liu Jing, who heads the State Council Office for Prevention and Handling of Cults, defended the ban once again. Reported Ian Johnson,

Mr. Liu spent much of the news conference dodging questions about Falun Dafa practitioners who, according to human-rights and United Nations officials, have died in police custody. He refused, for example, to say how many Falun Dafa practitioners are in so-called reform-through-labor camps. Instead, he gave a long defense of labor camps, saying the government cares for inmates like a parent looks after a child, or a doctor a patient . . . Although Mr. Liu's answers were elliptical, they hinted at problems facing the government. He said 103 people have committed suicide since the government banned the group in July 1999, but that 136 had killed themselves in the seven years previous to the ban—implying that the suicide rate had increased dramatically since the ban, and that the government's professed efforts to protect its people from an evil organization weren't working.

This point may have been too subtle for most of the media and the public. For media consumers, perception often trumps unclear realities. In a world where dramatic images overshadow complex issues, Falun Gong stands convicted of crazed cult behavior. Case closed!

Score a big one for Chinese President Jiang Zemin's crusade to "crush" and discredit a growing spiritual movement that continues to resist a state-ordered ban despite the detention of an estimated 50,000 practitioners and over 250 people reported dead while in government custody. When the *Financial Times* proclaimed, "Beijing Wins Propaganda War Against Falun Gong," the headline didn't refer to merely one skirmish in a protracted media war, but to the war itself.

Many other respected news organizations disseminated the same story in the same way even though they were unable to verify the reports independently. Instead, these agencies used accounts from Communist Party–controlled state media. Now, as new questions are raised and doubts expressed, it may turn out that the world media have been duped into becoming an uncritical transmission belt for Beijing's bullying.

The issue of Falun Gong inciting suicidal behavior was raised with me again and again during a recent four-city book tour. When I challenged the assumption that we know all the details, eyes glazed over. Perhaps that's because once people see "facts" that confirm their own assumptions, they don't want to hear more.

Hot images sear themselves into the brain; retractions and clarifications rarely do. In the *Tiananmen Papers,* journalist Orville Schell, dean of the journalism school at Berkeley, discusses the many forgeries and falsehoods the Chinese government and others have concocted and circulated over the years. The book preceded the publication in Beijing of a "diary" purportedly written by a Falun Gong defector. Its publication, given gobs of publicity in the state media, was treated far more skeptically by the Western press since such "diaries" have appeared before in politically charged disputes only to be discredited. Disinformation and misinformation are the trade craft of intelligence agencies in many countries, including China. It is not surprising that Beijing is denouncing the new documents in the *Tiananmen Papers* as fake. Clearly, this publication is embarrassing to the secretive rulers of China, especially President Jiang Zemin, whose hard-line role in the 1989 assault on student protesters has been revived in the official persecution of Falun Gong.

Where Are the Skeptics?

Why did the deeply ingrained, institutionalized skepticism of our own media crumble so quickly in the face of what smells like a stage-managed incident that's being blatantly exploited for political reasons? Why would so many American news outlets be so gullible? Is it because issues of spirituality and mysticism in a culture few of us understand make us uncomfortable in our journalistic practice?

In my investigation into Falun Gong, I document a disturbing pattern of US media outlets echoing China's charges. In some respects, the media in our own country also reflect a one-dimensional perspective, downplaying and denigrating a force that doesn't fit into simple left–right political categories—and which they may have trouble relating to because of its

Asian character and roots in a mix of a Buddhist cultivation practice, Taoism, and traditional qigong. Falun Gong is often treated like the classic "other," too weird to be taken seriously or shown sympathy.

At one of my bookstore appearances in Chicago, someone compared Falun Gong and the current situation in China to David Koresh's Branch Davidians and the fifty-one-day siege in 1993 by federal law enforcement officers in Waco, ostensibly to seize guns and protect children from abuse. This is a comparison that China has invoked to make the case that it is using the same tactics that the US government employed to combat its own dangerous cult. Another person at the bookstore jumped up to challenge the analogy, arguing that Koresh and company were anti-government and Falun Gong is not. He was right: There is no direct comparison, except in terms of the response to what happened. The far right has produced the most vehement attacks on the US government's brutal military intervention and FBI attacks in Waco, although journalists on the left such as Alexander Cockburn have also been outspoken on the abuse. Waco reminded me of the words of an American lieutenant following an attack on a village in Vietnam: "We had to destroy it in order to save it."

The lack of empathy toward the families under Koresh's mad control led to many rationalizations and, ultimately, silence regarding the bloody and illegal suppression that occurred in Waco. Once people are dehumanized in our eyes, we may lose compassion for them and turn away when their rights are violated, especially if we dislike their politics.

On February 17, more than a thousand Falun Gong practitioners protested nonviolently in Los Angeles against the persecution in China. Few media outlets showed up at their press conference, even though the Falun Gong story was then in the headlines worldwide. (I couldn't find any coverage of the protest the next day in the *Los Angeles Times,* although their Sunday book review carried a discussion of the events in Tiananmen Square in 1989.) Media indifference fans public indifference.

In light of the prominent media play the mass suicide story received, it is not too late to thoroughly investigate not only what happened but whether and why we were all taken in. The story was successful to the degree that it played to a suspicion of sects and cults already deeply imbedded in American culture.

The US–China spy-plane incident aroused nationalist sentiments on all sides. True to its apolitical nature, Falun Gong did not take a stand against China or the United States, but as the dispute hardened attitudes and polarized positions, the spiritual practice's sacrifices and struggles did find new, sympathetic voices. This is not to say that the press increased coverage—but many ordinary people were seeing the issue of human rights in China in a new way. Suddenly there were calls for boycotts of Chinese goods and a return to Cold-War rhetoric by the far right in America. The incident also illustrated how uninformed most Americans and American leaders remain about China—another sign of the poor job the media have been doing. "We do need intelligence about China," editorialized *The Nation,* "but not the kind gathered by spy planes." Indeed, we also need more coverage of the collusion of US companies doing business in China, and of the struggles of various other religious groups (Catholics, House Churches, and Muslims), as well as the Tibetans. It is my hope that such enhanced coverage will lead to more compassion for victims of human-rights abuses and solidarity with those who are fighting for freedom and individual dignity on every level.

As the spy-plane confrontation faded from view, the Falun Gong crisis moved back, however briefly, onto the world stage. In New York, the Pulitzer Prize jury honored the *Wall Street Journal's* Ian Johnson for his persistence and passion in covering the story in Beijing. In cities throughout the world, there were many new voices calling on the UN to debate China's human rights in Geneva—although the gains made there were, in fact, negligible.

If the *Journal* was recognized for the quality of its coverage, at least two other media conglomerates moved in an opposite diection—toward alignment with China. The first was Rupert Murdoch's News Corporation, which has a history of kowtowing to Beijing (as detailed in Chapter 7, "The Media Coverage"). James Murdoch, Rupert's son and head of the Hong Kong–based Star TV satellite system, lashed out at Falun Gong at a global affairs conference in Los Angeles in March 2001. Murdoch called on human rights activists to back down and to accept China's policies. Within weeks, it was announced that News Corporation would become the first foreign company permitted to invest in China's growing telecom industry.

On Human Rights Day—December 10, 2000—the Committee to Protect Journalists named Jiang Zemin the world's number-one violator of press freedom. Days later, Jiang keynoted a global business forum in Hong Kong mounted by *Fortune Magazine,* a publication in the AOL TimeWarner empire. In this instance, the media company was not just reporting news but *making* it, facilitating an event with Jiang aimed at luring foreign investment into China. (Ironically, AOL TimeWarner has been a contributor to the annual press freedom dinner organized by the Committee to Protect Journalists.)

Falun Gong contacted *Fortune* and AOL TimeWarner about speaking at the forum. Their bid was turned down. A *Fortune* editor told Falun Gong not to worry because Human Rights Watch would be represented. Falun Gong insisted on the right to speak for themselves—to no avail. They also asked the media chiefs to help bring dialogue between them and China. Again, no response.

Hong Kong was then transformed into an armed camp. Officials mobilized a small army of security personnel to "protect" Jiang and Bill Clinton, also a guest. Local newspapers detailed police brutality and "security overkill" in the attempts to stifle protest. According to a Falun Gong spokesperson in the United States, over one hundred practitioners from Taiwan and the US were denied entry into Hong Kong—turned away by immigration officials as "undesirable" and shipped out of town.

The forum was considered a test for freedom in Hong Kong as Beijing seeks to force the local government there to outlaw the practice of Falun Gong. The US-based media companies did not champion the rights of protesters. In the aftermath of the forum, Law Yuk-kai, director of Human Rights Monitor, stated, "We can't help but wonder if freedom of expression is being increasingly curbed."

AOL TimeWarner chairman Gerald Levin had introduced Jiang to the forum as his "friend." On June 4, 2001, that friendship paid off. The *Washington Post* reported a $200 million deal that ensued: "America Online plans an alliance with China's largest manufacturer of personal computers [in Hong Kong] to intensify its assault on the potentially vast but still unprofitable market for Internet services in China . . ."

In business, it is always good to have friends.

But in sharp contrast to the practice of these media companies, one of the region's top business publications, *Asiaweek,* named Falun Gong founder Li Hongzhi as its "Communicator of the Year." With no media company at his disposal, no satellites or TV stations to command, Li and his practitioners had managed, with a few websites and a great deal of spirited activism, to remain visible. They may not have always been able to disseminate their message under ideal conditions, but their presence and stature could not be ignored.

April 25, 2001

Two years had passed since the gathering in Beijing outside the leadership compound, the protest that shook the complacent Chinese government and put Falun Gong on the map of world attention (detailed in Chapter 6, "Promoting Falun Gong in China"). Two years had passed, but neither side had forgotten Falun Gong's significance. Extra squadrons of police moved into Tiananmen Square to contain expected protests as if the whole confrontation between Falun Gong and Beijing was choreographed by the ritual marking of anniversaries. Later, twenty-four practitioners who penetrated the security cordon would be arrested. Other protests were held around the world to mark the occasion. The Chinese government and Falun Gong by now were moving like scripted and pre-programmed chess pieces on a game board that had gone global. There were cycles of more demonstrations followed by still more denunciations. More deaths in the East prompted more outrage in the West.

To the Western press it seemed again as if the government's repression was working, eroding Falun Gong's support and momentum. CNN's Lisa Weaver reported:

> . . . the intensified search for Falun Gong practitioners slipping into the capital appears to have reduced the ranks of the most hard-core members committed to unfurling banners and shouting slogans on Tiananmen Square. The increasingly ragged appearance of some members attests to the marginalization from society of those who continue to practice in public . . . Two years on, the movement, publicly at least, appears to be losing steam.

In New York, on the same day, however, there was no such sense of defeatism. While scores of practitioners exercised on the veranda of St. Bart's Church on Park Avenue, Falun Gong held a breakfast press briefing to release a study documenting new cases of torture and sexual abuse against female practitioners. Their PR operation has been upgraded by a team of well-dressed and increasingly professional Chinese and Amercan practitioners, who are now publishing a magazine and newsletter, and producing solid press kits. But, significantly, new business was last on the briefing's agenda.

First, the practitioners wanted to deal with old business, and revisit the April 25, 1999 event because of new information, ostensibly from within the highest Chinese leadership circles. The details that emerged were intriguing. The 1999 protest, as reported in these pages, was prompted by police violence against practitioners who were complaining about unfair media coverage of Falun Gong. The new information suggests that the persecution had actually been building against Falun Gong well before that, over a period of three to four years. In short, Falun Gong's enemies had been criticizing them ever since a denunciation by the *Guangming Daily* in 1996. On July 24, 1996, three years and a day before the pivotal protest by Falun Gong in Beijing, the Chinese News Publications Office allegedly issued a circular banning all Falun Gong publications. Six months later, police agencies reportedly launched a nationwide investigation that was closed after reporting "no evidence found so far." It seems clear that some leaders wanted a crackdown, but Falun Gong had too much support among the people, and apparent protection by higher-ups. Another official investigation in 1998 is also said to have given Falun Gong a clean bill of health, because it "only benefits and does no harm to the Politburo and the nation."

When the ten-thousand-plus practitioners converged on Beijing in April 1999, they set out for the "appeal" office, which is actually two kilometers south of the main Xinhua gate of Zhongnanhai. According to Falun Gong's new report, they "never even intended" to go to the government compound. They insist the event was not highly organized but an outpouring of support from sympathetic fellow practitioners. Li Hongzhi was not there. Some report police directing them toward the compound, not away from it, suggesting there may have been a desire on the part of certain leaders to create a provocation that could be a pretense for a crack-down. This is still not clear. What *is* known is that Premier Zhu Rongi came out of the main entrance, the west entrance of the State Council, at about 8:30 in the morning, and crossed the street.

Was he shouted at? Did protesters challenge him? Quite the opposite, according to the report, which cites eyewitnesses claiming that he was applauded. In a document called "The Truth Behind the April 25th Incident," Premier Zhu is quoted as asking, "What are you here for? Who told you to come here?" A practitioner allegedly responded, "We've come here to report the situation regarding the Falun Gong issue. No one organized us." Premier Zhu then said, "Why don't you write letters to appeal? How come so many people are here?" Practitioners say they answered, "We've written letters until we're numb and we still haven't gotten a response."

What a scene this must have been, unprecedented in the history of the People's Republic of China. According to Falun Gong's report, Premier Zhu was skeptical at first, assuming that someone must have told them to congregate there.

Jiang Zemin had been locked in various internal wrangles in the past with Premier Zhu. Now, Jiang would use Zhu's willingness to meet with Falun Gong against him. According to information presented at the April 25, 2001 press conference, Falun Gong has access to secret documents suggesting that Jiang Zemin personally led the forces within the Party determined to wipe out the spiritual practice. Jiang is said to have indig-nantly asked, "How could this Falun Gong problem have appeared? How did it get so big? Obviously Li Hongzhi alone could not have amassed such power." He allegedly smelled a plot and asked to know if there were "senior insiders in the Chinese government that might be manipulating and directing the whole thing." Falun Gong claims to have evidence that he then forced Premier Zhu to "do self-criticism."

This is typical of China's Leninist, top-down approach to any and all challenges. Chinese leaders have been ideologically schooled and taught by history to suspect conspiracies and hostile internal political factions. The assumption is that people are incapable of organizing and mobilizing without someone in authority pulling the strings. (Sadly, this view is shared by many media analysts and politicians in the West.) Anxious to protect his power base against real or imagined enemies, Jiang Zemin cranked up his crackdown with propaganda, arguing later that all criti-cism of his view was "anti-government" and "anti-China." Like Mao before him, Jiang elevated himself above his own Party comrades, fellow leaders, and, of course, the people.

It was for this reason that more than a year ago Falun Gong began to focus its attacks not on China or Communism per se but on Jiang Zemin. Both sides of the conflict had personalized the battle; but in ways that neither anticipated, the conflict had grown beyond all expectations. The Chinese government felt forced to become more and more repressive after Jiang's ban on Falun Gong was rejected, ignored, and resisted. It had politicized an apolitical force, and had galvanized it into action, not only inside China, but across a globalized interdependent world. What had been solely a Chinese phenomenon blossomed into an international issue, and like many non-violent movements before it, Falun Gong's persistence and courage threatened to delegimatize a repressive government. Adrian Karanyncky, president of Freedom House, believes that Falun Gong's struggle must be compared to the struggles that triggered significant change in Poland, Argentina, and Yugoslavia. He feels that the protest is being heard by "people inside the Politburo who oppose the persecution of Falun Gong and who dissent from the Party line."

China is a great country with a great people. In historical terms, they have accomplished so much in so little time—and their own commitment to economic progress for their people offers lessons for other developing countries. China needed a revolution, but as we know, many revolutions implode. China is not wrong to challenge the hypocrisy of other countries in championing human rights—even if its motives are clearly self serving. China is also correct to be worried about those vitriolic anti-Communists and righteous defenders of free markets who rapidly dismantled Russia's economy and turned it over to the anarchy of organized crime. Those same privatizers and crooks are lining up to do the same in China if and when the situation permits. I was fascinated to learn that President G.W. Bush's uncle, Prescott Bush, happens to be the chairman of the US–China Chamber of Commerce. But it is not surprising that US business leaders who were so vocal in their support for the China trade bill have so little to say about human rights and labor rights in China. In fact, as China vied for the right to stage the 2008 Olympics, critics of China's human-rights record were vocal, but the US government maintained official silence while American corporations scurried to insure that they could cash in on the spoils. Human rights issues were downplayed, if well-covered, in the run up to the decision by the heavily lobbied International Olympic Committee.

This dispute handed Falun Gong a global news peg on a platter, although the group took no formal stand on the Olympics—consistent with its desire to be perceived as both apolitical and patriotic by the many other Chinese who were in a frenzy to get the games. A statement by a Falun Gong spokesperson charged that Beijing was distorting their actions: "The Chinese government is now spreading rumors throughout China that Falun Gong is working against Beijing's bid to host the 2008 Olympics. This rumor is completely without grounds, and is clearly engineered to breed hatred toward Falun Gong."

Practitioners reported that persecution was actually *escalating* in the period before the decision, resulting in several deaths. These rumors followed the imposition of still new laws classifying Falun Gong as "subversive" and calling for even harsher punishment that could, they fear, include execution—a common abuse in today's China. Falun Gong practitioners, citing their sources in China, told me that Jiang Zemin wanted "the problem taken care of." If true, the implications are ominous. "We hope that China will not see winning the Olympics as a license to kill," Falun Gong spokesman Erping Zhang said in a statement. "In just the past week, we have had two reports of mass killings of Falun Gong practitioners in Chinese labor camps. We do not want to see more."

Many Western leaders expressed the view that the very act of hosting the Olympics will transform China. Mark Bradley, a sports writer for the *Atlanta Journal-Constitution*, dissected the many illusions underlying that suggestion. "Maybe the man who stood in front of the tank can light the flame, assuming he's still alive. Maybe members of Falun Gong can carry the Olympic flag, assuming any are still alive. Maybe we on the outside can spew righteous indignation toward the IOC from now until 2008, and maybe we can delude ourselves into believing that the IOC actually cares. The Olympics do not change the world. The Olympics merely reflect it. The Olympics are a collision of political force and venal interest, pretty much like everyday life in every corner of the globe." In the *International Herald Tribune,* exiled Chinese investigative reporter Liu Binyan predicted that "the ruling Communist Party will spruce up Beijing for the Olympics . . . There will be no suicides of Falun Gong practitioners, for all suspected followers will either be expelled from Beijing or forbidden to enter the capital."

Countries like the United States forecast the coming of "democracy" as a result of global media events like the Olympics and China's orchestrated entry into the World Trade Organization. But two numbers tell the story best: China's share of world trade was $20 billion in the late 1970s, and by the year 2000 it had climbed to $475 billion; and in the first six months of 2001, as repression against Falun Gong intensified, direct foreign investment into China poured in unabated, up twenty percent from a year earlier. Wall Street analysts were bullish, with projections that such fresh investment will top $50 billion this year, setting a new record. Thanks to its vast market, China is booming; by mid-July 2001, its official growth rate was determined to be 7.9 percent. This economic might fortifies arrogance. Can the day be very far away when *Fortune Magazine* begins giving out new awards honoring Marx and Mao if that what it takes for them to kowtow for advance corporate interests? So far, Falun Gong has not tried to press the business world or mount campaigns demanding corporate responsibility, although it has now moved to the US courts to pursue human rights offenders in China.

China marked the July 22 anniversary of the banning with a massive display of might, according to the German Press Agency DPA, using "some of the heaviest security seen in Beijing's Tiananmen Square for the past year." Despite the cordon, a few practitioners slipped through. The *New*

York Times focused on the small turnout, not on its daring, asking with a headline, "Is Sect Fading?" A few days earlier, China escalated its own attack on the practice by opening a vast anti-cult exhibition in Beijing, called "Oppose Cults, Uphold Civilization," featuring, according to AP, "shockingly graphic photos of alleged members of the meditation group who committed suicide, mutilated themselves, or attacked others," as well as "video footage, text, and cartoons with a simple message: Healthy, intelligent people who begin practicing Falun Gong go crazy and hurt themselves and their families." On the eve of this opening, the government claimed once more that it has almost wiped out the practice. A few days later, Falun Gong responded that its ranks are actually growing.

The official propaganda offensive reinforces the allegations of suicide that continue to plague Falun Gong. Officially, Li Hongzhi and Falun Gong spokespeople deny Chinese accusations that they encourage or condone suicide. On July 4, 2001, China claimed ten practitioners in the Wanjia labor camp outside Harbin, in Heilongjiang Province, had killed themselves. For the first time, the Hong Kong–based Information Center for Human Rights appeared to confirm the charge. Craig Smith of the *New York Times,* who many in Falun Gong accuse of bias, appeared to accept the claim, too, while acknowledging that "it is impossible to determine which accounts are factual, and independent reporting on the subject is strictly forbidden." Vague and cryptic statements on Falun Gong websites do not make the job of reporters any easier.

The debate extends beyond who is telling the truth, since the definition of "truth" for a social movement under attack tends to be different than the definition sculpted in the offices of the *New York Times,* where journalists are expected to take a skeptical approach to all sides of any conflict. What is undeniable is that there has been a steady escalation in the death rate of practitioners in police custody. This pattern is likely to continue as the two sides talk past each other, appealing to different constituencies. The war of words is more about scoring points than settling differences. It is almost as if the anti–Falun Gong campaign in China has achieved a self-perpetuating momentum, with vast bureaucracies enlisted in the prosecution. Sadly, if one is to judge by the experience of the Tibetans, this could go on for decades; that is, unless something changes. Many in Falun Gong have hopes that a more sensible Chinese leadership might relax its crackdown when Jiang Zemin steps down in 2002.

A year after this book first appeared, the moral question remains: Who has the courage to speak out for justice and tolerance, for human rights and religious freedom? And when? After a bloody Tiananmen-like tragedy, or before?

Danny Schechter
September 10, 2001

INTRODUCTION TO HARDCOVER EDITION (JULY 2000)

"The picture doesn't add up. What I see here with these people and what they're doing, they seem very normal people. They're from all walks of life, all ages; and then on the other side you've got this picture that the Chinese government is painting, and the two just don't match."
—ADAM MONTANARO, FALUN GONG PRACTITIONER (USA)

On October 1, 1999, in the symbolic center of China at the vast square in Beijing called Tiananmen, with the Great Hall of the People on the west side, and the Gate of Heavenly Peace fronting the Forbidden City on the north, the People's Republic threw itself the mother of all parties to celebrate its fiftieth birthday.

Some half a million people turned out to dance, prance, and gawk at a massive four-mile-long parade of awesome military equipment. The subtext of this unprecedented ninety-float procession of marching soldiers in formation, jet fighters, ballistic missiles, and shiny tanks was an unspoken but hardly subliminal message: "We are strong: DON'T MESS WITH US!" Watching over the lavish and theatrical display of patriotic showboating was a color portrait, now on permanent display and still adored by millions: the image of the guerrilla fighter turned Great Helmsman and Chairman of the Chinese revolution, the late Mao Zedong. Fireworks cascading overhead were given names like "Chanting the Eulogy of the Motherland."

Tiananmen Square was an armed encampment that day, circled by army and police units and patrolled closely by squadrons of internal security forces on alert for possible disturbances. There had been fears that Muslim extremists from the northwest might throw bombs into the crowd. There were worries that the remnants of the protesters who had turned the same square into a worldwide symbol of shame and repression a decade earlier might resurface to embarrass the regime and spoil the party.

However, in 1999, there was a new and perhaps even more immediate danger, an insidious internal enemy, according to the Chinese Communist Party: *Meditators!*

Yes, meditators—people who practice distinctive-looking slow-motion physical exercises and proclaim loyalty to a movement reportedly larger than the Party itself. It is hard to believe that an unarmed, non-violent spiritual practice has been perceived as a grave threat to one of the world's most powerful nations. In the very month of China's greatest celebration, the government was engaging in a nationwide crackdown against a movement that is almost Gandhian in its breadth and historic in its proportions. It is ironic, because for decades China itself was viewed in the West as dangerous, a red menace and evil empire. Today, even as fears of Chinese aggression resurface in the United States, China is obsessed with an internal menace of its own, also deemed evil, an "evil cult." (Also ironic is China's charge that Falun Gong "brainwashes" adherents; this from a country that itself was accused of brainwashing captured US soldiers during the Korean war.) This development has perplexed China-watchers, foreign policy wonks, and journalists. "Has it come to this?" asked the *New York Times* front page in early November 1999, "That the Chinese Communist Party is terrified of retirees in tennis shoes who follow a spiritual master in Queens?"

But it is true. Commissars versus "cultists" has become a new fault-line in the fight for purity in the "New China." In truth, what the Central Committee is up against is not some fringe cult or marginal sect, but one of the fastest growing spiritual practices in the world. It is known as Falun Gong, or Falun Dafa (throughout the text of this book, these two terms are used interchangeably). Most worrisome for those in power is its claim of tens of millions of followers.

Unease about Falun Gong had been preoccupying the Chinese government in the period leading up to the fiftieth-anniversary spectacle. Two months earlier, President Jiang Zemin banned Falun Gong, ordering it "smashed." He demanded that its founder, Mr. Li Hongzhi, known honorifically by his followers as "Master Li," be returned from exile in the United States, arrested, and put on trial immediately. Every Chinese embassy, mission, and media outlet was enlisted in pursuing a crusade ordered at the very top of the power structure.

According to *Time* magazine, the seventy-two-year-old Jiang "has reportedly become obsessed with the sect and its ability to organize its activities in cyberspace." Jiang supposedly told aides at the time of the April 25 demonstration that he was impressed by the discipline of the vigil and by Falun Gong's capacity to mobilize so many so quickly. He personally was driven, according to press reports, hiding in a car with tinted windows, to watch Falun Gong in action. Upon reading about this covert mission, I was reminded of a baffling nocturnal visit by another seemingly paranoid president, the United States' own Richard Nixon—who slipped out of the White House in the middle of the morning to visit anti-war protesters camped on the Washington Mall. Like Nixon, Jiang was not content with secondhand reports by advisors. (Curiously, the *South China Morning Post* would later report that Jiang himself has, since 1992, consulted with the master of another qigong movement, Zhong Gong, to cure his arthritis and back problems. In February 2000, Zhong Gong was also banned. There was no report on the status of the President's maladies.)

And just in case anyone in China missed President Jiang's hard-line message, Beijing unleashed a vitriolic media campaign to demonize Falun Gong and turn the country against it. It was a saturation-propaganda offensive, reminiscent in its intensity to the strident sloganeering of the Cultural Revolution, in which millions were punished for being of the wrong class or consciousness. China's state-owned media went into overdrive. Newscasts were lengthened from thirty minutes to an hour, in order to make more time for a steady drumbeat of reports on the fight against this new threat. The leadership ordered the imprisonment of Falun Gong practitioners, while those who resisted harsh government-enforced "re-education" were tortured or worse. The *New York Times* quoted one Beijing citizen as saying, "It is as if we are reliving a bad dream."

Despite the severe crackdown by a powerful state apparatus, there was still anxiety in high places after intelligence agencies uncovered Falun Gong practitioners continuing to defy government orders and not going quietly into the night. Trains into Beijing were searched because police suspected that practitioners were on their way to file complaints with the government. In one bizarre incident, Beijing police raided a conceptual art exhibit because of a neighbor's tip that Falun Gong would be there. They seized the artwork, including a display of repainted lobsters, on suspicion that it was somehow linked. The artists, who had nothing to with Falun Gong, were shocked. It took them a long time to get their lobsters back.

Meanwhile, in the days leading up to the October 1 national celebration, Tiananmen Square and the surrounding areas were sealed off from traffic and the public. Residents nearby were instructed to stay in their homes for three days. In security parlance, this is called "freezing" a zone, but this one wasn't frozen for long. Two days before a massive display of colorful fireworks would ignite the skies over Beijing, and just hours before 100,000 singers and dancers would flood the capital, a handful of Falun Gong practitioners managed to slip into the well-guarded square to commit what is now considered a serious crime against the government: a silent display of physical exercises beginning with the raising of arms above the head in a graceful gesture known as "Buddha showing a thousand hands." It is intended to open up the energy channels and increase circulation in the body by stretching gradually and relaxing suddenly. It usually takes three minutes.

In less time than they were able to finish a cycle of five exercises, a swarm of security men surrounded them as they stood at the epicenter of official China. Some reporters compared it to an incident years earlier when a young German managed to fly a small plane through the Soviet

Union's prodigious air radar system and land in the center of Moscow's Red Square, right next door to the Kremlin.

As one press account had it, "four or five people in their twenties or thirties sat down cross-legged together on the pavement in a meditation pose typical of the Falun Gong group. When the protesters refused to stand, police dragged them away. About two hours later, a man in his twenties . . . began doing Falun Gong–type meditation exercises on the square. He also was escorted away by police."

The event, reported by the wire services, was a small item on a busy news day, and went largely unnoticed. Yet it was, in its own way, an act of bravery comparable to that heroic, unknown Chinese citizen who put himself in front of a line of tanks then crushing the protests of 1989. That image was broadcast the world over as a representation of the lone individual standing up against the brutal state. It became a universal symbol of freedom.

But what differentiated these two gestures was much more than a decade. The students in 1989 were originally campaigning to reform the government and renew the Party (not overthrow it, as was erroneously thought by many abroad). They soon became international human rights martyrs as their protests were bathed in worldwide media attention. The Falun Gong practitioners, on the other hand, are non-political. They just want the government to leave them alone. The former student protesters became dissidents fighting for political freedom, while the Falun Gong practitioners, many of whom are loyal to the ruling Communist Party, are standing up for their personal beliefs and the right to practice Falun Gong. Yet in China a seemingly personal act can quickly become political, or be perceived that way by nervous officials. Unlike the 1989 protests, Falun Gong's efforts have been followed only episodically in the world press. The international responses to these two movements have been quite different, and it is that difference which this book explores.

What is Falun Gong?

Why are as many as 100 million people drawn to it?

Why is China marshaling all of its resources to crush non-violent and non-political spiritual practitioners?

Is it a dangerous cult, as its detractors insist, or a beneficial practice promising health benefits and spiritual growth?

How is this practice able to communicate its message and belief system so widely in a country where the government controls communications? What role does the Internet play in the spread of Falun Gong, both within China and across the world?

Who is Falun Gong founder Li Hongzhi, a man whom some Chinese newspapers are even denouncing as a reincarnation of Adolf Hitler? Does he have political aspirations, or is he simply a charismatic figure whose ideas happen to have mass evangelical appeal?

The Chinese government is insisting it will prosecute the so-called Falun Gong "leaders" even though Falun Gong says it has no leaders. (They consider the exiled founder, Li Hongzhi, their "teacher.") Most of those prosecuted are not permitted a legal defense. Many are now in prison, while others have been brutalized and even reportedly killed as a result of prison torture or hunger strikes.

How is it that resistance continues despite predictions by "experts" that the practice would be crushed in weeks?

What is the real story?

CHAPTER 1
UNDERSTANDING CHINA

This is a complex story for a socially conscious journalist, based in New York, to attempt. It is not a report from China nor a scholarly study. I am not a China expert nor booster of this or any other spiritual practice. I have been producing stories on human rights issues in China and elsewhere for a decade and have worked on several TV reports dealing with the aftermath of the Tiananmen Square protests. Later, I came to know some of the student leaders and have followed the debates about how their own youth and inexperience may have partially provoked the Chinese leadership to smash their historic movement. Yet I still have admiration for them and the democratic ideals for which they struggled.

I've also been to Beijing, at the invitation of Beijing Television, and later worked with Chinese colleagues on a television project. In 1999, I was again invited by an institution in China to speak at an international media symposium, only to be disinvited after NATO planes "accidentally" bombed the Chinese embassy in Belgrade. "The time is not right for an American to come," I was told. This logic angered me and I fired off an e-mail, protesting that I was not responsible for the bombing. In fact, I insisted, I was very disturbed by it. I noted that even at the height of the Vietnam War, I was allowed to report from Hanoi, because the Vietnamese government correctly drew a distinction between the American government and its people. I asked the organizing committee in Beijing to raise my concerns at a higher level and to reconsider. I expected no response. To my surprise, the Chinese authorities reversed themselves and re-invited me, although, by that time, I had made other plans. But the incident and their flexibility was more evidence to me that I was not dealing with unyielding ideologues.

China is a land of intense contradictions. Thanks to nationwide sacrifices, not all of them voluntary, the country has in recent years rapidly developed its economy to the benefit of ordinary people. Chinese citizens now enjoy a higher standard of living, with better health, nutrition, and education than ever before in their history. So, in fact, the People's Republic did have much to celebrate on its fiftieth anniversary, especially given China's long history of foreign imperial oppression, humiliation, and internal savagery. It has survived long years of hostility and isolation from much of the world. Shaken by war and revolution, China has gone through cycles of crisis and change. Today, in relative terms, it is prospering, although economic progress remains on shaky ground, with rapidly increasing unemployment, a widening urban-rural economic divide, and serious corruption running largely unchecked.

When I visited in late 1997, I came to feel the confusion that China expert Orville Schell expresses so well: "On the one hand I felt a kind of admiration for China trying to do something different and going it alone—on the other hand, there was no doubt in my mind that something was hideously wrong with the place." He speaks of a discontinuity between ideals and accomplishments. "I think many revolutions fail when disillusionment sets in. A sense of having been betrayed by false ideology leads people to banish all idealism and often even a concern for values that stress the commonwealth," he says.

Years earlier, I had silently praised an unpopular president, Richard Nixon, when he went to China, finally reversing America's ostrich-like policy of denying the existence of mainland—or "Red"—China for so many years. I hoped that at long last we could learn more about a people and nation we were taught to hate. Cheer as I might, I certainly did not trust Nixon's larger designs nor those of his National Security Advisor, Henry Kissinger; they were both pursuing their own Metternichian geopolitical strategy. (In transcripts released of the secret meetings between the Americans and Chinese, it was clear Mao didn't trust them either.) Today, many modern-day Nixonians in the ranks of Republicans and Democrats alike vacillate between coveting China's market and bashing China's policies. Few seem genuinely concerned about human rights or workers' rights there, or to have much respect for the country or its culture. Many still seem locked into the hostile containment thinking that kept the Cold War alive for so many years. Fear and loathing of China has a long history in the United States.

As an activist affected by the revolutionary spirit of the 1960s, I was enamored with the Chinese revolution and its emphasis on fighting colonialism and championing communal values and the needs of the poor. While never a Communist myself, I was certainly sympathetic to their commitment to radically transform a poor and exploited country. In London in 1966, I met Chinese students carrying the "little red book" of Mao's quotations and heard their denunciations of "the capitalist road." I could identify with their aspirations. Their campaign, seen from afar, seemed romantic and bold, mobilizing millions of young people to shake up a stagnant Asian form of Stalinism, challenge a bureaucratic system, and revitalize socialism.

Was I ever wrong: without knowing it at the time, I had experienced a classic disconnect between theory and practice.

CHAPTER 2
FROM CULTURAL REVOLUTION TO CAPITALIST REACTION

Despite its name, and however well-intentioned or radical the impulse, the Cultural Revolution was reactionary to the core. Following Mao's call to challenge the existing Party bureaucracy and eradicate remnants of China's traditional culture, his most extreme supporters were given official license to break the law in the name of revolution. With the support of the People's Liberation Army, teenage Red Guards destroyed property and homes, and humiliated, beat, and sometimes killed anyone they designated as being against the revolution, including their teachers and parents. Millions died and millions more suffered. Soon Mao's militant cult of personality was disgraced throughout the world and, after his death and the end of the Cultural Revolution in 1976, in China itself (although he is still highly respected by many as the founder of the People's Republic). But at the time, few in China could challenge those excesses, or his increasingly erratic personality. They lived in fear.

I am compelled to note that economic development in the West was, as Mao himself would say, "no dinner party." It was built on the backs of colonialism, slavery, and intense labor exploitation. Those Americans who point their finger at the People's Republic's mistakes and murderous mobilizations often fail to acknowledge our own shameful historical legacy. China's revolution was fought against a background of war, despotism, foreign intervention, and crushing underdevelopment. Hard times like that, in an environment that never knew a democratic culture, tend to produce hardened people and hard-line policies. China clearly went too far into the worship of a totalitarian mechanistic Marxist-Leninism. Its top-down system relied upon ordering people rather than persuading them. Grassroots initiatives and dissent were discouraged, by force when necessary.

After Mao died, the country went through intense internal political convulsions. Top leaders, many of whom had been supported by Mao, lost political battles and, in some cases, their lives. Mao's wife and her cronies, denounced as the "Gang of Four," were blamed for the excesses of the Cultural Revolution, and their 1976 arrest sidelined some of the more extreme hard-liners. In their place emerged modernizers, led by Deng Xiaoping, who launched the country on a campaign to build what is now called "socialism with Chinese characteristics." His Marxist-Leninism soon devolved into a form of "market"-Leninism.

As China slowly opened its markets to foreign investment and trade, a new ethic was legitimized. Indigenous businessmen were urged to make money because, in Deng's words, "to get rich is glorious." Soon, inevitably, sharp inequalities emerged, unemployment spread, and unrest surfaced. Corruption became pervasive, often implicating the top ranks of the Party, government, and their children, many of whom were educated in the West. These "princelings," as they are known, left as the sons and daughters of Communists and returned as aspiring capitalists, helped along by their positions of privilege in the new economic order. Their know-who proved as important as their know-how.

More significantly, in a country in which the Party line embraced atheism, spiritual voices were few. For a population just recovering from the recent wounds of the Cultural Revolution, enforced, top-down socialism had lost its mass appeal and few traditional religions or organs of civil society were in place to fill the spiritual void at the national or personal level. The thick and suffocating political rhetoric that had mobilized generations of poor and illiterate Chinese slowly lost its hold as the country modernized and produced a more educated population.

As gaps between Communist rhetoric and Chinese reality turned into cracks and then chasms, intellectuals, students, and workers alike started speaking out. Many who had, in effect, worshipped at the Church of Marxism, were becoming disillusioned as corruption became more apparent and economic changes shattered community building, collective work, and job security. A small democracy movement sputtered along, spearheaded by the 1978–79 "Democracy Wall," where individuals, such as dissident Wei Jingsheng, publicly posted their grievances in the center of Beijing.

Citizens were also unhappy with the condition of state services. As China's people began living longer, the country's health-care system proved inadequate. In addition, free medical services for workers in state enterprises have been slashed in recent years, leading many to seek out alternative health-care regimens. Older people in particular began searching out new treatment methods. They flocked to traditional Chinese medicine and qigong—an exercise system that taps internal energy forces, or qi—after they became popular again once the reform era started in 1979. (In the 1950s, many Communist leaders had practiced qigong but later abandoned it as un-Marxist.) In the early 1990s, many discovered a new movement: Falun Gong. It seemed to offer something that would meet a widely perceived practical need as well as fill a spiritual vacuum. It spoke to the body and the mind.

Falun Gong's appeal to the older population may be particularly worrying to the government for reasons not yet expressed: the "graying" of China. "In 1998, ten percent of the population was over sixty; by 2020, the figure is expected to rise to sixteen percent," reports James Watson in *Foreign Affairs*. "Like their counterparts in the American Association of

Retired Persons, future retirees in China are likely to be a vociferous, aggressive lot who will demand more state resources." This amounts to an aging population of 274 million, more than the total US population. And this is a group that has lived through revolution and repeated political mobilizations. It is many of these older people who have embraced Falun Gong in large numbers.

Former *New York Times* Beijing Bureau staffer, Chinese journalist W. Huang offered his elderly mother's experience as an example of the appeal of Falun Gong. She turned to the practice, he wrote, because she was both physically sick, and sick at heart about what was happening to China. "Society is deteriorating," she told her son. "Rampant corruption among the Communist Party, rising crime rates, drug abuse among young people. People don't have any goal except to earn money."

Remarkably, her practice of Falun Gong led to what her reporter son called a "miraculous recovery." "As more and more people like my mother become disillusioned, they search for something to fill the ideological and spiritual void," he wrote in the *Christian Science Monitor*. "Falun Gong meets the spiritual needs of ordinary Chinese because it has familiar Buddhist and Taoist roots."

German correspondent Harold Maass has also argued that home-grown spirituality is replacing socialism in today's China. "After two decades of a policy of openness, the heirs to Mao Zedong are sensing that control of the giant country is slipping away from them. This time, it is neither idealistic students nor democrats who are testing the CCP's power monopoly; it is the Chinese people, on a quest for spiritual leadership," he wrote in a February 11 *Frankfurter Runsdschau* report. "The Chinese have been turning again to religion and superstition since the Cultural Revolution (1966–76), when the only prayer allowed was to the great Chairman Mao. The official religions count more than 200 million believers. Taoist masters, teachers of meditation, quacks, and fortune-tellers are as popular today as in Imperial China."

There has been a debate among China experts about how to understand the widespread interest in Falun Gong in China and the government's harsh response. UCLA's Patsy Rahn thinks China's reaction has less to do with the size of Falun Gong than its symbolic importance. This view is spelled out in an Internet posting:

> The CCP is nervous about Li because they recognize him, they see in him a reversed mirror reflection of themselves; whereas you had Mao the materialist, you now have Li the spiritualist. I think it's also possible that Li is the first sign of "revenge" for the Cultural Revolution that China has had to face. The Chinese people suffered traumatic treatment in the Cultural Revolution, everything was bad, everything was unsafe. To join Li's Falun Gong movement is to be told you are good,

and that you are safe. Not only are you good, but Falun Gong can change the entire degenerate world (not just the degenerated CCP) into a good world if only everyone would become a FLG practitioner. It's as if the Chinese people are saying they want to be good, they want to be spiritual, and they want the CCP to officially recognize them as such.

There's also a more material view, as articulated by a policy analysis group who posted this assessment at Stratford.com:

China is in deepening economic depression. The reason China is so concerned is because the Chinese know that there is no solution to their economic problems. Therefore, they are bracing for the social and political consequences of long-term economic failure. Beijing understands that in times of misery, seemingly harmless groups can suddenly challenge the regime. The crackdown on Falun Gong expresses Beijing's deep-seated insecurity. If China's economy can't recover, can the regime survive? President Jiang Zemin intends to do whatever is necessary to make certain it can.

Throughout Chinese history, citizens have turned to spiritual practices as a means of expressing dissatisfaction with larger societal problems. Sometimes turning violent, these movements could lead to fierce battles with official troops, and several times came close to toppling the Qing Dynasty. In 1774, for example, a martial arts and herbal healing expert named Wang Lun preached an underground folk Buddhism called White Lotus, attracting the support of the poor and marginalized in a corrupt and highly stratified society. Their subsequent revolt was crushed by Qing Dynasty forces, but it nevertheless reflected social problems that ultimately led to the fall of the dynasty. In describing Wang Lun's movement, historian Jonathan Spence could well be talking about Falun Gong: "We cannot say that Wang Lun had a firm political agenda . . . His followers rose in rebellion not in response to some specific political program for social and economic amelioration, but from general feelings of antagonism to the dominant forces in society, reinforced by simple forms of spiritual euphoria."

In implementing their crackdown on Falun Gong, China's current leaders undoubtedly are aware of the movement's historical significance, and may even see it as a harbinger of their own downfall.

Yet, as their testimonials in Part II show, Falun Gong practitioners themselves strictly adhere to a policy of non-violence, and claim self-improvement and spiritual fulfillment as their only motives. They do not cite historical parallels or threaten to topple the state.[†]

[†]Much of my information about Falun Gong has come from practitioners. Clearly, their news releases should be held to the same standards of verification that we expect of other sources. In a paper presented to the American Family Foundation, Patsy Rahn notes:

Whatever the outcome of Falun Gong's challenge to China, there are reasons to believe that the disaffections expressed by practitioners echo throughout society. Journalist James Mann points to deeply embedded contradictions within China itself that are likely to fuel more conflict. "The gaps are becoming ever greater in China between rich and poor, between the developing eastern coastline and the poor inland, between the cosmopolitan elites of Shanghai and the tradition-minded cadres in the small towns and countryside," Mann writes in his analysis of Western illusions about China in the *American Prospect*. "And China does not have, of course, a political system that can easily accommodate dissent or balance competing interests. At some point, the many millions of Chinese who have not gotten rich from the boom of the 1990s (retirees, bureaucracts, factory workers, teachers) could find common cause for political action . . . "

Although Mann does not specifically mention Falun Gong, it seems likely that it and other spiritual practices will continue to grow in an economic climate that is certain to be turbulent in the near future, with widespread layoffs and intensifying social inequalities.

A major source of information to the Western press has been the Falun Gong office in New York through the Rachlin Management and Media Group, owned by Falun Gong spokeswoman Gail Rachlin, who is a practitioner. Information is provided via press releases, interviews with Li Hongzhi (interviews with Li have been discontinued since the summer of 1999), and information provided on the Falun Gong website. The information from this source is understandably biased and serving self-interests. This raises the larger question of the use of the Internet for information and the absence of any standard of accuracy, verification, or accountability for information provided on personal and interest-group websites, as well as the websites' impact on individual Internet users, the news media, and political policy.

Many of the allegations made against Falun Gong by the Chinese government and the Chinese state-controlled media have not been verified by independent third parties; similarly, many of the reports and statements from practitioners inside China that I have culled from Falun Gong websites have not been verified by independent sources.

CHAPTER 3
WHAT DOES FALUN GONG BELIEVE?

Falun Gong, which can be translated as "the practice of the wheel of law," is a branch of qigong, which, together with acupuncture, massage, and herbal medicine, is one of the four pillars of Chinese traditional medicine. Qigong has a long history dating back, Chinese scholars say, some 7,000 years. It is rooted in a culture fed by three streams of religious thought: Confucianism, Buddhism, and Taoism, although some people claim that qigong practices actually predate the introduction of religion to China. The Chinese have long believed in cosmic forces that circulate both within the body and through the world. The notion that masters can see inside you, or help you understand the flux that is at the center of all life and nature, has been around since at least the year 100. The geomancers of another age live on in the popular and common Chinese belief in feng shui, which people rely on to find the correct location for their homes, offices, and other spaces they live within.

Qigong fuses qi and gong: qi is defined as vital energy or life force, while gong means practice or cultivation. There have been different approaches to the practice of qigong, with Falun Gong based in what's known as the Buddha School. As Erping Zhang, a US-based spokesperson for Falun Gong, explains it, "The martial arts qigong enhances the strength, endurance, and spirit of the warrior. The medical qigong can be used to heal diseases. Most spiritual qigong is focused on self-cultivation, ethical development, and refinement of personal temperament. The Taoist qigong is aimed at alchemical transmutation, merging with nature, longevity, and immortality. The Buddhist qigong seeks refinement of mind, transcending the world of illusion and salvation of all living things." Some of these practices are open to all, others just to devotees or disciples of different masters. Some are theoretical and complex to grasp, others more simple, practical, and easy to access.

Falun Gong stresses the importance of working on mind, body, and spirit at the same time. Zhang explained to an audience at New York's China Institute: "Falun Gong practitioners have found that Falun Gong . . . is a science for life because of its merits in cultivating both mind and body. The ultimate goal of practicing Falun Gong is not for simply healing one's illnesses, though practicing its exercises can bring health to the practitioners. More importantly, it provides a way of life that complies with the law of the universe for people to elevate themselves toward the spiritual goal of enlightenment."

Falun Gong is based upon five sets of exercises, accompanied by the study of a moral code, what are collectively described as "universal laws and principles." The exercises are graceful, and impact, practitioners say, on the circulation of energy in the body. Falun Gong literature calls its exercise regime "smooth, natural, suitable for people of all ages and safe to practice. One can practice them at any time, any place, and in any order."

Here are the exercises, as their literature explains them:

1. Buddha Showing a Thousand Hands: This involves a series of simple stretches with the arms and hands. It usually takes three minutes from start to finish. Its aim is "to open all the energy channels and mobilize energy circulation in the body by stretching the body gradually and relaxing it suddenly."

2. Falun Standing Stance: This is "a tranquil standing exercise composed of four wheel-embracing movements . . . Frequent practice of the Falun Standing Stance will enable the entire body to open up and enhance the energy potency . . . The duration of each movement may differ from person to person; the longer, the better."

3. Penetrating the Two Cosmic Extremes: "To purify the human body by mixing and exchanging energy from the cosmos using simple up and down hand movements. Length: three minutes."

4. Falun Heavenly Circulation: "To rectify the abnormal conditions of the human body by enabling energy in the body to circulate over large areas. Slow and natural movements. Length: three minutes."

5. Strengthening Divine Powers: "A sitting tranquil (meditation with empty mind) exercise to strengthen supernormal (or instinctual) powers and energy potency. No requirement on duration, but the longer, the more effective."

Falun Gong echoes a traditional Chinese belief that all of us are connected to the universe through our minds and our bodies. Practitioners claim there is a "law wheel," referring to Buddhist notions of the laws of the universe, or what they simply call the "fa." It is rotating, they believe, within another dimension, in the lower parts of our abdomens. Tapping its power offers profound personal benefits such as the ability to cure diseases and prevent the deterioration of our bodies. Their exercises, they contend, influence the energy, or life forces, circulating on the inside that then intersect with this wheel, resulting in a beneficial outcome.

According to followers, the spiritual practice impacts on several levels at once. By balancing and enhancing natural healing resources in the body, by stimulating the function of qi, it has physiological effects, spurring the delivery of oxygen to the tissues, speeding the elimination of waste products, and strengthening immune cells through the lymph system. It works on the chemistry of the brain and the nervous system, they claim. "Patients who use qigong faithfully need less medication, less acupuncture, and heal faster," contends Zhang. Qigong focuses less on sickness than wellness, emphasizing prevention, nutrition, and positive thinking.

Falun Gong literature states that "by complying, synchronizing, and assimilating to the law of the universe, one is able through doing the exercise to eliminate the negative energies or karma and be able to truly follow the course of nature." Falun Gong founder Li Hongzhi suggests that the more one practices, the more one's body actually changes. He writes in *China Falun Gong*, a book of his teachings (excerpted in Part II), that there are channels in the body that can be opened:

> The objective of opening channels is to allow energy to circulate, to change the molecular components of cells and to transform them toward the high-energy substance. The channels of non-practitioners are clogged and very narrow. The channels of practitioners will gradually brighten, clearing out the clogged areas . . . They will widen even further when cultivating at higher levels. Some people have channels as wide as a finger . . . Through practice, the channels will be brightened and widened, and eventually they will connect to become one large piece.

In developing Falun Gong, Li Hongzhi reconnected the physical exercises of traditional qigong with their historical spiritual base. Using familiar Buddhist and Taoist terms, Falun Gong promotes three key principles: Zhen—truth and truthfulness; Shan—compassion, kindness, benevolence; Ren—tolerance and forbearance.

The philosophy behind this is explained in two books written by Li Hongzhi, *China Falun Gong* (title later changed to *Falun Gong*) and *Zhuan Falun*. All practitioners at one time could buy them for two dollars in China, twelve in America. The teachings are also available for free on the Internet (www.falundafa.org). *Zhuan Falun*, which is composed of nine lectures, is often taught in nine-session classes, and is read ardently by practitioners and often discussed in small groups.

Li Hongzhi's ideas offer his own interpretation of Buddha's "laws and principles." He explicitly challenges what he calls "conventional mentality." He sets out to unveil myths of the universe, time-space, and the human body. "If mankind can take a fresh look at itself as well as at the universe and change its rigid mentality, it will take a leap forward," he writes. He calls on those he attracts to approach his writing as ideas to discuss, just as his practice is based on process—"cultivating" one's mind through physical exercises and spiritual ideas.

Asking humanity to take a "fresh look" at itself is a tall order. Perhaps that is why elements of mankind, especially governments and media institutions which operate in a more grounded and pragmatic reality, can't make much sense of ideas that explicitly seek to transcend that reality and reject its conventional thinking. They approach these ideas literally—seeking proof and evidence, as if that is even possible. There is a lot about Falun Gong's belief system that is difficult to penetrate; on the other hand, that may not be the point.

Adam Montanaro, a US practitioner, says: "There's a whole other aspect to Falun Gong. It's not just the physical exercises . . . It teaches you about certain things, like virtues . . . It's very hard to find examples of that in the modern world. If you work in New York City, you can go the whole day and not see anybody doing much of anything nice for anybody else." My friend Gail Rachlin seconds this emotion: "When I do Falun Dafa, there's twenty-four hours a day that my energy is balanced. Even when I hit critical points, I know how to be within myself and literally live through the principles of truthfulness, forbearance, and compassion."

"It seems like such a simple thing. You open the book, it teaches about compassion, and this changes your life? Wait a second," remarks software professional Levi Browde, who came to Falun Gong after six years of studying with a more traditional Buddhist teacher. "But when I look at all the other practices I've tried in my life, it is the first practice that breaks things down to a very simple exercise and a very simple idea of Truth, Compassion, and Forbearance. And just because it's simple doesn't necessarily mean that it's not powerful."

Among those simple but powerful ideas is to give up "attachments" like fame, greed, selfishness, ego, and sentimentality. Falun Gong does not oppose fame or sentimentality per se, just the "mental attachments" that people form to them. One practitioner explained: "As a form of self-cultivation, Falun Gong is intended to help an individual develop his/her mind-body-spirit principles. As a person's practice deepens, they gradually learn to take more lightly the desires and ambitions that ordinarily rule human life."

According to Rebecca Weiner in *Tikkun*, among the things practitioners should give up are "attachments to money, things, ideas, even people which distract them from their own cultivation. This concept is not taken to the extremes of some groups; followers are encouraged to hold jobs, marry, have families and lead normal lives." She quotes Gail Rachlin as calling Falun Gong "three systems in one: it's an exercise system, a meditation practice, and a system of moral guidance." All of these elements are woven together.

People who practice Falun Gong point to concrete benefits and a value system they say fulfills their lives. Maria Sahlin, a Swedish practitioner, is typical: "When I found this . . . it influenced all parts of my life—my work and my everyday life. It helps me be more sure of what I'm doing and I can distinguish right from wrong more easily now." Another practitioner insists, "It is a rational decision . . . Just because our value system and way of reasoning is different, doesn't mean we are irrational or superstitious. The principles work for us. The question of whether or not it promotes health is not the real issue."

* * *

Nevertheless, many people do claim to have experienced improvements in their physical health from practicing Falun Gong. Mrs. Zhu, a practitioner living in New York's Chinatown, pointed to her husband and told me, "He got severely sick for quite a while and he tried a lot of other qigong exercises but none of them helped him. So once he started to practice Falun Gong his health improved greatly, and since his practice of Falun Gong, the problem never came back to him."

Women and men with chronic fatigue syndrome told me that it eased or disappeared once they began exercising. William Woodton, another American practitioner, claimed it was helping him address a serious malady: "I just couldn't sleep. Every time I lay down I would have pain . . . The doctor told me I had some clogged arteries . . . I don't know if [Falun Gong] is going to cure what my problem is, but I do know that it makes me feel better . . . Maybe it's the flow. I wanted better circulation, but the flow is real . . . it's no joke."

The link between Falun Gong exercises and better health has yet to be proven in any Western scientific studies of which I am aware, although some Chinese studies chronicle a number of health benefits. One must remember that traditional Chinese medicine has been treating problems that elude Western medicine for thousands of years. Some linkage between mind and body, once scoffed at, is now basically accepted by health experts. There has even been a White House Conference on Energy Medicine, and Falun Gong practitioners say that the National Institutes of Health is now funding studies of qigong, as is the American Foundation of Traditional Chinese Medicine. Alternative health and medicine has become a big industry in America, appealing to millions of people, although some within the medical establishment remain dismissive.

One of the Chinese government's main charges against the practice is that Falun Gong irresponsibly encourages people to stop taking medicine, leading to premature deaths. China claims that more than 1,500 practitioners have died as a result of their Falun Gong practice—some by suicide, others because they wouldn't take medicine or go to the hospital. Some details of the cases have been produced by the government, with photographs and short comments or, on TV, emotional soundbites from family members.

Li Hongzhi denies that he instructs practitioners to refuse medical treatment. "What I'm doing is telling people the relationship between practicing and cultivation and medicine-taking," he says. One of Li's protégés told me: "One can look into all of Falun Gong's books and Mr. Li's lectures and never find that Mr. Li says that one cannot take medicine. The charge that Mr. Li forbids people from taking medicine is easily proven as being groundless and wrong by reading his books. It is always an individual choice whether one should take medicine or not."

At the same time, however, Li's writing strongly discourages practitioners from seeking medical treatment, stating that once a practitioner has reached a certain level of cultivation, he or she will not get sick. Sickness, in his view, is a result of a "karmic debt," which manifests itself in the form of a virus or physical malady. Medication merely postpones the symptoms of serious illness but does not eradicate it, according to Li. Practice of Falun Gong then eradicates the root cause of the illness by eliminating the negative karma. When a practitioner asks whether or not he or she should take medicine while practicing, Li responds in *China Falun Gong* that "you should think and decide for yourself." Yet he also writes that "taking medication during cultivation implies that you do not believe in the disease-curing effects of cultivation. If you believed in it, why would you take medication?"

While the government claims that Falun Gong somehow encourages suicide, in reality Li Hongzhi opposes the practice in his writing, stating that "one must be able to suffer the toughest hardships of all . . . Many people just live to prove their points and will hang themselves when they cannot deal with things anymore. Therefore, we must practice cultivation in this complex environment and be able to endure the toughest hardships of all." Furthermore, people who have known mental illness are discouraged from taking up the practice. One practitioner explains that "if the person's own spirit cannot control his or her body and cannot make conscious judgments of his own, he simply cannot practice Falun Gong . . . If they cannot follow the teaching of Falun Gong, and cause some trouble for themselves, Falun Gong or its founder should not be held responsible for their actions."

As for many "suicide" cases cited by China, no independent analyst has reviewed the medical records or case histories they are based on. However, the case of one of the people on the list renders part of, if not the whole list, suspect. It was written by Jin You-Ming in late January 2000 about his mother, Ma Jinxiu, who was on China's list of suicides, and whose case was publicized by the government. According to her son, she actually had died of a long-term illness.

In 1981 when I went to middle school, my mother got diabetes . . . She often had heart palpitations. Believing that she might die very soon, she entrusted me to Aunt Hua, asking her to take care of my brother, my sister, and especially me as I would be so young after she died. For more than ten years, she was plagued by her diseases. Although she took more than thirty prescribed pills daily, her health got worse and worse . . . My mother was on the verge of death . . .

My mother's health showed no improvement until she learned [of] Falun Dafa in 1996. After she watched Master Li's videotapes, she thought that Falun Dafa was so good that she would like to practice cultivation. Shortly, my mother's health improved miraculously. She stopped taking medicine . . . [Two years later] she was sent to the hospital soon after she felt uncomfortable, without delay, and hence, received adequate medical treatment. She took medicine. She was given injections. There does not exist the problem of refusing medical treatment. What about the outcome? She still died. We all know that the hospital can treat one's illnesses but can not save one's life if one is to die.

The Chinese government's focus on the alleged suicides seems consistent with its view that Falun Gong practitioners are mentally unbalanced. But there is a political dimension to this as well. To the Chinese state, it appears that anyone who challenges its authority is acting in a de facto suicidal manner. Curiously, this view is often mirrored in American media accounts. In the *New York Times* on April 30, 2000, Craig S. Smith wrote: "Little light has been cast on why so many people feel Falun Gong worth dying for." This implies that the death of practitioners in prison or state custody was somehow voluntary, when in fact, as far as we know, reported deaths have been primarily due to torture. In any case, the idea that people would die for their beliefs has a long and proud history. Some societies honor martyrdom, while others honor those who fight against unjust systems.

In response to government allegations, Falun Gong spokesperson Erping Zhang says, "Certainly there are patients who practiced Falun Gong and still died. What is so strange about it? Falun Gong never guarantees that people do not die simply because they practice Falun Gong. Hospitals, t'ai ch'i, yoga, jogging, physical exercises, medical doctors do not guarantee that either. Should they be sinners as well?"

In an even-handed assessment in *China Rights Forum*, Columbia University China scholar James Seymour explains, "Practitioners are not encouraged to enter Chinese hospitals (which often are institutions most would want to avoid anyway). But in general [Li] and his colleagues try not to let claims get out of hand or dominate the movement's ethos. Practitioners say that they are free to do what they want, and many do seek out doctors and hospitals." (Seymour's full article, "The Wheel of Law and the Rule of Law," is reprinted in Part II.)

Falun Gong practitioners claim to have evidence that the practice "works," and its rapid spread is undoubtedly due in part to the widespread perception that it has health benefits. Practitioners cite several health surveys, including one allegedly of 10,000 practitioners in Beijing: "Our results show that Falun Gong's disease healing rate is 99.1 percent with a cure rate of 58.5 percent; improvement rate is 80.3 percent in physical health and 96.5 percent in mental health." Furthermore, in *Zhuan Falun*, Li claims that 80–90 percent of practitioners will have their illnesses healed through the practice of Falun Gong. There is an aspect of faith here—you believe you will get well, and so you do. This leads to an environment within Falun Gong that is hostile to conventional medicine, but I know many people who feel the same way and do not practice Falun Gong.

Significantly, China's official government TV stations initially credited Falun Gong with reducing the country's expensive health-care burden. In one typical report, a Falun Gong practitioner was honored: "She used to spend over 2,000 yuan on medical expenses every year . . . Now with the exercises, she not only doesn't spend a cent but was awarded a healthy citizen award by the government."

Another report on Beijing TV showed Falun Gong practitioners in the park, stating that "Since Falun Gong is becoming more recognized in China, people are filling parks and gardens to practice it. Falun Gong is beneficial to health and is beneficial to society as well, making society healthier and more productive."

* * *

In addition to medical benefits, Li and his followers believe that intense study and practice can take one to "higher levels." Li says that this can lead to "supernormal capabilities" and "special powers," even levitation, although he also makes clear that such abilities should never be the aim of cultivation. Newspaper accounts claim Li postulates that gravity may be controlled by deities that practitioners can visualize at work in their own bodies. Like most media, the *Wall Street Journal* called these "strange pronouncements," reporting that Li "teaches followers, for example, that practicing Falun Dafa will transform their bodies into 'high energy matter' at the sub-molecular level and allow some of them to fly, bodily, to heaven." Clearly there are mystical aspects of Falun Gong, as there are in many traditional Chinese spiritual practices and other widely recognized religions. (As I write, the Vatican has just revealed the "third mystery of Fatima." The press reported the story widely, but without seeking to debunk it or ridicule those who embrace its vision.)

Another example from *China Falun Gong*:

> After going through the adjustment of the physical body, students of
> Falun Gong have reached the state that is suitable for cultivation of the
> Dafa (Great Law), which is the state of "Milk White Body." Gong
> (cultivation energy) will develop only after this state has been reached.
> People with Tianmu (third eye) at a high level can see that Gong devel-
> ops on the surface of a person's skin, then is absorbed into the body of
> the practitioner. This process of Gong generation and absorption
> keeps repeating itself, going through layer by layer, sometimes very
> rapidly. This is Gong of the first round. After the first round, the body
> of the practitioner is no longer a regular one. After reaching "Milk
> White Body," one will never get sick again.

I asked spokesperson Erping Zhang about the concept of "higher consciousness" in Falun Gong. His response: "Higher consciousness is a commonly used term in Eastern cultivation of mind and Western psychology.
In Eastern cultivation, either in Buddhism or Taoism, one can reach a
higher level of consciousness via meditation. Higher consciousness may
also refer to consciousness beyond this physical dimension. Levitation is a
phenomenon or a byproduct of one's cultivation of mind and body. One
could find color photos of this phenomenon on Eastern cultivation practices; e.g., Indian yoga, Chinese Taoist and Buddhist practices, etc. The
central message of Falun Gong is to teach people to follow 'truth, compassion, and tolerance.' "

Falun Gong also draws on an interpretation of physics and other sciences to argue that energies are more important than substances in understanding the dimensions in which we live. Explains Zhang, drawing on the
work of Li Hongzhi, "Chinese philosophies and the ancient personal transformation traditions of the original cultures have always held that the
world we experience through our senses is but a fragment of what 'is.' In
addition, an individual's energy field is proposed to be more central to who
they are than their physical body. As Western science digs itself out from
under its 'seeing-is-believing' position, what occurs is a profound valida-
tion of ideas and traditions that were called 'mysterious,' 'unscientific,' and
'primitive' as little as a decade ago."

In *China Falun Gong*, Li Hongzhi explains:

> Dimensions, from our perspective, are very complicated. Mankind only
> knows about the dimension in which human beings currently exist, and
> other dimensions have not yet been explored or detected. When it comes
> to other dimensions, we Qigong masters have already seen dozens of lev-
> els of dimensions, which can also be explained in theory, but yet to be
> proved by science.

Some of Li Hongzhi's viewpoints don't sit well with Western readers, such as when he blames "homosexuality and sexual freedom" for interfering with practitioners' cultivation. He also in his books speaks out against "phony" qigong masters, and even tells stories of how he used his powers to injure other masters. When relating the story of how another qigong master had both his legs broken, Li explains, somewhat ambiguously, "Because he always committed bad deeds and interfered with my teaching of the Dafa, I then eliminated him completely." While such attitudes are worthy of our skepticism, they do not seem to be central to Li's philosophy or teachings.

This is also the case with a theme popular media loves: aliens. For a short period I produced for a popular TV program called *Strange Universe* that catered to the large number of Americans who believe in subjects like UFOs, aliens, and other strange phenomena. So, it appears, does Li Hongzhi. David Van Biema of the Asian edition of *Time* magazine focused on this subject of popular fascination and derision in an interview with Li conducted before the April 25 events in China. Li told him that aliens have begun to invade the human mind and its ideology and culture.

> *Time*: Where do they come from?

> Li: The aliens come from other planets. The names that I use for these planets are different. Some are from dimensions that human beings have not yet discovered. The key is how they have corrupted mankind. Everyone knows that from the beginning until now, there has never been a development of culture like today. Although it has been several thousand years, it has never been like now.

There appear to be as many people in China as in other parts of the world who believe in the possibility of extraterrestrial life. In December 1999, reports of UFO sightings over Shanghai were covered on TV, and discussed widely. Scientists scoffed at them, but as in the United States, government denials have led to charges of cover-ups. China scholar David Cowhig reported on the H-ASIA listserv that the magazine *Feidie Yanjiu* (Flying Saucer Research) of Lanzhou, China, boasts of having the highest circulation of any flying-saucer magazine in the world.

The conflict between the government and public opinion on this issue was pointed out by UCLA's Patsy Rahn: "In regards to China, the present official ideology, with its highly rational attempt at scientific materialism, has left no room for the (healthy) emotional, spiritual, or irrational. By attempting to forcibly deny the irrational (e.g., Falun Gong and others, who offer to fill the insatiable hunger for anything extraordinary), 'ideal,' or emotional aspects of life, the CCP has added to the problem, if not helped to create it."

A few newspaper accounts, such as a highly skeptical and condescending *Washington Post* feature by Peter Carlson, emphasize Falun Gong's unconventional beliefs. Carlson quotes one practitioner as saying, "The other spiritual paths I've done—Christian things—were all related to earth and this planetary sphere, but Master Li is beyond this planetary sphere . . . He has gotten permission—put that word in quotes—from the higher world to do what he does. You cannot bring that kind of truth to the world without permission. He would be killed. He would be destroyed. The fact that he has been able to do this shows that he has support from above." Carlson goes on to ask, "Clairvoyant? . . . Supernatural powers? . . . Beyond this planetary sphere? It sounds strange, but strange things are said about Master Li Hongzhi—sometimes by his followers, sometimes by his enemies, sometimes by Li himself."

Suffice it to say, despite such polished skepticism, I met many people in Falun Gong who insist that they have never felt healthier and credit the exercises, meditation, and moral philosophy for their well-being. They strike me as grounded, serious, and thoughtful people, not nutty fanatics. They look pretty good, seem rational, and to be honest, alas, are probably in better shape than I am.

CHAPTER 4
EVIL CULT?

In its 1999 statement upholding religious freedom worldwide, the US government points to a growing tendency by governments around the world to "stigmatize religions by wrongfully associating them with dangerous 'cults' or 'sects.' " In this case, it is a spiritual practice that is being so stigmatized by the Chinese government. Chinese authorities have compared Falun Gong to the Branch Davidians, who were burned alive in Waco, Texas, in 1993, and the Aum Shinrikyo cult that staged a nerve-gas attack on the Tokyo subway. These misleading parallels are then invoked to justify a crackdown on what they declare to be a dangerous threat.

Recently, a few observers in the West have also termed Falun Gong a cult. At a Seattle conference in May 2000 on "Cults and Millennium," Margaret Singer, a Berkeley, California, psychologist and critic of authoritarian religious groups, told the *San Francisco Chronicle* that she has been contacted forty-four times by parents of Falun Gong practitioners who were worried about their children's devotion to Li Hongzhi's teachings. "Their children have begun talking to them in memorized jargon, reading from the words of Master Li," Singer said. In the same month, an American Fundamentalist preacher denounced Falun Gong in similar terms, almost parroting the Chinese government line.

Yet Falun Gong stresses that it is not a cult, or a sect, or even a religion. There is no organization to join. There are no priests, temples, or churches. There are no rituals or worship services. I have been told there are no dues or mandatory tithing. In these respects, Falun Gong cannot be compared to most cults, which are organized around a charismatic leader who draws followers in, demands complete veneration, and often exploits members by controlling their money and other possessions.

Liu Binyan, a non-practitioner and a respected dissident Chinese journalist formerly with the *People's Daily*, writes in *China Rights Forum*, "The way the Chinese government is attacking Falun Gong teachings as unscientific is unreasonable. Of course this does not mean one cannot pose challenges to the teachings and to Li Hongzhi himself, but this is not an acceptable reason to negate Falun Gong. The group's followers have not demonstrated any destructive fanaticism; indeed their behavior has been peaceful, rational, and constructive. The CCP's (Chinese Communist Party) smear tactics of calling Falun Gong a cult are just absurd."

Ken Roth, Executive Director of Human Rights Watch, made the same point when I asked him about it. "If you look at what Falun Gong is, it's just ordinary people. This is not a cult in the sense of brainwashed people intent on doing some harm to society or themselves. These are people who want to go out and exercise as a group, who have a certain, perhaps mystical view of healing, which is harmless to anyone. This is not the kind of cult that legitimately is repressed. This is . . . a group of ordinary people that deserves to be able to band together as they've chosen to do—but that in and of itself is so threatening to the Chinese government that it resorts to this name calling."

People who practice Falun Gong say they do so voluntarily. Mrs. Zhu, a Chinese woman I spoke to on a park bench in Queens, New York, was matter-of-fact about it: "I have no obligation to anybody when I practice Falun Gong. If one day I say well, I want to do something else, I want to go shopping, I want to take the day off, I can just go. I don't have to report to anybody."

The Chinese government tried to mock Li Hongzhi by claiming that he had warned practitioners that the end of the world was at hand. He denies making any such apocalyptic predictions and, at a talk he gave in New York, he said: "I can proclaim here to everyone in all earnestness that all of those so-called catastrophes of the earth or of the universe and things of this kind in the year 1999 simply do not exist." Practitioners say that he has always discouraged theories forecasting the end of the world or doomsday scenarios common in many religious circles.

China has not paid any attention to his denials, as Stephen D. O'Leary explained in a piece about Falun Gong and the Internet in June 2000. "If Li is the archetypal doomsday cult leader, and his followers are deluded, superstitious victims of sophisticated psychological coercion, then any measures taken by the government would seem to be justifiable," he noted. "These allusions to the Western ideas of a doomsday cult figure are clearly an attempt by the Chinese government to seek sympathy and empathy from Western countries, particularly from America, where Li now resides" (O'Leary's full article can be read in Part II).

The practice's approach to making money is another example of how un-cultlike Falun Gong is. The Chinese government contends that Li Hongzhi is getting rich off of Falun Gong and is busy investigating the sale of his books and videos. He says, "I make a comfortable living off my books." Indeed, if he has 70 to 100 million followers, and each one buys a book, even for a small amount, that's a lot of money. Writing in *Tikkun*, Rebecca Weiner reports that Li personally owns the publishing company. She quotes a Chinese marketing specialist as saying, "the key in China is cheap, cheap, cheap. Slash margins mercilessly. As long as you are making a little each time China's sheer volumes will make you rich." If Falun Gong is as wealthy as she implies, why isn't it spending more money on advertising or high-power lobbying?

Practitioners deny that greed is a factor. "I promise you that if you are approached for money or pressure to do or say something against your will, it is not a genuine Falun Dafa site or practitioner," asserts Eric Allen. "We simply do not behave this way." The Chinese government disagrees, making detailed accusations suggesting large-scale diversions of funds. These charges, as far as I know, have never been examined in a court or evaluated by third parties.

There are certainly wealthy people in Falun Gong, but if they donate money, they seem to do so voluntarily to support various projects. The *Wall Street Journal* ran an exposé regarding a luxury home in Princeton, New Jersey, that one wealthy practitioner allegedly presented to Li Hongzhi and his family, but in his wife's name. Ironically, Li reportedly turned it down. But is this so surprising? The controversy reminded me of a debate in South Africa over Nelson Mandela's decision to move into a fancy suburban home that some supporters bought for him after he was released from prison. They wanted him to be secure and treated in a presidential manner. Others thought it "looked bad" for him to leave his small Soweto house and move away from the community that loved him. After twenty-seven years confined in a tiny cell, Mandela opted for the bigger spread. It was understandable. Yet Li did not. According to an ABC-TV report, "Li says he seldom watches movies or television or even leaves home, except for occasional trips with his wife to the mall on weekends." Most of his time is said to be spent studying his cultivation practice.

Falun Gong is also quite forthcoming about practicing in public parks, not in secret. This is an early-morning tradition in China, rapidly spreading in America and across the world. In park after park, we can now add Falun Gong practitioners to the joggers and the walkers. Explains Adam Montanaro, a young American professional in his twenties, "They are very open about what they do and they want people to see that they can try it if they are interested. That is why you practice publicly in the park, and you put up a sign that says, 'Hey, we're doing Falun Gong. If you're interested come on by, it's free and you can stop by any time and learn it.'"

One of the people who did just that was Sterling Campbell, who was walking in New York's Central Park and stopped to watch the exercises for a long time, before asking for information. A professional musician with a number of well-known rock bands, he had been fighting against drug addiction for years. He told me, "I tried yoga and I tried other qigong practices. I was looking for something but I always kind of felt, you know, like I'm forking out $400 here and $500 there and when you have to pay for salvation, there's something wrong. That's another thing that struck me, that it's for free." It also seems to reinforce a sense of community among the practitioners. Says Gail Rachlin: "I find that in doing the practice in the park together, we are really basically bonded together."

"We are not interested in politics," insists twenty-seven-year-old Feng Keran. "We do not have political intentions. We are not against the government. We just try to live for ourselves; cultivate our hearts. Try to be good people." While Falun Gong practitioners have not been actively political, the Chinese government is in effect politicizing them through its continuing assaults.

The practitioners' aversion to politics may be understandable given the widespread fatigue with China's overheated political environment. China expert Orville Schell blames the Party for encouraging people to become self-centered and self-aggrandizing, to get rich and abandon politics. Falun Gong's apolitical stance constitutes a rejection of both this political correctness from above and the spread of materialism below. The experience of many Falun Gong practitioners with the Cultural Revolution soured them as well, and is frequently cited whenever anyone suggests that Falun Gong is a cult. "We have known cults of personality well," one told me in a veiled reference to the cult of Mao. "And this is not one."

All of these developments have been transpiring against the backdrop of mounting Party concern over the growth of a weird assortment of other alleged cults throughout China, including the "Cry Out Faction," "the Shouters," "The Master of God" group, and the "Disciples." In March 2000, Amnesty International reported that even before the crackdown on Falun Gong started, the Chinese government had arrested 21,000 people in a two-year campaign against so-called superstitious activities. Human Rights Watch obtained and republished an internal document that first appeared in the theoretical journal of the Chinese Communist Party (*Qiushi* 5, 1996) contending that 500,000 people were under the "deceptive influence" of cults. Author Luo Shuze explained the danger to Party discipline: "They incite people to subvert the government, rave about 'fostering powerful centrifugal forces in the broad countryside where the Chinese Communists find it most difficult to control' . . . Some raised the slogan, 'Seize church power first and then take over political power.'" Significantly, this report did not cite Falun Gong—which was legal at the time—as a cult.[†] In October 1999, Liu Jiaguo, accused of leading the "Master of God" cult, was executed for allegedly raping eleven women, including two under the age of fourteen. The Chinese media reported that Liu and his cohorts told women followers that they must sacrifice their bodies to God, saying that members of their families would get sick and die if they did not have sex with them. The report of this incident in the Chinese media mentioned Falun Gong, even though the two movements seemingly had nothing in common.

[†]Human Rights in China, in a July 1999 statement condemning the crackdown on Falun Gong, pointed out that "over the last twenty years, among the harshest sentences for 'counterrevolutionary crimes' have been imposed on those accused of using reactionary sects or secret societies for counterrevolutionary purposes. To our knowledge, almost all of the 'counterrevolutionaries' sentenced to death in this period have been in this category."

Following the Falun Gong crackdown, at least three other qigong practices were denounced by the government as "cults," including Zhong Gong, which was founded in 1988. Zhong Gong has some similarities to Falun Gong on the surface in that it couples qigong practices with a philosophy, created by its leader Zhang Hongbao, that combines Buddhism and Taoism. By July 2000, the government had reportedly closed 3,000 Zhong Gong training centers and arrested 600 members.

CHAPTER 5
LI HONGZHI AND THE FALUN GONG "NETWORK"

Li Hongzhi's family was originally from Manchuria. He has said he started learning qigong from monks at age four. "The older monk looked at me," he recalls, "and then said, 'You are the one I have been looking for.' "

His practitioners refer to him honorifically as "Master Li" because he is considered a master of the practice he founded. This is common among various qigong practices. He claims to have learned at the hands of his own masters, and that his role has been hyped beyond recognition. "Were the real cultivators in the cultivation community to know that I was ranked among the most influential people in the world, they would most likely laugh," he told the *New York Times*. He doesn't accept the idea of rankings or such status designations.

Yet practitioners' deference to him is obvious. Writes Rebecca Weiner in *Tikkun*: "It seems that the only attachment followers are encouraged to make is to Li Hongzhi himself . . . [Followers] spoke of him in terms that could only be called rapturous." The practitioners I asked all spoke of their "gratitude" to him but never in godlike terms. (I am told that some of the less-educated Chinese practitioners consider him a messiah, even though he doesn't claim such a status.) Throughout the world, qigong practices routinely have masters, and students tend to be deferential to such teachers. Falun Gong clearly is not, however, a democracy or a collective. Its followers treat their "master" worshipfully, and in ways that Westerners skeptical of Eastern practices would be uncomfortable with.

I met with Li in lower Manhattan just after Falun Gong's banning in July 1999. He struck me as rather shy, and uncomfortable playing the role of an internationally recognized leader. He seems to have encouraged followers to stop calling him Master because the term is misunderstood in America as suggesting genuflection to his every word. It is significant that even as the crisis in China escalated and news outlets sought comments from him, he chose to remain out of public view. This may be for security reasons—but it certainly indicates that he is not an obsessed publicity-seeker.

He grew up in poverty like many ordinary Chinese, and graduated from high school during the Cultural Revolution, when higher education was essentially abolished. He later served in the army, working with horses at an army stud farm, and then as a clerk for the Changchun

Municipal Cereals and Oils Company. He played trumpet in a provincial police band of the Forestry Corps.

There is a dispute over Li's correct birth date. The Chinese government claims he was born on July 7, 1952, but he claims he was born on May 13, 1951, in the lunar calendar, which is also the birthday of Siddhartha Gautama, the Buddha. The government says Li altered the date so that it would coincide with Buddha's birthday. He told me that it had been doctored originally, like many official records, during the Cultural Revolution, and that he had simply corrected it. Practitioners also say that Li could not have changed his birth date without proof, and certainly not without the approval of the appropriate government office. (A biography assembled by practitioners is included in Part II.)

China's propagandists say Li has fabricated his life story, using commentary like this: "Many of Li's former schoolmates, teachers, and neighbors, when interviewed, all said Li Hongzhi was no more than an ordinary child obtaining average marks in his studies. In their reaction to his fabricated story of 'spiritual cultivation,' their answers were either 'nonsense' or 'impossible,' or 'I have never seen or heard of that.'"

Li began developing his ideas in the late 1980s, when a qigong revival was well under way. His first book, *China Falun Gong*, spelled out his spiritual discoveries. He had to borrow money to get it published. He soon authored another book, *Zhuan Falun*, which was published legally in January 1994, and had a formal publication number assigned to it. *Beijing Youth Daily* reviewed it as one of the top ten sellers. The book followed a national speaking tour, between the years 1992 and 1994, with Li "giving fifty week-long lectures," according to a Congressional Research Service report prepared for the US Congress (this report is reprinted in Part II). He lectured at police universities and health expos, where he was sometimes presented with awards, which practitioners cite as evidence of their legitimacy.[†] His message quickly became very popular, and the government began to notice.

Not long after *Zhuan Falun* became a bestseller, it was banned. In 1996, for reasons that haven't been fully explained, Li, who speaks only Chinese,

---

[†]Falun Gong seems very eager to win commendations and recognition from prominent people and politicians, perhaps because of the way they have been demonized and marginalized. The credentials and status of their supporters are often cited prominently. UCLA Professor Patsy Rahn, a Falun Gong critic, sees this as deliberate fraud, noting on the H-ASIA listserv:

> . . . these "awards" are documents routinely obtained by groups from public officials and elected bodies for public relations purposes. All you have to do, for instance with the CA Governors office, is call and leave a message as to whether you want a "proclamation" or a "commendation" and what day you need it by. You can also fax in your request, sending them a sample proclamation, which they will then use . . . I wonder if the mainland Chinese practitioners see these documents in a different context than we do in our free-market, press-relations savvy way. Might they see these documents as official and meaningful support of Li Hongzhi?

Another scholar, Barend ter Haar, is less exercised putting it into a cultural context, stating that "the public endorsement by figures with official status is a fundamental aspect of socio-political organization in modern China, as it was in the past."

traveled to the United States. He moved first to Houston, and then to New York, on a permanent visa status with his wife and daughter. He told me that his daughter wanted to go to an American high school. His presence in the United States has led to Chinese attacks on the United States for encouraging Falun Gong, calling it a US pawn, and Li a US "spy."

When I met with Li, he wore a business suit over a crisp white shirt, and spoke softly with occasional passionate flourishes. He stands just under six feet tall, with brown eyes and a warm but intense personality. He was at the time giving press interview after interview, but didn't seem to be enjoying it. Having been around a lot of politicians and officials, I was surprised by how unpracticed and uninterested he seemed in the art of the sound bite, taking time to explain his views to journalists who clearly only wanted a quick quote. That awkwardness appeared to be an indication of sincerity, as he didn't seem to be pushing himself or his ideas.

The charisma I'd seen in videos of his talks was subdued, as he called on China to dialogue with him and try to resolve the crisis. According to an ABC report, he "mixes a degree of modesty with a clear desire for firm control of his movement." I sensed his deep concern for what was happening in China. He was, above all, calm, centered, and focused.

I didn't have time to ask him personal questions but he did talk a bit about his life in America with Jonathan Landreth and J.S. Greenberg for the *New York Times*. "I need to have a quiet and calm place to concentrate on the practice," he said. "So I don't watch TV and movies often. But I know they have created irreversible pollution to the world . . . Because of the language barrier, and because of my personal practice, I seldom walk down the street. Sometimes on weekends, we go to the mall. You know, sometimes I help my wife do the grocery shopping. I love that I can get Chinese sauces in New York."

The apartment where we met, borrowed from a practitioner, was covered with color posters of him being cheered in China and other countries, and materials introducing the practice. Clearly, his image is projected as the personification of Falun Gong, although practitioners insist his emphasis and theirs is on self-cultivation and personal improvement. A recent picture of him on Falun Gong websites shows him meditating on a scenic mountaintop. The caption reads, "Master Li quietly watching his disciples and people in the world from the mountains after leaving New York last July." The *Washington Post's* Peter Carlson wrote about the picture: "It's the first news about Li since he dropped out of sight last July and it caused quite a stir among practitioners. They've been printing it, framing it, sending it all over the world via the Internet, and speculating endlessly on what it might mean." He quotes conflicting interpretations from practitioners, mocking their beliefs, concluding with sarcasm: "Master Li says nothing, of course. He just sits there with his eyes closed, looking serene, inscrutable, mysterious."

There are several ways to interpret the picture, as well as Li's role. He had been out of the public eye for months, so a sighting would at least confirm he was alive, although I was told by Gail Rachlin that the photo published in January 2000 was actually taken in the summer of 1999 during a trip to the western United States. In April 2000, I met a ninety-six-year-old practitioner who told me that Master Li dropped by to see him recently and was in good health. Some critics speculate that Li has stayed out of the spotlight during the crackdown to conceal his lack of real power. On the other hand, an absence from the public spotlight reinforces his mystique of power by presenting the image that he is above the fray, not bothered by the mundane minutiae of China's charges. Practitioners certainly feared for his life and circulated suggestions that a "hit squad" from China has been dispatched to kill him.

Yet if he is the leader, what is his movement? The seeming absence of a structured organization is striking, although Falun Gong does have practice centers and a worldwide network of volunteer "contacts." They also maintain websites in many languages, using the Internet and e-mail as key communication and educational tools (see Chapter 19: Internet Resource Guide). As one practitioner noted on a website posting: "To fully appreciate the role of technology in the April 25 protest and similar Falun Gong events, one does not have to look further than the recent Tiananmen protest during the Chinese New Year: over 2,000 managed to participate at a time when all of the 'leaders' had been imprisoned and their organization jeopardized."

Stephen D. O'Leary of the *Online Journalism Review* was amazed by how sophisticated Falun Gong is on the net. "The list of Falun Dafa websites that is provided in one of the links is staggering," he writes,

> Lists of volunteers all over the world provide the email addresses and contact numbers of individual members representing groups who practice together. The number of groups in China is claimed to be so large that a disclaimer, almost a boast, is given: "Too many to be listed . . . " The Internet is clearly being used as a means to keep contact and mobilize members. One comes away from the various Falun Gong websites with a distinct impression of an effective global network that is indeed organized and connected by virtue of the Internet.

China is trying to monitor and disrupt this network. In November, 1999, Zhang Ji, a twenty-year-old student practitioner at Qiqihar University in northeast China was jailed for "using the Internet to spread subversive information."

The Chinese government has "filtered," blocked, and hacked into many of Falun Gong's websites, waging a virtual electronic war against them. In April 2000, a series of "Smurf" attacks, similar to the attacks that temporarily paralyzed Yahoo and eBay earlier in the year, were carried out against major Falun Gong sites. The editor of one of the sites claims to have received an advance e-mail warning of the attacks, stating that they would be carried out by hackers from two major security companies in China. Some practitioners have had their e-mail accounts attacked as well. The global website that I edit, MEDIAchannel.org, is no longer accessible in China, according to friends there, possibly because it has reported on the media's role in the Falun Gong crackdown.

The Chinese government clearly believes Falun Gong's movement is highly organized, and even alleges that there were thirty-nine general instruction offices, 1,900 ordinary instruction offices, and 28,000 practice sites. How such a vastly intricate apparatus was allowed to be built over seven years under the all-observant eyes of the security police is not explained. This structure is accused of "all sorts of law breaking activities," ranging from charges of disrupting public order to economic crimes such as tax evasion and money laundering. By presenting Li and Falun Gong practitioners as criminals, the Chinese government deflects attention from the blatantly political character of its campaign against them.

Other observers have also marveled over Falun Gong's ability to organize and sustain protests. At first, it all seemed amorphous and non-bureaucratic to me, perhaps in reaction to China's many overgrown leaden bureaucracies. There is no visible rank or hierarchy and Li doesn't seem to have any one assistant or aide. High-profile practitioners say they don't know where he is most of the time and are not in touch. As one Chinese practitioner put it, "Falun Gong has always been taking a way of no-formality." Even the PR people refer to themselves as volunteers and practitioners.

China scholar W.T. Liu calls Falun Gong a "non-organization organization." His essay in the pamphlet, "The Mystery of China's Falun Gong," cites the group's use of the Internet to faciliate "a core of believers directing a mass of followers." He adds that the elusive structure of Falun Gong "has created an unprecedented fear for the leaders in Beijing. Communist cadres know how to deal with organizations . . . But how does one deal with a non-group?"

The practice's apparent decentralization may be deliberate and may, in fact, be responsible for its remarkable survival in the face of such organized government attacks. A highly centralized organization is easier to penetrate and disrupt than a fluid non-organized entity held together by shared beliefs. Nonetheless, I have been told that many spies have been detected in Falun Gong's midst.

I was impressed by the diversity and geographical diffusion of this Falun Gong network. They are now in over thirty countries, forty US states, and 104 cities and towns. They come from many walks of life, young, very young, and old alike, from varied racial, cultural, and religious groups. And despite the government crackdown, Falun Gong is continuing to grow internationally.

CHAPTER 6
PROMOTING FALUN GONG IN CHINA

Li Hongzhi introduced Falun Gong to the Chinese public in 1992, but at the time it only directly reached a few thousand people, not millions. "He personally taught his practice only about two and a half years in China, from May 1992 until the end of 1994," recounts Erping Zhang, who was in China at the time. "And probably about 20,000 people actually listened to his lectures in person, in China. After that he stopped teaching the practice personally; for the past four years really, people learned his practice through word of mouth, because in China, everybody practices the exercises early in the morning in the parks. That's how people really get started." Practitioners who gather in parks to practice often display Falun Gong banners and free literature to attract newcomers.

China is an organizational society, highly structured by the long hand of government. All social groups and organizations must register with the government before being allowed to operate. For years, China has had an official China Qigong Research Society, a government-approved structure for coordinating and controlling the various qigong practices. Unlike some of the other masters, Li Hongzhi decided to focus his energies on teaching Falun Gong at the bottom of society, first in the public parks in the city of Changchun. He started by making his ideas accessible and affordable to the poor. As it became popular, it was quickly recognized, and co-opted, by the qigong establishment, which began profiting from it. A report by Falun Gong practitioners states that fees for Li's lectures and demonstrations were charged by the China Qigong Research Society, not by Li himself, and that Falun Gong only received forty percent of the profits, with the official association receiving the other sixty percent.

"After three years of teaching I withdrew from the China Qigong Research Society," Li told freelancer J.S. Greenberg for ABC News. "I thought at the time that all the qigong society did is try to make money off the qigong masters, and they didn't do any research on qigong." His alternative was to encourage people to read his book and learn on their own.

That decision later would become a factor in his estrangement from one official structure, especially after he cut his fees and offered free lectures. At that time, a nine- or ten-day class cost forty yuan (about five US dollars); others were only twenty yuan. This proved very popular with the people, but upset many of the other qigong masters, who complained that

Falun Gong was undercutting their prices and competing unfairly. According to Li, the society asked him to hike his tuition. He refused— and soon afterwards left the society, which was going through a period of political in-fighting. The formal-sounding Falun Dafa Research Society had been set up as the entity that allowed him to be part of the qigong establishment, and created contact posts and training centers to spread the word. This association was automatically dissolved in 1995 when Li pulled out. The business dispute would soon spill over into politics. In 1999, the government would dramatically ban the Falun Dafa Research Society, although it ostensibly no longer existed.

The apparent consequence of this conflict was that Li Hongzhi had unintentionally created enemies as well as friends. He had alienated a group of people who he felt wanted to cash in on Falun Gong or at least use it to their own advantage. Unsuccessful in convincing him to work with them, they turned against him. According to Falun Gong sources, a small number of these individuals started attacking Falun Gong and lobbied the government to intervene against its growth. I was told that these people started spreading rumors against Li Hongzhi, questioning his bona fides, even recently calling him a "spy for America." As one Chinese practitioner explained anonymously in a detailed analysis published on a Falun Gong Internet site, "The hazardous fact is: these pure slanders from a few turned into the mistake of the central government."

One problem for the government: Many members of the Communist Party had become practitioners, including high-level military and intelligence officers, and reportedly even the wives of Cabinet Ministers. Perhaps that is why there was no open conflict earlier. "It was just a year ago (1998), that we saw so many positive reports from the media—the statewide media in China—about the benefits of Falun Gong," noted Erping Zhang. In fact, in the February 1999 issue of *US News & World Report*, when asked, "Why are you not banning it?" a health official said, "Why should we? We save millions of dollars a year in health care." In 1993, Falun Gong and Li Hongzhi received commendations from security organizations. Li often spoke at educational institutions that served the police and army.

Veteran Chinese journalist Liu Binyan, writing in *China Rights Forum*, explains, "Of course the participation and support of powerful cadres at the top and middle levels of the CCP hierarchy, people with high social status and strong political influence, also increased the legitimacy and appeal of Falun Gong. There is no basis for the claim that these people have any political ambitions. However it is true that many old and retired officials feel dissatisfied with current CCP policy, official corruption, and the state of society. For them, strengthening a movement like Falun Gong could be seen as a way of cleansing the spirit of society, and thus appeared to be a way of addressing some of their concerns" (Liu Binyan's full article,

"Unprecedented Courage in the Face of Cultural Revolution–Style Persecution," is reprinted in Part II).

Tikkun magazine quotes Dr. Philip Zimbardo, an expert on cults and religious movements as saying: "Our search for meaning should begin at the beginning. What was so appealing about this group that so many people were recruited/seduced into joining it voluntarily? . . . We want to know also what needs was this group fulfilling that were not being met by traditional society."

* * *

Li Hongzhi's students became a transmission belt, spreading the word, reaching others . . . and they others, and the number of people involved multiplied exponentially. While some local TV stations in China carried positive stories, the world media paid little attention—that is, until April 25, 1999. On that day, suddenly, silently, this new practice so oriented to individual well-being and personal transformation dramatically burst onto the world scene as a significant collective social force.

It transpired without any public advance notice and sent a shockwave through Chinese society. In recent years China has experienced disruptive localized labor protests and small-scale riots, but after the Tiananmen protests of 1989, large-scale challenges to the central government were considered a thing of the past. The government, its police, and army are, above all, committed to preserving what they call social stability. That attitude is well-known by the public at large, which is, for the most part, intimidated by the power of the State. In response to any direct challenges to the system, labor and democracy activists are routinely thrown in prison.

Yet on that April day, 10,000-15,000 Falun Gong practitioners quietly surrounded Zhongnanhai, the government leadership compound in the heart of Beijing, not far from Tiananmen Square. They lined the streets, sometimes eight deep, quietly, and without placards. They shouted no slogans. They just stood or sat there for twelve hours, with great dignity but little expressiveness. Some meditated. Others read books.

It began as a media protest. When asked, the practitioners explained that they were there to file a complaint—what the Chinese call "an appeal"[†]—with the government against what they considered an inaccurate, even slanderous, attack on Falun Gong launched by He Zuoxiu, a physicist and member of the Chinese Academy of Sciences. One of his denunciations took the form of an esssay, "Why I Am Opposed to Qigong Practice by Teenagers," which appeared in *Teenage*

[†]A report by Falun Gong practitioners explains the term "appeal" this way: "Public appeals efforts have played an important role in Chinese history. A feudal empire of over 2,500 years, China has always found it hard to accept a legal system based on Western principles of rule of law. China's feudal system was not replaced until as late as 1911. Thus, the old thinking and appeals form remains prevalent in society today."

Science-Technology Outlook, a state-sponsored magazine. In the short piece, he challenged Falun Gong's claims of being scientific and reported that a "post graduate in my institute had two relapses of mental disorder after he practiced Falun Gong." This article was one of several he wrote critiquing Falun Gong. He also appeared on Beijing Television citing the story of his student practitioner. Falun Gong practitioners rallied at the TV station when that show was broadcast.†

According to He Zuoxiu, who was later quoted widely by the Chinese government, Falun Gong responded by sending practitioners to his door to challenge his views and mailing letters to attack him. He claims Li Hongzhi personally denounced him in a speech in Sydney, Australia, on June 2, 1999, branding him a "scientific scoundrel." In response, He Zuoxiu turned his personal pique into a political broadside. In an article titled "How Falun Gong Harassed Me and My Family," reprinted in a government propaganda pamphlet, he concludes, "I think Falun Gong, under the control of Li Hongzhi, is an organization purely intent on disrupting public order of the society. Its theory and acts are very similar to heretical cults in the West." This language was soon co-opted by the government.

Falun Gong practitioners believed that He Zuoxiu had unfairly maligned their spiritual practice with the first magazine article. According to one supporter, when the magazine would not agree to carry a response, practitioners gathered at the editorial offices in Tianjin. By April 22, several days later, their numbers had grown to a few thousand. Riot police were dispatched to the scene, where they beat demonstrators and arrested forty-five people. A small group of shocked practitioners complained about this treatment to local authorities, who told them that those arrested could only be released with the approval of Beijing authorities. They were told to take their appeal to the central government in Beijing, an hour and a half away. And they did.

What soon mushroomed into a small army of practitioners then went to the public-complaint bureau located in the heart of the power center in Beijing. Word of the protest spread through Falun Gong's information network, and soon thousands had gathered at the gates of Zhongnanhai. The right to appeal is guaranteed in the Chinese constitution (excerpted in Part II)—and they exercised it. These practitioners came, seemingly out of nowhere, and vanished after some of their number met with government officials. They presented the officials with a letter seeking official recognition and the release of practitioners imprisoned in Tianjin, and specifically asked that the government allow "a legal and non-hostile environment for

---

†This incident was recounted by Craig Smith in the *New York Times* in April 2000, in a way that portrayed protests against Chinese state-owned media, which is well-known for broadcasting propaganda posing as news, as "intolerance" toward the press. "Falun Gong is no more tolerant of the Western press," he added, citing calls and e-mails he received after publishing an account in the *Wall Street Journal* of a gift of a house presented to Li Hongzhi (which Li reportedly turned down). This reveals how thin-skinned media outlets can be—in both China and the United States—when those discontented with their coverage dare to challenge them.

practicing Falun Dafa in China." The content of their specific message—
their reasons for being there—was soon overshadowed by the audacity and
scale of their gesture.

Unlike the Tiananmen demonstrators a decade earlier, this crowd was
not composed of students, and there was little anger or spirit of confrontation. Many older people and workers drawn from every level of the
society took part. Indignation may be the best term for the collective feeling. They felt they had every right to ask their government for help, insisting they were acting within the law.

That is not, of course, the way China's rulers saw it. According to
China scholar James Seymour, the protest unnerved the leadership. "They
were just so afraid of what they saw out there," he told me. "I suppose it
was very eerie, with thousands of people just sitting there silently . . . or
surrounding the compound where the officials lived. They've never seen
anything like this before. And they just didn't know how to deal with it."

"The regime was particularly scared by the failure of its intellegence
service to prevent the demonstration, and by membership in Falun Gong
by some medium-level political and military leaders," surmises Massimo
Introvigne of Italy's Center for the Study of New Religions.

Another perspective is found in "The Mystery of China's Falun Gong,"
published by Singapore University Press. In the pamphlet, scholar John
Wong states:

> According to one source, the Chinese Public Security services started to
> watch this sect as early as 1996 under the order of the then Secretary
> General of the State Council, Luo Gan. But the police did not stop this
> demonstration partly because the crowd largely made up of many old
> folks and women, was genuinely peaceful and orderly, and partly
> because several leaders of the group were known to be respectable mem-
> bers of the establishment . . . In fact, of the five Falun Gong leaders at
> the sit-in who made representations to Premier Zhu, one was report-
> edly a retired Public Security Officer and one was a serving officer
> from Beijing's Supervisory Bureau.

Xinhua, the official Chinese news agency, echoed what was to become
a strident official line: "The Falun Gong cult had evil intentions and endangered society and the country as a whole. Among the examples was the April
25 siege of the central leadership compound, Zhongnanhai, by over 10,000
Falun Gong practitioners from Beijing, Tianjin, Hebei, and elsewhere in the
country. This incident seriously disrupted the work of government departments and the daily routine of the general public, threatened social stability, and had negative political consequences." That vague and
undocumented assertion foreshadowed a harsh and ongoing crackdown.

* * *

Between May and June 1999, in the aftermath of the Beijing protest, the Communist Party leadership was divided on how to respond. Some, like Premier Zhu Rongji, were reportedly sympathetic to Falun Gong. According to one practitioner, during the April 25 protest, Zhu came out of his office in the morning and met inside Zhongnanhai with several participants. Some practitioners applauded him for this, and many within Falun Gong believe that as a result President Jiang became wary, later criticizing Zhu. President Jiang, who also heads the Communist Party apparatus, apparently feared a loss of Party authority. An internal debate raged at an annual top-level party conference at the oceanside resort of Beidaihe. An analysis in Hong Kong's *South China Morning Post* reported, "The leadership is facing its toughest test since the Cultural Revolution," and spoke of "the Party's inadequacy and perhaps even impending irrelevance."

The hard-liners, led by Jiang, came out on top in this dispute. In that period, Jiang was attempting to catapult his own persona into the pantheon of China's patriarchs like Mao and Deng. In the aftermath of the NATO bombing of the Chinese embassy in Belgrade, he personally whipped up nationwide protests, appealing to a base but deep-rooted nationalism, while projecting himself domestically as *the* Chinese leader who could stand up to the world. Soon, Falun Gong became another convenient "threat" with which to mobilize support inside the Party and the government. His campaign against Falun Gong was a useful way to further distract people from deepening economic problems and the slowdown in growth. "This conflict has always been about power, not principle," says one Falun Gong practitioner, "They know we are not a direct threat, but it is in their interest to make it appear that way. They are using us for their own purposes."

"The decision to crack down on Falun Gong was made by a few people at the top, at the urging of their more conservative advisors and ideologues," James Seymour told me. "Chinese Communist politics is impossible to predict. You just never know who's going to emerge. It's something that cannot be seen, the process cannot be observed from the outside world. And it's just a lot of people elbowing each other aside, and the tough guy will win. And unfortunately, that tough guy winning scenario does not produce benign leaders."

In July 1999, the leadership formally reversed the legal status of Falun Gong for the first time, denouncing it as an "evil cult." On July 22, the Chinese government announced its crackdown on Falun Gong with this announcement:

> The Department of Civil Affairs of the People's Republic of China
> declares that the Falun Dafa Research Society and the Falun Gong
> Organization under its control are illegal organizations that should be

banned. It is hereby prohibited for anyone in any circumstances to distribute books, video/audio tapes or any other materials that propagate Falun Dafa (Falun Gong). It is prohibited to hold gatherings or demonstrations that uphold or propagate Falun Gong such as sit-ins or appeals. It is prohibited for anyone to organize, coordinate, or direct any activities that go against the government.

An arrest order was then issued for Li Hongzhi, turning him in effect into Public Enemy #1. It read, in part: "Wanted for disturbing public order: Li Hongzhi; Gender: Male; Ethnicity: Han; Speaks Mandarin with a northeastern accent; Eyebrows slope to the middle of his brow." The government put up a $6000 reward for his capture. Interpol, the international police agency, refused to serve the warrant because there was no criminal wrongdoing and because they considered China's request blatantly political.

Up until that point, some high-level government officials had given assurances that Falun Gong could operate freely, while still others contradicted them by outlawing their activities. This is not unusual in China, where Party factions often vie for influence and control. The leadership conflict played itself out in different ways around the country, provoking practitioner protests in a number of cities. The party was being encouraged to crack down, even as Falun Gong was appealing to local officials to get off its back. Parts of the government claimed they were "under siege." Later, government officials cited 307 such "sieges" between April 25 and August. This figure was not reported by practitioners, nor confirmed by outside experts, but if true suggests the extent of Falun Gong's pervasiveness and strength. In all of these instances, Falun Gong was presumably appealing to the government to reconsider its hostility. But the pressure seems to have had the reverse effect. Authorities, unaccustomed to being challenged by their own people, became more suspicious, hostile, and then aggressive. "The Falun Gong movement was not originally political, and probably still isn't political, but it has taken on a political character simply because the government has decided to perceive it as political, and that has become a self-fulfilling prophecy," explains James Seymour.

According to a March 2000 report issued by Falun Gong practitioners, officials of the State Council were saying in June 1999 that there would be no punishment. At first this position was wrongly interpreted as an indication that political reforms were permitting more tolerance. But, while China's public face projected openness, a crackdown was being plotted behind the scenes at a higher level. Falun Gong practitioners say in the report that the Chinese government was "widely speculated to have been misled by some self-serving officials."

This pattern of tolerance in some quarters and hostility in others continued to intensify in the period before the crackdown. The People's

Liberation Army was the first institution to try to purge Falun Gong influence, according to one posting from China on a Falun Gong website:

> Inside the military force, the new rules of the Chinese Military Committee and the new regulation of the troops were widely announced. It is said in the document and regulation that "First of all, all the troop staff are forbidden to take part in practicing Falun Gong (including staff and workers, army family members, retired cadres, and army enterprise members). Second, it is forbidden to practice Falun Gong in the barracks. Third, it is forbidden for all military enterprises to print books of Falun Gong." In addition, units in various places monitored practitioners. All kinds of national news agencies went out of their way to make propaganda of the "Three Talks" and "Upholding Science, Breaking Superstition" education. Furthermore, under the manipulation of some governmental departments, a few mean people from Wuhan TV Station and a few plotters from Changchun colluded and fabricated a videotape called "An Exposé of Falun Gong." All of the above actions paved the way for the large-scale arrests of Falun Gong practitioners after July 19 and for the consequent ban of Falun Gong.

Falun Gong might have been temporarily spared the fate meted out to other groups deemed superstitious because it had friends and practitioners in military and intelligence bureaucracies. Later, some of these friends would reportedly tip them about the government's plans, and a few would even be tried and sentenced for "stealing state secrets."

* * *

Many outside observers didn't think Falun Gong would or could resist the crackdown. In the United States, the Chinese-language newspaper *World Journal* made a point that clearly reflected official thinking in Beijing: "With the force of the entire state machine against them, even if Falun Gong members number in the tens of millions, they will find it virtually impossible to resist."

"Many people, including myself, agreed with that sentiment at that time," admits long-time *People's Daily* journalist Liu Binyan in his *China Rights Forum* article. "I did not believe that Falun Gong would be totally exterminated but that it would become an underground movement. But the reality proved me wrong."

Liu was not the only one who was dismissive, assuming that state power would crush emerging people power. But two factors were missed: the growing boldness of the Chinese people as a whole, and the deep beliefs shared by Falun Gong practitioners. According to veteran

Guardian China-watcher John Gittings, "Falun Gong reflects a grassroots mood in China of greater assertiveness: interest groups, whether they be peasants complaining of corruption or laid-off workers seeking benefits they've been denied, are more prepared to protest. As Chinese society becomes more differentiated and more vocal, this is a growing trend with which the Communist Party has to come to terms."

Although non-political, Falun Gong members were willing to take to the streets. Ironically, many supported and even worked for the government. At all times, they considered themselves "good people." They sincerely believed they would be heard. The following Internet report provides insight into their collective consciousness:

> At the risky moment, Falun Gong practitioners took to the street to appeal to higher authorities with their benevolent hearts. They hoped that the government would see through the conspiracies and schemes of the very few people, would consider the facts and the will of Falun Gong practitioners, and would not be blinded by those people with ulterior motives. Unfortunately, the government regarded the genuine appeal from practitioners as opposition to the government.

The government saw the April "appeal" and subsequent mobilization as a threat, while Falun Gong viewed it as a right. As an Internet-circulated Falun Gong position paper explained, "In these practitioners' minds they did not believe it was wrong to report facts and express opinions to the central government directly. They believed that Falun Gong was beneficial to the country and the people and they were obligated to let the people know this. Moreover, in a socialist country, it is both the citizens' privilege and obligation to report truth to the government. They believed that the central government's leaders would carefully listen to their own people." Practitioners were apparently surprised by the government's reaction—which focused on the size of the vigil, not its content—and suggested that they could "have brought a million people if a massive show of force was their real goal."

Li Hongzhi himself made this point in a message he called "some thoughts of mine" on June 2, 1999, more than a month before the government acted to outlaw his practice. "In fact, the number of people who went [to Zhongnanhai] was not large at all. Think about it, everyone: There are over 100 million people practicing Falun Gong, and only over 10,000 people showed up. How can that be considered a large number? There was no need to mobilize practitioners. Among 100 million practitioners, since you wanted to go and he wanted to go, in a short while, over 10,000 people would be there. They did not have any slogans or any signs, nor was there any improper conduct. Furthermore, they were not against the government. They merely wished to present the facts to the government. What was wrong with that? Please allow me to ask: Have there ever been such well-behaved demonstrators? Shouldn't one be moved by such a sight?"

Nevertheless, the Chinese government saw the appeal as an omen, and a demonstration of Falun Gong's organizing ability. The leadership was reportedly further shocked when one of their own surveys confirmed that as many as 70 to 100 million Chinese citizens had taken up the practice. An analysis delved into who these people were and why they were attracted: "A high percentage of practitioners are highly educated intellectuals and officials from the Party, the government agencies, and the army . . . many of them have been searching so hard for a piece of land where 'superstition' and political struggle do not exist. To them Falun Gong is such a piece of pure land." For the record, the Party later downplayed these numbers, officially tallying Falun Gong's support at only two million.

The Chinese government insists that Li Hongzhi has been a major force in organizing the protests, even personally pulling the strings during the events of April 25. Li denies it: "The Chinese government has always believed that I have been behind all this. I want to state once again: I have not been involved in any of these activities." The government cites phone calls they tapped to prove Li was in China in the days before the protest, and Xinhua news agency claimed, "Li Hongzhi came to China in the capacity of a businessman but devoted his forty-four-hour stay here totally to planning the illegal gathering near Zhongnanhai." But Li says he was only in Beijing to change planes and was not in touch with any organizers. One astute practitioner pointed out that in government footage of an interview with a former practitioner that was used to "prove" Li's involvement with the protest, the video captions did not match what was actually being said.

"If the country really wants to eradicate Falun Gong, that's only because there are a great number of people who are practicing Falun Gong," Li Hongzhi told me. "Some reporters told me the number of people who are practicing outnumber the Communist Party members so the government is kind of nervous about it, but they shouldn't be." Li believed that the government should view his efforts positively in order to avoid negative consequences for the leadership itself. In his June 2 statement, he wrote:

> I, Li Hongzhi, unconditionally help practitioners improve their moral quality and keep people healthy, and this in turn stabilizes society. Additionally, with their healthy bodies, people can better serve society. Isn't this bringing good fortune to the people in power? In reality, this has indeed been achieved. Why, instead of recognizing this and showing me appreciation, do they want to estrange more than 100 million people from the government? . . . Furthermore, among these 100 million people, who doesn't have a family and children, relatives and

friends? Is it merely an issue of 100 million people? So the number of
people they are going against could be even more. What has actually
happened to the leadership of my beloved country?

To the leadership of his "beloved country," this line of thinking must
have sounded quite illogical and even naïve. China Central Television, the
official network, reported, "The practice of Falun Gong and its effects have
severely affected the stability of the entire country, as well as the proper
functioning of people's lives and work. The outcome of Falun Gong's
harmful effects and the widespread influence have brought about significant adverse impact on society."

At the heart of the government's concern is the implicit political chal-
lenge. Suisheng Zhao, who teaches about China at Colby College, told the
New York Times, "Logically they had to do this . . . For the Communist
Party, the greatest threat is a nationally organized force." Added Harvard's
Roderick MacFarquar, a senior China scholar, "The Party cannot allow the
existence of a rival mass organization with control over the hearts and souls
of the ordinary people—and exposing their own ideological vacuum." The
Los Angeles Times made this same point editorially late in December 1999:
"Falun Gong's true threat isn't to state security but to the Communist
Party's monopoly on power."

Writing in the Fall 1999 *Religion in the News*, a publication of the
American Enterprise Institute, Michael Lestz argues that the State's
response "is the Party's natural reaction to any form of dissent it interprets
as antagonistic. When the Party identifies a target for destruction, it readily flips into a Stalinist/Maoist mode of operation to isolate and destroy the
enemy . . . To destroy an 'antagonistic' ideology, you first need to prove that
it is immoral, a fraud, empty, heterodox, and especially destructive of the
good order provided by the State . . . The State's suppression of Falun Gong
has to do with a generalized intolerance of any group that flaunts itself in
the Party's face."

Jacques DeLisle, a law professor and member of the Foreign Policy
Research Institute, catalogued various reasons for the harsh government
reaction, emphasizing an economic factor that other analysts missed:

> The reform-era Chinese leadership has defined itself largely as direct-
> ing a developmental state, thereby claiming legitimacy on the basis
> of the rising levels of material prosperity that have been the defining
> achievement of the Deng and post-Deng era. Groups like Falun
> Gong point unnervingly to two possible weaknesses in this strategy.
> Most simply, the group's popularity among those who have not done
> particularly well under the reforms underscores the perils of betting
> too heavily on economic growth. Falun Gong's rapid ascension sug-
> gests that mechanisms could emerge quickly to channel and amplify

discontent arising from general or sectoral economic pain—hardly an idle worry for generally pro-reform leaders facing problems that include the unresolved plight of the losers in previous rounds of reform, the current leveling off of growth rates in even the booming coastal cities, and the soon-unavoidable costs of restructuring state-owned industries and banks . . . The apparent popular demand for Falun Gong could indicate dangerous stresses in the structure of "market-Leninism."

As resistance mounted, China's top leaders became more convinced that they were facing a political threat—and that they had to act decisively. In February, Hong Kong's *South China Morning Post* reported that "President Jiang Zemin has warned that the Falun Gong sect poses as much of a threat to the Communist Party as the Solidarity movement did to the Communists in Poland in the 1980s. In a discussion with senior aides, Mr. Jiang cited the Falun Gong movement, unemployed farmers and workers, and 'splittists' among ethnic minorities, as the most destabilizing factors in society. A source said yesterday that Mr. Jiang stressed the party must never underestimate the threat of the Falun Gong because of its 'ability to infiltrate society' and win the hearts and minds of the people."

In Poland, the Communist government declared martial law to try to crush Solidarity. Its repressive campaign failed. Yet how real a threat is Falun Gong to China's government? Not very, says David Holm, a Professor at the University of Melbourne in Australia, who is a specialist on popular religions in China. "It probably challenges the Party only so much at this point as the Party itself chooses to be challenged. This is not a movement which advocates either overthrow of the Communist Party or anything remotely like it." Other experts who have studied the issue say there is little substantiation of government claims that Falun Gong "uses illegal organizations to engage in political activities."

I spoke to one long-time member of the Chinese Communist Party about any conflict he may have felt between his Party and his Falun Gong practice:

Q: Is Falun Gong against the government?

A: Never thought about it. I am a Communist Party member. How can I be against the government or against the Communist Party?

Q: Have you been a member of the Communist Party for many years?

A: I've been a Party member for forty-seven years.

Q: Forty-seven years in the Communist Party. Are you trying to overthrow the Communist Party?

A: How can I overthrow myself? Overthrow myself? I don't understand.

At the same time, Falun Gong's resistance, as it deepens, in journalist Liu Binyan's well-informed perspective, "has far-reaching significance and will have a variety of social and political consequences." He believes the Chinese people as a whole will become more sympathetic to Falun Gong—not the government—the longer the confrontation continues. He views the government as ineffective and at risk because of its own behavior. "Recently Jiang Zemin said, 'I don't believe we can't deal with Falun Gong.' But when Chinese people used this construction, 'I don't believe/I can't . . . ' on the one hand they are indicating their determination to deal with the matters, and on the other, they are acknowledging that they face serious obstacles to achieving their aims." Most telling, he believes that Jiang "has picked up the stone which will crush his own foot; this campaign may be one of the factors which brings his rule to an end."

Some scholars offer a more negative scenario. In "The Mystery of China's Falun Gong," a pamphlet published by Singapore University Press, John Wong writes: "After the mass arrests and other tough government measures, it now seems clear that Falun Gong in China, either as a quasi-religious sect or as a social movement, has been effectively curbed . . . The sect is therefore set to decline in China." However, on June 26th, 2000, many months after that was written, Associated Press reported that 1,200 practitioners had been arrested in the previous week alone, dispelling any notion that an irreversible "decline" of Falun Gong had been set in motion.

Andrew Nathan, professor of political science at Columbia University and author of *China's Transition*, told China Online why he believed the government views Falun Gong as a threat: "The leaders are allergic to any kind of autonomous organization that they can't control, the bigger it is the worse . . . I of course have no personal knowledge of this, but approaching the issue from the standpoint of the CCP [Chinese Communist Party] leadership, they have no way of being sure that the group would not have ambitions that, to them at least, would seem political." When asked if he believed China's crackdown would be sucessful, he said he thought not because "the administrative methods available to the government are not effective in suppressing belief systems."

If that is the case and if the Communist Party cannot prevail, what will that mean for its own future? A number of commmentators have speculated that the unsuccesful crackdown poses more of a threat than Falun Gong itself. "The ban of Falun Gong is a mistake by the Chinese government and is a clear sign of its weakness and great fear," writes Sven Hansen for a German publicaton. Hansen continues:

What can people in China still believe in today? Surely not in the Communist Party. Their members have long ago betrayed their former ideals and would rather dedicate themselves to Deng Xiaoping's slogan: "Becoming rich is glorious." Earlier, in the times of civil war in the 1930s and 1940s, the Communist Party itself was a strong, moral power in comparison to the corrupt and increasingly degenerate reigning Kuo Min Tang. Cadres of the Communist Party used to be regarded as models who lived up to their ideals and did not indulge in materialism. This role, today, is claimed by Falun Gong.

So, in many ways it is capitalism in China that is exacerbating these tensions, not traditional Communism; most of the American media would prefer to avoid commenting on this. "Like it or not, the Falun Gong is a by-product of today's more materialistic China," the Hong Kong-based *South China Morning Post* noted in a recent editorial. "The collapse of the ideological basis for Communist rule in the rush towards a free-market economy has left a spiritual void."

Historically, spiritual movements and rebellions have shaken China and signaled the end of failing dynasties. That history has been cited in a variety of Western press accounts of Falun Gong, though Michael Lestz believes journalists were mostly misled on this point by China experts. "Throughout China's dynastic history," he writes, "religious groups following what the State considered to be 'heterodox' paths appeared at regular intervals. Most did not in any way threaten the State." Perhaps a stronger, but unmentioned, possibility is more universal—how non-violent activism has helped to bring down repressive regimes in many countries. When Martin Luther King Jr. mounted protests against racial segregation in America, he didn't do it only as a leader of black Baptists, although he was one. He was viewed primarily as a civil rights leader. Falun Gong praciti-tioners, however apolitical, have become de facto human rights activists.

* * *

For Falun Gong, defending its rights has become a battle, albeit a non-violent one. Denigrated and accused of crimes they haven't committed, they have become determined to prove their sincerity as "good people" and try to change the regime's position. Their resistance was not expressed solely in brave and quickly crushed public protests but also in unreported instances of resistance in institutions and workplaces throughout the country. Two examples are cases in point. Students and teachers resisted the crackdown on college campuses, as this appeal letter from students at Beijing's elite Qinghua University explained:

After the Chinese government denounced Falun Gong and made it illegal on July 22, 1999, some of our prominent members were requested to break away from Falun Gong, while the students were ordered to discontinue the practice and hand in Falun Gong books and materials. However, the majority of the student practitioners went on practicing. The university administration put most of the students who were determined in their practice of Falun Gong on suspension and forced them to go home after the Chinese government further declared Falun Gong an "evil religion." The university also asked parents to participate in transforming their children so as to "keep pace with the Central Communist Committee." At the same time, some of the teachers were either suspended from work for "introspection" or sent to "reform." These people could not resume their education or work unless they took a stand against Falun Gong and promised not to practice any more. Under pressure from both the university and parents, some of us wrote the "confession" unwillingly. Those who refused were put under house confinement to achieve "mind changing." [In April 2000, China announced it would not permit students who practice Falun Gong to take national exams, effectively ending their academic mobility.]

This Orwellian Big Brother "mind changing" was also resisted by workers. Chinese journalist Liu Binyan points to events in the Jiang'an Locomotive Factory in Wuhan, the scene of the renowned "February 7" strike launched by Communist Party members in the 1920s. So many workers there practiced Falun Gong that the government labeled it the "worst hit disaster area." Liu reports that elements of the working class, long championed in Communist theory, were opposing the state. "The crackdown . . . had little effect there," he explains. "As soon as workers who had been detained were released, they continued all of their activities. The authorities ordered the managers of the factory to re-educate those workers who are Falun Gong members, but that also did not change anything. Most of the Falun Gong members in the factory are known to be honest, hardworking people who are dissatisfied with the current social environment."

It is hard to know how widespread the resistance has been in other factories, because few reports have appeared in the press overseas or in China itself. But Falun Gong's resistance campaign is, like an iceberg, only partially visible above the surface. In May 2000, I spoke with a practitioner who had just returned from China. He said that many practitioners there are still active—but indoors, not in the parks.

After months of this assault, the Party began admitting publicly that it was failing to wipe out the practice. In November 1999, newspapers like the *People's Daily*, the mouthpiece of the Party, began speaking of a threat of "long-term" resistance that was not just confined to a handful of top leaders. In April 2000, a year after the Zhongnanhai protest, the official Xinhua news agency acknowledged that government attempts to wipe out Falun Gong had failed, stating, "the cult group led by Li Hongzhi has not recognized its defeat and continues to cause trouble." Agence France-Presse also quoted a Chinese official as saying that the "ongoing crackdown on the outlawed Falun Gong spiritual sect will be a long-term and complicated struggle."

Overseas commentators took note of Falun Gong's tenacity. "Falun Gong is being forced underground. But it's highly unlikely that its appeal will fade," noted a *Los Angeles Times* editorial in late December. "The strength of the movement is that it fills a need the regime refuses to address or even acknowledge. That all but guarantees its survival."

The deepening of this one-sided offensive is not a good omen for a peaceful resolution of the conflict. Instead of a dialogue, there has been a hardening of positions—with China officially brushing off all complaints about widespread human rights violations. Indeed, human rights groups say that 1999 was the most repressive year in China since 1989.

The danger for President Jiang, as English journalist John Gittings noted, "is that this campaign will be interpreted by Chinese as a sign of the Communist Party's weakness rather than its strength." Leaders have become concerned that Falun Gong represents a loss of allegiance to the Party, and they have acted to reassert a position of socialist superiority. On April 2, 2000, China's official media released the text of a January 14 speech by Jiang Zemin to Communist Party disciplinary officials, in which he stated, "We must cherish the socialist regime built upon the blood and sacrifices of countless martyrs."

Later the same month, a campaign was launched within the army to strengthen loyalty to the Party. Military analysts told the *South China Morning Post* that, in launching the campaign, President Jiang was particularly worried about the spread of Falun Gong in the ranks. But some experts have pointed out that such reactions from the government only make more clear its own failings. As a report by the International Institute for Strategic Studies noted in May 2000, "The [Falun Gong] sect's success at spreading its message at home and abroad, and the nervous and ham-fisted response by the regime, including Jiang Zemin personally, showed how far the Communist Party's capacity to control society had been diluted."

In New York, as the crackdown progressed, Li Hongzhi asked for international help, charging that the human rights of 100 million people were at risk. "I hope all the people who have a kind heart and the various governments will step in to assist in the resolution of this issue." At that time, the US government and the UN were silent. Human rights groups issued press releases but no demonstrations or solidarity meetings were called. Perhaps that's because the groups feel more comfortable supporting political dissidents than a spiritual movement. That's not true in the case of Tibet—but then Tibet is a very distinct issue, an exception to the rule, which Tibetans have spent years educating people in the West about. Falun Gong is new and not well understood.

After an initial period of waiting and watching, the human rights community did begin to speak out. Human Rights Watch criticized the crackdown as an illegal attempt to try to control all organizations—religious, civil, social, and economic. The group pointed out that "the number of members, their ability to organize, and their use of modern tools of communication have made Falun Gong especially threatening. Concerns about social instability, fed by . . . a stagnant rural economy and the demoralizing effects of pervasive unemployment, add to the leadership's need to ensure that the Chinese people's first loyalties remain with the Chinese Communist Party."

Human Rights Watch Director Ken Roth was passionate on the issue when I spoke with him, stating: "We are deeply concerned about the fate of the Falun Gong members. It's clear that some of them are facing quite severe abuse. There have been unconfirmed reports of torture, possibly even deaths in custody . . . It's clear that all the tools, all the weapons in the government's arsenal are being deployed to try to stop this seemingly innocuous popular collection of ordinary people who simply want to do their own thing, who don't . . . have an area of their life that the government doesn't control."

Amnesty International in London finally issued a detailed report on March 23, 2000, putting Falun Gong in the context of a broader crackdown on so-called "heretical organizations." The human rights organization was forthright:

> Amnesty International is calling on the Chinese government to stop the mass arbitrary detentions, unfair trials, and other human rights violations resulting from the crackdown on the Falun Gong and other groups branded by the government as "heretical organizations."

> All the information available indicates that the crackdown is politically motivated, with legislation being used retroactively to convict people on politically driven charges, and new regulations introduced to further restrict fundamental freedoms . . .

> Tens of thousands of Falun Gong practitioners have been arbitrarily detained by police, some of them repeatedly for short periods, and put under pressure to renounce their beliefs. Many of them are reported to have been tortured or ill-treated in detention . . .

> While it is difficult to estimate accurately the number of Falun Gong practitioners currently detained or imprisoned—notably due to the

continuous succession of arrests and releases—the information available indicates that the number is likely to be in the thousands. Some have been charged with crimes and tried, while others have been sent to labor camps without trial . . . Unfair trials have continued and arrests and detentions of practitioners continue to be reported every day. Amnesty International is concerned that the detention and prosecution of members of Falun Gong are politically motivated, and that many of those held in police custody, sent to labor camps without trial, or sentenced to prison terms under the Criminal Law are being held arbitrarily for the peaceful exercise of fundamental human rights. [More excerpts from this report are reprinted in Part II.]

China did not respond directly to the demands of, or documents amassed by, various human rights groups. It took a different approach. Inside China, Li Hongzhi was being demonized by a dawn-to-dusk slander campaign driven by propaganda TV shows and even a vicious, nationally distributed comic book. Some newspapers compared him to Adolf Hitler. In branding Falun Gong a "cult of evil," TV shows routinely feature excerpts from news footage of mass suicides by cults like the Jim Jones People's Temple. Images of cults in Japan and other countries are intercut with images of Falun Gong practitioners. The government then justifies its crackdown on the grounds that it is acting in the public interest to protect practitioners from a similar fate.

Li was never given a chance to respond to the relentless accusations: the perspective of loyal practitioners was simply not covered in the Chinese media. "I feel sorry that the Chinese government has taken such steps," Li told me. "But whatever the Chinese government will do, I'm not going to oppose the government and I don't want to get involved in politics. They can be unfair to us but we can never treat others with the same approach."

I asked Li if he thought he represented a threat to the Chinese government. He responded: "Maybe they have seen me as a threat, but this is because they do not understand me well enough. For this I cannot blame them. If they have felt threatened by Falun Gong for so long, then why haven't they contacted me in the first place and contacted me directly? If we had communicated directly, we could have eliminated misunderstanding before it started. If we had done something wrong I could have corrected it, I could mend it."

* * *

Each week seems to bring new charges and new claims from both sides of the struggle. Falun Gong books are banned and burned, a process which has continued for months. On October 21, 1999, a stepped-up crackdown reportedly seized a total of 7.8 million books and 4.9 million videotapes in the Chinese cities of Wuhan and Jinan alone. The army and the police have rounded up many practitioners, even forcing them into detention in stadiums, a chilling parallel with the aftermath of the coup in Chile years earlier. (Fortunately, the captives were not murdered or "disappeared" as they were in Pinochet's Chile.)

The brutality of Chinese police and security forces is well-known, and even admitted by high-level officials. On November 4, 1999, Li Peng, the second-in-command of the Communist Party, denounced corruption by the police as well as "unjust enforcement of the law, illegal handling of cases, crimes committed during law enforcement, and a brutal work style." Two days later, Cabinet Secretary Li Bing insisted that "there have been no beatings or inhumane treatment." On the previous day, Falun Gong had reported that in just one city, 500 practitioners had been sent to re-education–through–labor camps, where the accused can be sentenced to up to three years without trial.

Throughout the winter and spring of 2000, China's repression escalated along with Falun Gong's resistance. In April 2000, the Chinese government acknowledged that protests by Falun Gong practitioners in Tiananmen Square had been near-daily occurrences since July 22, 1999, when Falun Gong was officially banned. According to human rights groups, 35,000 people in all were arrested in the Beijing area alone from July to December 1999. In one week in February 2000, during the Chinese New Year, 2,000 people were arrested; then in June 2000, another 1,200 practitioners were arrested in a single week. While many of those arrested were released and sent back to their home provinces, others were held in various forms of detention and some were sentenced to long prison terms. Several Americans and Australians were swept up in the net. Some were held but most were released, while the Chinese practitioners faced crueler treatment.

People have been imprisoned on charges of "illegal business practices" for selling Falun Gong publications, even books that had been officially approved by the government. The parents of two managers of a Beijing bookstore overseen by China's Ministry of Culture drafted a detailed point-by-point appeal challenging the fairness and legality of their sentences of six and seven years in prison. "Finding them guilty of a crime is an illegal judgment and we will not accept it," the parents state in their appeal, which was published in *China Rights Forum* in Spring 2000. They add this personal detail which in many ways tells the story of agony and confusion of so many in China with the crackdown:

> Our daughters Li Xiaomei and Li Xiaobing were born and grew up in
> the military and we took care of them throughout their upbringing.
> They also worked in the countryside as sent down youth. They have

good hearts and are generous to others, and neither have any criminal intentions or carried out any illegal activity. As we are both retired veteran cadres, we wonder was the purpose of our revolution nothing more than penalizing good, ordinary people? What has happened to this society? Will this kind of judgment stand the test of history?

In April 2000, the government stated that 2,591 Falun Gong–related cases were being processed in the courts. Of those, ninety-nine had concluded, resulting in eighty-four sentences. At the same time, human rights groups said that at least 5,000 practitioners were being held in re-education camps. Many practitioners from the provinces who travel to Beijing are reportedly held under Custody and Repatriation, a form of administrative detention that can last up to several months and does not require the detainee to be charged with any crime. There are many accounts of what has happened to those arrested, written by the prisoners themselves and then posted on Falun Gong websites (some of which appear in Part II). Here is one typical testimonial:

> The guards dragged all of us out while beating and kicking us madly. They dragged us to the yard downstairs and ordered us to squat down. Then they ordered us one-by-one into a room and conducted a thorough body search. Later we were separately detained in different cells with criminals. I was assigned to the sixth cell. I found a practitioner from Jiangxi in that cell, plus six criminals. One of the criminals immediately came over with a bowl of cereal and persuaded me to eat. She said that this was the task assigned to them and they would be punished if they could not succeed in persuading us to eat. I said that I would tell the guards that it had nothing to do with them. After a short while, the officer in charge of female prisoners came over and asked whether I had eaten or not, and threatened to fill me with salt water if I refused to eat. The inmates all told me that it was a very terrible thing to be filled with salt water. Meanwhile, I heard someone screaming in another cell. They told me that it must be someone being filled with salt water. The officer then ordered four to five male criminals to come over. One of them carried a tool for filling salt water, which is a long glass tube attached with a soft and thin tube and some other stuff. I sat on the ground and was close to the wall. The officer approached me and asked whether I still refused to eat. I asked him why I was arrested since I had not committed any crime; and up to now I had not seen the arrest certificate. He became extremely angry and kicked my right breast heavily, yelling, "Who do you think you are?" He then said to the criminals, "Fill her with salt water."

Several male criminals came over and dragged me on the ground to the door, pushed me down, and put shackles on me. I felt somebody squeezing my nose and I could not breathe. Then something big was squeezed into my mouth. My mouth was immediately full of salt water. Since I could not breathe I had to swallow. It was high-density salt water. My throat felt like what I swallowed were all grains of salt, or a lot of salt plus a tiny bit of water. I wanted to struggle but my hands and feet were forcefully held. I could not move at all. After a long time, I still heard the officer order, "Fill more." I thought that I would suffocate to death if they continued to do that. After another three to four minutes, they let me go. But I could not breath freely for a long time. I felt like I would be suffocated to death. Then my stomach felt terrible. I wanted to drink water. I could not speak. My inmates held a bowl of cereal and fed me. But after a short while, all the cereals were thrown up. I had to constantly drink water and throw up. My clothes were full of water and dirty stuff. Ms. Ye could not help crying upon seeing me like that.

Practitioners have lost jobs, property, and even their homes when neighbors are ordered to spy and report on them. Their mail has been censored, e-mails checked and blocked, and phone calls monitored. Some practitioners have been forced to make daily reports of their activities to local police stations. Supporters of Falun Gong reportedly have also been assigned "guarantors," usually family members, who are held responsible if the practitioners go to Beijing to appeal. Family members who do not practice Falun Gong have in that way been fired from their jobs or dismissed from school. Even a judge and a policeman were arrested in February for covertly practicing Falun Gong.

As the crackdown progressed, authorities came up with a new tactic: throwing those they arrested into mental hospitals, like the Russians used to do with their dissidents. Official media reports cited unnamed doctors at the Beijing University School of Medical Science to the effect that "since 1992, the number of patients with psychiatric disorders caused by practicing Falun Gong has increased markedly to 10.2 percent of all patients suffering from mental disorders caused by practicing qigong exercises." That number supposedly increased to 42.1 percent by 1999. Accounts from inside the hospitals are chilling, including this one from Huang Jinchun, a former judicial officer from Beihai, Guangxi Province:

On November 15, two police officers came to my home and asked me to go with them. Assuming that it might just be another routine interrogation, I followed them. However, they drove me directly to the Long-xiang-shan Mental Hospital in the Zhuang Nationality Autonomous Region of Guang-xi Province. I asked them why they sent me here. They said, "It is the order of the officials of Department of Public Security. They want you to take a rest here for a few days."

Since then, I have been detained in this mental hospital. This is a medical institute of forced treatment. If the patient does not comply, the staff members will resort to violence by beating or roping the patient. Only those patients who have been in the hospital for a long time are allowed to be outside in the fresh air for two hours every day. After I was detained, I was forced to take medicines and injections. I asked the doctors and nurses why they treated me like that as I did not have any mental or physical illnesses nor had they conducted any medical examinations on me. They asked, "then how come you end up here if you have no illnesses?" I told them that I was sent here by the police officers. They then said, "that means that you have illnesses; otherwise, they would not send you here." I felt this was really ridiculous.

There are no longer working ethics in the hospital. If the police send a person to the hospital, then that person is deemed to have illnesses with no need for medical examinations. When the medicines were taking effect, I felt very weak all over my body. I felt sleepy and anxious for days. The doctors and nurses even made fun of me: "Aren't you practicing Falun Gong? Let us see which is stronger, Falun Gong or our medicines."

The use of psychiatric institutions to involuntarily imprison Falun Gong practitioners is becoming an international issue. The American Psychiatric Association, at its May 2000 meeting in Chicago, discussed this concern. The Committee on Misuse and Abuse in Psychiatry unanimously passed a resolution asking that the American Psychiatric Association leadership request the World Psychiatric Association to investigate this problem. That body's intervention helped end a similar practice in the Soviet Union in the 1970s and '80s.

Dr. Abraham Halpern, a professor emeritus of psychiatry at New York Medical College and a former civil rights activist who worked with Dr. Martin Luther King Jr. in Alabama in 1965, has taken the lead. He told me that he believes "the [Chinese] government needs to hospitalize, wrongfully, non–mentally ill dissidents because this will help them in their effort to paint the Falun Gong practitioners as not being against government policy, but as being mentally ill. So even if they were to hospitalize a small number, word would soon spread that Falun Gong practitioners are crazy."

He is calling on his colleagues worldwide to speak out. "Deliberate hospitalization, wrongful hospitalization, is only part of the problem. They then make it very difficult for the practitioners to get out of the hospital by demanding that their families pay exorbitant amounts of money for their 'treatment' in the hospital. So there's no question that this type of conduct, government-sanctioned, is a serious violation of human rights. And we'd like to stop it early rather than wait until large numbers of dissidents are placed in the hospitals, as occurred in the case of Soviet Union."

* * *

The death toll of detainees continues to rise. According to foreign media reports, by September 2001, at least 270 practitioners had died in government custody due to beatings or hunger strikes. The Information Center for Human Rights and Democratic Movements, a Hong Kong–based human rights group, claimed that one practitioner, who was in a coma following beatings, was forcibly removed from the hospital and brought to a crematorium. The group believes it is possible he was still alive while he was cremated. The *Wall Street Journal* ran an exposé on April 20, 2000, of a fifty-eight-year-old woman, Chen Zixiu, who was beaten and tortured to death in prison, all the while refusing to denounce Falun Gong. Her daughter, a non-practitioner who had been interviewed by the *Wall Street Journal*, was later arrested, but soon released, apparently because of media attention.

Torture of detained practitioners appears to be officially sanctioned and is reportedly widespread. According to statements from detainees, means of persecution and torture vary, ranging from physical abuse (such as denying food, sleep, and the use of a toilet, exposure to extreme hot or cold weather, forced labor, forced feeding of those on hunger strike, beating, dragging by hair, etc.) to torturing with instruments like lighted cigarettes, electric batons, and handcuffs. Chen Zixiu had been severely beaten and made to run barefoot through the snow before she died. According to the *Wall Street Journal* account of her death: "Two days of torture had left her legs bruised and her short black hair matted with pus and blood . . . She crawled outside, vomited, and collapsed. She never regained consciousness." In a statement to the UN Committee Against Torture, the Chinese government later denied that Falun Gong practitioners had been tortured, saying that Chen Zixiu had died of a heart attack.

James Seymour, who has written a book about Chinese prisons, was not surprised to hear these stories:

> To some extent the police in China are out of control. But of course, they are, in a way, following the signals that are sent down from above. Now officially there have been something like 2,500 cases of individuals who are undergoing the judicial procedures. But, of course, for everybody who gets his case in court, there are many other cases that are just sort of handled by the local precinct. So we're probably dealing with thousands. And we have confirmed information on a dozen

or so people who have been killed, and the government admits this—they say that they were suicides or natural deaths, but at any rate Falun Gong people who have died in prison. And probably many more that we don't know about. There is a lot of this that goes on, a lot of abuse in Chinese prisons and jails.

Thirteen or more practitioners have been tried for "stealing state secrets," a notoriously vague charge that can be applied in a very subjective manner and is often used against political dissidents. The Information Center for Human Rights and Democratic Movements put this charge in perspective: "The so-called 'state secrets' that Falun Gong members disseminated are fundamentally different from the true classified state information. Those 'state secrets' are all related to the secret plans and police orders that the government used to crack down on Falun Gong. Making such secret orders is by itself against the Chinese constitution, because the government encourages the police to go by direct 'secret orders' rather than by the law. Such conduct of 'power bypassing the law' is against the Chinese constitution."

Public announcements, like this one posted on the Internet and alleged to be issued by the local Committee of the Communist Party in a rural village, have been used to threaten practitioners:

Comrade Villagers,

The Falun Gong "organization" has been charged with the crime of "overturning the state power" by the authorities, and whoever refuses to give up Falun Gong will be deemed as a criminal. According to the principle set by the authorities, from now on, any Falun Gong practitioner who has gone out of town to appeal to any governmental department beyond the township and to make trouble will be fined 10,000 yuan after being escorted back by the police. His/Her water supply, electricity, and telephone will be cut off. All his/her certificates will be confiscated too.

He/She will be severely punished by law. All backbone members of Falun Gong must write a pledge of breaking up with XXX and Falun Gong, turn in their ID cards, and pay a deposit of 5,000 yuan. The township government will hold a class for those who refuse to break up with the Falun Gong "organization" until they write the pledge and pay the deposit in full.

If one refuses to break up with Falun Gong, the police department will confiscate all his/her certificates issued by the state. Moreover, the village will not issue any certificates to him/her, or provide any service. All his/her directly-related family members will be expelled from

school, kindergarten, or state-run workplace until he/she breaks up
with Falun Gong.

Committee of Xiao-jia Village
December 18, 1999
(With Official Seal)

Officials have even tried to control the activities of practitioners overseas
as they become increasingly organized and outspoken. For example, in April
2000, over 1,500 practitioners gathered for an experience-sharing conference
in the imperial ballroom of the Sheraton Hotel in New York. At lunch, the
whole crowd performed Falun Gong exercises for the media and onlookers,
while both Chinese and English speakers described the personal benefits they
derived from the practice and denounced arrests of practitioners in China.

One woman's description of her experience in a cold and crowded
Beijing jail cell brought members of the audience to tears. The conference
itself worried Chinese officials, and managers of the Sheraton Center were
approached directly by two Chinese consular officials—Qu Zhongwen, the
Consul, and his Vice Consul, Zheng Lu—who boldly urged them to cancel
the event. The officials even sent a package of official propaganda to the
hotel, including a videotape and CD-roms in English called *Falun Gong:
Cult of Evil*, along with a 150-page booklet on Li Hongzhi's "heretical fallacies." Organizers shrugged at the crudeness of the attempt and the hotel went
ahead with a lucrative booking, which packed its biggest ballroom. A day
later, an American practitioner who had allowed his e-mail address to be used
for public contact, said that someone in China had targeted his computer
with a "mail bomb"–style attack, which consists of flooding an e-mail
account with thousands of messages as a means to disable the target account
and/or network. The administrators responsible for the China-based service
provider that launched the attack did not reply to requests to have the attack
stopped, and eventually the site was blocked by US administrators.

The trials, detentions, sentences, and harassment of Falun Gong practitioners have been denounced internationally as substituting political criteria for legal standards. As the group Human Rights in China pointed out in
a December 1999 statement: "There are no checks and balances on law-
makers and no effective way of challenging government-imposed regulations, even those so overly vague and broad as to be inherently arbitrary." In
addition, the Chinese government has violated international human rights
covenants to which they are a signatory, including the International
Covenant on Civil and Political Rights and the International Covenant on
Economic, Social, and Cultural Rights. By depriving citizens of their rights
to freedom of religion, freedom of assembly, freedom of speech, and freedom from torture and unlawful detention, the Chinese government is making plain their disregard for basic international human rights standards.

Nonetheless, China's crusade against Falun Gong has taken a toll. It has forced many practitioners underground and caused others, for survival, to disavow any affiliation, and in some instances to confess to prescripted statements drafted by government propagandists. In Hong Kong, a year after the crackdown began, one group of practitioners became divided, with a small number breaking away in a doctrinal dispute. Some journalists in China reported that a hardcore activist group had taken over power. Yet, as in all movements for change, external pressure can lead to more internal fortitude.

In Falun Gong's case, a strong sense of moral purpose and spiritual community has, in many cases, strengthened practitioners' commitment. Internationally, as overseas Chinese and others become involved in what had been a domestic phenomenon, the dimensions of the problem for the government, as well as opportunities for Falun Gong, have grown as well. The Internet has become a tool for sharing information and reinforcing a sense, albeit virtual, that Falun Gong is a force that will not be crushed, which is why Chinese authorities repeatedly target its websites. Like the Chinese Communists themselves, who after repeated batterings by opponents only got stronger, Falun Gong will not give up easily. It is rooted in that same tradition.

This commitment has not gone unnoticed by China scholars like Barend ter Haar, who posted the following on his University of Heidelberg website:

> The continued perseverance of Falun Gong adherents/practitioners even inside the People's Republic of China in publicly expressing their resistance to the prohibition and persecution of their movement is remarkable, and easily (mis-)understood as fanaticism. I would hesitate to apply this label, given its obvious negative associations and because I do not know how to objectively measure "fanaticism" independently of our own preconceptions . . . [Falun Gong's] public expression reflects the urban and text-based nature of the movement, which more or less prescribes this form of visible resistance.

Yet as the crackdown has intensified, and as Falun Gong has continued to fight back, most of the world still looks on without saying much, and doing even less.

Years ago, journalists cited a lack of access as reason for not reporting on certain sensitive stories from China, like what went on behind prison walls. It took the courage of former prisoner Harry Wu to courageously slip back into the country to spotlight conditions in the gulags. But today, thanks to the Internet, revealing stories about what is happening in China are increasingly available and often can be confirmed.

And yet they aren't widely disseminated.

Why?

CHAPTER 7
THE MEDIA COVERAGE

How much of this story made its way into the press? And how has it been reported? There was scant coverage in the West until the protest in Beijing in April 1999, which got play as a one-day story. But it was only after the Chinese government banned Falun Gong and began persecuting practitioners that it was certified "a real story."

While I believe the US media has not given Falun Gong the attention it deserves, I also acknowledge that I rely on this same media as a primary source in the Falun Gong story. When following developments of the story within China, I have no choice in this. Nonetheless, it is my view that US journalists have largely failed to provide in-depth, consistent, and objective reports on Falun Gong; wars and confrontations are media genre that rate ongoing coverage. European wire services like Agence France-Presse (AFP) and Reuters were way ahead of the American news outlets, but their copy is not heavily used by large US newspapers. Partly that's a function of overall shrinking coverage of international stories in the American media, and partly a problem of access.

But in this case perhaps there was another factor involved—a conscious decision by media executives to downplay stories that upset the Chinese government.

Years ago, media mogul Rupert Murdoch dropped BBC from one of his satellites over China for that very reason. He reiterated his stance on this issue in a speech on May 23, 2000, at a conference on doing business in Asia. While his focus was primarily on his movie business, the implications for news are clear, as is his economic interest in China. "We can strike a balance by deferring to our host's views into what we may broadcast in countries in which we are guests, while refusing to distort what we are able to broadcast," he stated. "If a film is unacceptable in a country in which we operate, we don't show it. If a TV program covers forbidden ground, we will have no choice but to delete it from our broadcast." The reasons for his willingness to censor his own progamming? "My own company, News Corporation, has been engaged in China for some two decades. We acquired Star TV in 1993, and have built a business from zero revenues to one enjoying total revenues of $200 million . . . We have key sports rights and have extensive local content production producing and commissioning over 9,000 hours of contemporary programming in greater China every year. And we have unique distribution on mainland China."

Other executives share similar perspectives. On September 28, 1999, in the midst of the Falun Gong crackdown, Sumner Redstone, who was about to merge the giant Viacom corporation with CBS, was in Shanghai for a conference organized by the US-based *Fortune Magazine* and keynoted by President Jiang Zemin. To the delight of the Beijing government, Redstone called for American press restraint in the coverage of China. The media, he said, should report the truth but avoid being "unnecessarily offensive" to foreign governments. "As they expand their global reach, media companies must be aware of the politics and attitudes of the governments where we operate . . . Journalistic integrity must prevail in the final analysis. But that doesn't mean that journalistic integrity should be exercised in a way that is unnecessarily offensive to the countries in which you operate," he said.

Signals like this by leaders of the American media industry set the tone for news coverage and are viewed as an indication of what resources will be devoted to that coverage. Redstone, like Murdoch before him, was predictably silent on human rights abuses in China. Earlier, human rights advocates had formally appealed to business leaders who planned to attend the *Fortune* conference to speak out on the issue. They didn't. Falun Gong practitioners were then in prison, but their plight was not discussed or reported upon at this media-organized event. Ironically, the Chinese then brazenly censored a *Time* magazine special on China, published by Time-Warner, the same company that paid for the event. As one news report explained, "the edition, whose masthead was emblazoned with the headline 'China's Amazing Half-Century,' fell foul of Chinese censors by including articles written by exiled dissidents Wei Jingsheng, Wang Dan, and the Tibetan Dalai Lama."

Falun Gong's perspective was often missing from news stories, not only after Chinese practitioners were silenced, but also for institutional reasons and due to the structure of overseas news coverage. Few news organizations solicit comments in the United States for China-based stories. So if voices are silenced in China, they are rarely heard because what human rights groups or Falun Gong followers overseas report is not usually considered part of a China-correspondent's beat.

Another problem has to do with language, and how stories are framed. In the case of Falun Gong, many news outlets, perhaps unconsciously, used the very same language that the Chinese state media used—labeling Falun Gong a cult or a sect, and sometimes both in the same story. One Reuters story didn't know how to identify them so used the term "mishmash." (A Chinese practitioner asked me what the word meant.) In England, after a complaint was filed with a press oversight body regarding the use of the term "cult," an editor told me with a chuckle, "Well, we just voluntarily stopped using it. Then we just began calling them a sect."

Human Rights Watch Director Ken Roth told me that "the American press doesn't know quite what to call Falun Gong. It's not a religion. It's not really just an exercise group. It's some kind of mystical combination of things that doesn't fit into an easy label. And so perhaps out of laziness, many Western journalists have simply started using the Chinese government's terminology, which is that of cult. It's another example—if you repeat a lie often enough, it's taken as the truth. And that's something that's happening."

Falun Gong supporters actively sought to encourage media outlets to use less pejorative language and a more neutral tone. Sometimes they were successful. In one instance, the early edition of the Sunday *New York Times* carried a front-page reference to Falun Gong as a "cult." A timely phone call with an explanation to an attentive editor led to a change to "spiritual practice" for the late and more widely circulated edition. The group's volunteer media team in New York were dismayed when the Chinese media would not seek out their views, but even more piqued when the US media paid only scant attention or ran poorly researched stories.

United States coverage has also been limited by problems of access that still exist for foreign journalists in China. (In February 2000, for example, when 20,000 laid-off miners rioted for days in a northeastern Chinese city, setting fire to cars and looting and destroying public property, it took a month for the story to trickle down to foreign media circles in Beijing.) When reporting on the Chen Zixiu torture case, the *Wall Street Journal* relied on accounts smuggled out of jail by fellow inmates, allowing the paper unusual access to heavily guarded information. This story made page one of the *Journal* but I have seen few similar accounts based on interviews with practitioners and their families. The *Journal* demonstrated that this type of reporting is possible, even if it is very difficult for journalists whose activities are frequently monitored and with whom many Chinese are afraid to speak.

So it is not easy to report on human rights in China, and the situation is made more complicated when Western news agencies put business interests above their journalistic responsibilities. Beatrice Turpin, a producer for Associated Press Television News (APTN), believes her committment to covering the Falun Gong story led to her dismissal and subsequent expulsion from China. She wrote her story as a whistle-blower for the MEDIAchannel.org website:

> The question of why APTN acted in such a horrendous fashion toward me raises some troublesome points. First, APTN has major business interests in China. Apart from selling contracts to various Chinese television stations (all government-controlled) to use APTN material from other parts of the world, the APTN Beijing office had earlier managed to convince the government and Chinese Central

Television (CCTV) to organize satellite feeds directly from the APTN bureau. In the past, all broadcasters and agencies were obliged to take a long trip to the western part of Beijing in order to do satellite feeds. Reuters has since been granted this privilege also, but APTN was first, giving it an obvious commercial advantage.

Another worrying element is a conversation I overheard in the APTN Beijing office while I was still employed there. A marketing executive had stated that the new APTN policy was to concentrate on broadcast services and business more than on news. Why was APTN so reluctant to stand up for me in the face of police harassment? Why did they deny that a problem even existed? The only possible answer, as I see it, is that they feared that this would negatively affect their business interests in China.

Later, APTN, which had promised to sell footage of Falun Gong's secret press conference in Beijing to Falun Gong for a documentary, reversed itself without explanation.

CNN did take the Falun Gong story seriously, covering the crackdown, but often with what appeared to be Chinese TV–supplied footage. The network showed practitioners in detention in stadiums, but without any interviews or explanatory background. Again, it was a one-day story with little follow-up. ABC's *Nightline* offered a half-hour report just after the crackdown in July 1999, which was probably the longest single program about Falun Gong on American TV that year. Spokesperson Erping Zhang was invited on the show along with a Chinese official who refused to be interviewed in the same segment. The show's host, Ted Koppel, seemed peeved that Li Hongzhi, then in hiding after rumors circulated that hit-men were on the way from China to track him down, was not available.

Zhang thought he would get a chance to appeal for help for those detained in China, but host Koppel stopped him, aggressively going after him on other issues. He focused on whether or not Zhang would go to the hospital if he were sick, picking up on a typical charge made by the Chinese government and, it appeared, seeking to discredit the movement or unmask a fanatic. When Falun Gong's spokesperson tried to bring the conversation back around to the crackdown, Koppel told him curtly that he would decide what subjects could be discussed.

The Chinese official was treated far kindlier, with Koppel pressing him to allow ABC News more access to the story. The official seemed most upset with Falun Gong's alleged threat to social order. "They have mobilized so-called demonstrations throughout the country in all thirty cities. They are interrupting traffic, blocking traffic and social order," he steamed.

* * *

The Western media initially covered the story as one of repression, not resistance. Few journalists followed it with any regularity and even most of the alternative media seemed uninterested. The United Nations Correspondents Association did invite Falun Gong supporters to present their views over the objection of Chinese diplomats. The *New York Times* sent a photographer and a correspondent to the event but nothing appeared in the paper. CNN, however, did cover the press conference.

In late October 1999, this minimal coverage pattern began to change when Falun Gong practitioners in China, reacting to an imminent decision by the Chinese Parliament to officially brand Falun Gong a cult, decided on a more aggressive course of action. They mounted daily protests in Tiananmen Square and dramatically called a secret press conference, an unusual event in China. The story broke on the front page of the *New York Times*, which reported that "a far wider and more profound confrontation appears to be building between clearly unnerved authorities and an uncrushed movement that, with astonishing speed, drew in millions of ordinary, seemingly non-political Chinese, creating an unexpected challenge to Communist authority." (An insider at AP in New York confessed to me later that his organization had missed covering several days of protests. "We blew it," he confided.)

The *New York Times* reported that "The group's defiance continued Friday morning, as followers, unbowed by tighter security, staged two protests around Beijing's Tiananmen Square. Plainclothes and uniformed police immediately tackled the protesters, with at least one being dragged by her hair. China's Communist Party, meanwhile, promised it would show no mercy to what it now called 'the devil cult.' The fervor and flair for secret organization displayed at the news conference underscored the difficulties the government faces in eradicating the Falun Gong."

In response to the press conference, the police mounted a massive manhunt, tracking down the location and ultimately arresting some of the principals. But they didn't stop there. Five Western reporters who covered the unprecedented October 28 event had their press accreditation cards seized and were warned against covering illegal events.

One journalist described what happened:

> The police reaction to the press conference was organized and, unfortunately, efficient. Journalists known to have covered the event were followed everywhere, making further contact with Falun Gong members or work on other sensitive topics almost impossible. A few days later, five of the journalists present at the press conference were called in for an interrogation worthy of a bad spy novel. We were placed in one of various rooms accessed by a long corridor, and the police

demanded that we describe to them in detail the circumstances surrounding the Falun Gong's audacious attempt at reaching out to the world. Our papers were confiscated and I, for one, was again threatened with expulsion. I continued to refuse to cooperate.

Foreign journalists in China were caught off-guard, and began bickering among themselves about whether or not to name the Falun Gong practitioners who put themselves at risk by organizing the clandestine press conference. Reported Oliver August of London's *Sunday Times*:

> Chinese authorities are trying to exploit differences of opinion among foreign journalists over how to report the Falun Gong crackdown to justify the arrest of members of the spiritual movement . . . Followers interviewed by journalists have asked to be identified by name to demonstrate their determination. Journalists working for the *New York Times*, Reuters, and other media have named the followers, possibly risking their imprisonment. Other correspondents have sharply attacked the practice. One Chinese official said: "This only proves how divisive Falun Gong can be . . . Even the foreign journalists cannot agree how to deal with this group . . . They obviously want to be arrested to become martyrs. Journalists are their tool."

In an open letter to Beijing-based correspondents, Floris-Jan van Luyn, of the Dutch newspaper *NRC Handelsblad*, wrote: "Some Falun Gong members might have requested their names to be used but I believe that we as foreign journalists should more seriously consider the risk of complete openness." He considered the practitioners "naïve."

These journalists were united, however, when it came to responding to Chinese threats against *them*. The Foreign Correspondents Club of China issued a statement condemning "intimidation and harassment . . . Our members have been followed, detained, interrogated, and threatened," it said. "We find this worrisome and unacceptable," they wrote in a letter to the Foreign Ministry and Cabinet press spokesman. "Such harassment is completely out of line with international practice. It impedes our legitimate journalistic work and violates the private lives of our members and their families." Some Chinese officials argued that because Falun Gong is illegal, journalists shouldn't cover it.

While the coverage whipsawed between the protests and the reaction, Falun Gong adherents in other countries began to travel to China to get involved. Like the Mississippi officials who during the 1960s civil rights movement in the United States told "outside agitators" to mind their own business and stay home, China denounced interference in its "internal affairs." Few media outlets drew this parallel, or any parallel with other non-violent movements—in America, India, or South Africa—that resisted police violence.

All too often, this story has continued to be played as "China vs. the Cult," although when Americans were arrested, local US media outlets offered a home-town angle that humanized the issue in a way that most daily news reports did not. This was the case when a Chinese-American practitioner, an airline stewardess, was detained after taking a photo of practitioners in Tiananmen Square.

* * *

Meanwhile, in China, the government-controlled media has been particularly egregious in ignoring and distorting the crackdown. A constant procession of reports has claimed that various sectors of Chinese society are rallying behind the government to condemn cults. Government officials who abandoned Falun Gong are widely quoted; one typical comment embraced the Party line: "The Party's decision is very wise, very correct, and very timely." (See Chapter 12 for a detailed analysis of the Chinese media's coverage of the crisis.)

When the crackdown was first announced in July, articles about Falun Gong dominated the media; in the *People's Daily* on one typical day there were four stories about Falun Gong on the front page and four more with criticism and confessions of practitioners on the second page, as well as an entire page of anti–Falun Gong photographs. "I see but do not hear," one shop clerk told the *South China Morning Post* about similar television news reports. "They have been doing this daily for two weeks, saying the same things again and again. We are numbed."

UCLA China scholar Tomas DuBois reported from Tianjin on the H-ASIA listserv that the propaganda campaign was not working: "This campaign is very closely modeled on the 1951 campaign against Yiguandao, which was directed at a more credulous population. What I have seen in Tianjin (Tianjin remains one of the centers of the teaching), however, is open cynicism towards the campaign itself. Everyone seems to know someone (brother, cousin, neighbor) who follows Falun Gong, and most insist that it is just a form of qigong. Innocent inquiries such as 'I see Falun Gong is in the news again' are answered by often bitter tirades about the campaign itself. Many even accuse the government of launching the campaign as a way of directing public attention away from more pressing problems at home. In other words, it has been written off by many as a political tool and is at least considered highly suspect by many more."†

---

†There has been no survey of Chinese public opinion on this subject, but an e-mail poll of Chinese in America conducted by the Michigan-based Voices of Chinese website found that the overall view of respondents regarding the Chinese government's actions toward Falun Gong leans toward the negative: "Twenty-five percent of the respondents stipulated that the government should take other alternative approaches to solve the problems with Falun Gong. People commented that the government over-reacted to Falun Gong, and the government should adopt more

Nevertheless, the government's efforts were hardly a total failure, as Phillip Cunningham, an American journalist with extensive China experience, explained in a letter from Beijing published on MEDIAchannel.org:

> Students on Beijing campuses who I have spoken to about this are generally critical of the cult and repeat things they've heard on TV about how dangerous it is. But one sarcastically remarked that "they must be doing something right to get this kind of attention." There has been a relentless media barrage on the evils of Falun Gong in the state-controlled media, sometimes dominating the entire news hour, pre-empting all other national and international coverage. TV viewers of the respectable CCTV evening news at 7:00 have been shown mutilated corpses of alleged Falun Gong–inspired suicides, tearful denunciations, and gut-wrenching accounts of mental disturbances blamed on the cult, all on prime-time TV. One reason this footage is especially shocking is because normally criminal acts and suicides go unreported or are deliberately under-reported, and generally TV and newspapers are in the "good news about China" business, so there's no familiarity, as there is on American TV, with the blood and guts side of the news.

Clearly, many in China bought into the ceaseless one-sided propaganda. I heard one Chinese practitioner in New York describe a conversation with her parents in China, who had been supportive of Falun Gong before the crackdown. Now, she revealed, they dismissed her concerns, parroting the government line—probably out of fear, possibly out of conviction.

In one instance, Chinese authorities were forced to admit that one of their widely-circulated "exposés" was fabricated. That story was reported out of Los Angeles on the Voice of America by Hai Tao and circulated by Falun Gong:

> Since the Chinese government started to crack down on Falun Gong in July 1999, all state-run media agencies started to attack Falun Gong, its founder, and its key members. On November 28, a special report authored by Li Xin-gang was published in the newspaper *Xi'an Workers*. The article "reported" that "Zhi-wen Zhang," who was a lady living in Wei-nan region of Shan-xi Province, burned her six-month-old daughter and then committed suicide by setting herself on fire, in protest of the government's crackdown on Falun Gong. This report made a stir in the country and has been reprinted by many newspapers in Shen-zhen, Harbin, Shanghai, and other places. Recently, the Hong Kong Information Center for Human Rights and Democratic Movements conducted an investigation and

---

dialogues and education. People also frequently commented the government should let laws make judgments and focus on real criminals." This same poll found a majority disapproving of Falun Gong as well.

found out that the report was a total fabrication. The center said, by quoting Chinese officials, that the people, location, time, and the story in that report were all fabricated. An official in the Wei-nan Communist Political and Law Committee of Shan-xi Province named Wu testified that there was absolutely no fire-suicide event and moreover there did not exist a lady named Zhi-wen Zhang at all. In addition, many news agencies in China called them for verification and got the same answer.

Still, the virulent anti–Falun Gong language emanating from China helped Falun Gong win sympathy in the West. "The campaign the Chinese government has taken on is a very vicious campaign and so unnecessary. It's almost as if in a few instances on TV and in the media—the written media—they've made fools of themselves," said practitioner Gail Rachlin. After Chinese state media "journalists" invaded a Falun Gong press conference in Geneva, a local newspaper called them "ridiculous."

The Chinese government has also tightened its already stringent control of the media since the crackdown began. The Press and Publications Administration announced in early January 2000 that twenty-seven newspapers and publications had been punished for violating press regulations. The Information Center for Human Rights and Democratic Movements in China revealed in December 1999 that 200 local newspapers, accounting for ten percent of the country's total, would be shut down in the year 2000 to allow the central government to reassert control over a press that might be deviating from the Party line.

Increasingly, the Falun Gong conflict has become a communications tragedy: China cannot hear the appeals of its own citizens, while the world media does not hear, or make a serious commitment to report, the ongoing cries of this significant new spiritual force. After a closer look at coverage of Falun Gong, it is easy to see that the American media and the Chinese media are not as different as they first appear to be. All too often, the world of news and the world of newsmakers are far apart.

CHAPTER 8
A TEPID RESPONSE IN THE WEST

Practitioners in the United States, where many forms of protest are permitted, have responded to China's barrage of charges and abuse. In New York, some have, on their own, brought their practice and passion to the United Nations. In Washington, they've assembled at the Chinese embassy and at the US Congress. Other practitioners have taken similar actions in Canada, Britain, Australia, and New Zealand.

While trying to maintain a non-political stance within China, practitioners in the United States have quickly learned the ins and outs of the American political system in order to get their voices heard. Some, like Allen Zeng, flew to Washington at their own expense. "I'm a software engineer. I flew in to try to help out the situation in China," Zeng explained. "A lot of people are suffering a lot of severe infringements on human rights. A lot of people are arrested and detained. I wish the American people, including American senators, could understand this more."

Zeng met Senator Richard Durbin of Illinois, who was impressed. "Certainly what they've done to these people, as I understand, very innocent people practicing their own beliefs, expressing themselves in a very peaceful, non-political way, is clearly an overreaction, and I hope the Chinese come to realize that."

Eventually, twenty-four US Senators from both parties appealed to China to "uphold the rights of practitioners to freedom of expression and assembly." As protests continued in China, Congress finally woke up—drafting a much stronger stand. Some on the liberal side sympathized with the human rights concerns while others on the right saw an opportunity to tie the issues to its campaign to promote religious freedom in China, an issue first raised by fundamentalist Christians but then endorsed by the Catholic Church. In early November 1999, New Jersey Congressman Chris Smith introduced a resolution supported by the bipartisan Congressional Human Rights Caucus led by Congressmen John Porter and Tom Lantos. On the Senate side, Arkansas Senator Tim Hutchinson took the lead and others joined. China issued an angry response. Eventually, a resolution affirming religious freedom passed in both legislative chambers.

During this period, the Clinton Administration kept a low profile on the issue, most likely because of its pledge to help win China entry into the

World Trade Organization (WTO). Lucrative trade deals and a growing trade deficit with China were never far in the background. This contradiction between what the US government was saying and doing finally prompted a strong editorial in the *Washington Post*: "You wouldn't know it from listening to deferential Clinton administration officials, but China is carrying out one of its more ferocious assaults against freedom of speech and freedom of association in recent years. Just since September 30, the regime has arrested an estimated 3,000 practitioners of Falun Gong . . . Given the absence of a free press, it's impossible to know how many have been arrested and how many have died in custody."

The *Los Angeles Times* was even more forceful at year's end, asking: "Has America lost all sense of outrage over China's human rights abuses? That question must be asked as China completes what is, by any reckoning, its worst year in human rights since the beginning of the 1990s."

It had taken months for official Washington and the media to wake up to what was happening in China and to respond, although mostly in a tepid manner.

When the crackdown began, the US government was low-profiling its criticisms, dutifully calling on China to stop persecuting Falun Gong practitioners. Only low-level officials were involved. For its part, China took this as a conciliatory signal. On November 3, 1999, Beijing agreed to resume military cooperation with the United States, which had been suspended after the NATO bombing of the Chinese embassy in Belgrade. Amidst all of this wheeling and dealing, State Department spokespeople issued banalities like, "no one should be persecuted for peaceful assembly, association, or peaceful expression of their views."

As the crisis deepened, however, President Clinton flew off to New Zealand to meet President Jiang Zemin at a regional summit. Jiang, ever obsessed by Falun Gong, presented him with a government propaganda tract against Falun Gong. The two were pictured smiling with each other. Some local practitioners later gave Clinton a copy of one of Li Hongzhi's books. A waffling Clinton smiled at them too, but said nothing.

At one point during the summit, Jiang delayed attending the official dinner for heads of state for three hours until Falun Gong posters outside the hall were taken down. In response to Chinese pressure, local police officials were ordered to move the protesters out of view. The cops were embarrassed at doing China's bidding and told the practitioners, "Just turn your music up." The same pattern of Western "cooperation" with Chinese requests took place in England and France, where security officials blocked protests and shielded the traveling Chinese President from their view. Headlined the *Guardian*: "Police Criticized for Their Tough Handling of Demonstrations Against China's Human Rights Record." Demonstrators were, the paper reported, "prevented from waving flags and unfurling banners while police vans were parked in front of protesters to hide them from

Mr. Jiang's view." In these instances, not only did Western governments fail to challenge China's hostility to free speech, they emulated it.

Other countries followed the American lead. The Canadian government mildly condemned China's crackdown on Falun Gong. Miles Kupa, Australia's Deputy Foreign Secretary, was also understated: "The ban on Falun Gong does raise some serious questions about China's international commitments relating to freedom of assembly."

The countries doing business with China continued to put their business interests first, refusing to link trade with human rights concerns. During the week of a particularly intense confrontation between China and Falun Gong practitioners, the White House was proudly putting the final touches on its trade deal with China.

Human rights groups also issued statements. Amnesty International said that the crackdown in China "marks the beginning of another cycle of stifled dissent and repression." Human Rights Watch called on China to end the ban because "the Chinese people have a right to exercise their faiths peacefully." There were many words like these, but little action. Few human rights activists publicly advocated on behalf of Falun Gong or staged solidarity protests. Falun Gong wrote to Human Rights Watch protesting its perfunctory stance on the issue. In response, a stronger statement was issued.

It was in this period, nearly four months after the crackdown was first promulgated, that foreign governments began to receive confirmed reports of deaths of Falun Gong practitioners in prisons. They were presented with photographs documenting vicious tortures, including the brutalization of old women. They also knew that practitioners were being fired from jobs and that their property was being confiscated. While the press may have been reporting this only episodically, the embassies in Beijing had better sources. Falun Gong representatives flooded Western governments with evidence, asking for action. A State Department country report cited some specifics:

> Tens of thousands of members of the Falun Gong spiritual movement were detained after the movement was banned in July; several leaders of the movement were sentenced to long prison terms in late December and hundreds of others were sentenced administratively to re-education through labor in the fall. Late in the year, according to some reports, the Government started confining some Falun Gong adherents to psychiatric hospitals. The Government continued to commit widespread and well-documented human rights abuses, in violation of internationally accepted norms. These abuses stemmed from the authorities' extremely limited tolerance of public dissent aimed at the Government, fear of unrest, and the limited scope or inadequate implementation of laws protecting basic freedoms.

In the United States, Falun Gong representatives met with State Department officials and members of the White House's national security advisory team. They rejoiced when President Clinton finally issued a strong statement in January 2000. But, beyond the rhetoric, there was a more complicated dance under way, as the *Washington Post* revealed on January 17:

> The wondrous contradictions of the Clinton administration's China policy were on full display last week. On Monday President Clinton announced an "all-out" campaign to lobby Congress to pass permanent most-favored-nation status for China. The lobbying will be rough, with a fully mobilized American business community working as the iron fist inside the administration's velvet glove. The same day Clinton kicked off his new campaign, US Chamber of Commerce President Thomas Donohue warned, on cue, that members of Congress who oppose permanent trade status for China "will find themselves in an unhappy situation with the business community."

> Then on Tuesday the Clinton administration announced its intention to introduce a resolution condemning China's human rights abuses at the UN this March. The administration suddenly wants to shine a "spotlight" on what State Department spokesman Jamie Rubin called the "serious deterioration in [China's] human rights situation . . . "

> Some may find the juxtaposition of the two announcements a bit odd. The Clinton administration inaugurates a big push to grant China the biggest prize in the history of US–Chinese economic relations and, in the next breath, singles China out for special condemnation as a world-class violator of human rights. But there was nothing coincidental about last week's announcements. The administration's tougher public stance on China's human rights abuses is an essential component of its "all-out" campaign to win congressional approval for the trade deal. The administration has a high-stakes and high-risk battle on its hands.

In March 2000, at the annual meeting of the UN Human Rights Commission in Geneva, the United States did introduce a resolution against China and worked to get European support. Secretary of State Madeleine Albright delivered a fifteen-minute speech to the Commission criticizing Serbia, Russia, and Cuba, along with China. It was the first time in that UN body's history (it was formed in 1946) that such a high-ranking American official had paid a visit. Albright declared that China has "always fallen well short" of UN human rights standards, even though it is one of five permanent members on the UN Security Council. In the past year, China's human rights record has "deteriorated markedly," she said, adding that the US resolution would cite "widespread denials of political, cultural, labor, and religious freedom in China." Chinese authorities have made "widespread arrests of those seeking to exercise their right to peaceful political expression," she continued, and went on to criticize the detention of thousands of members of Falun Gong. The speech to a standing-room-only crowd was not exactly a passionate barn-burner, and the wires reported that "Her audience listened attentively and applauded only once, at the end of the speech" (AP).

The Chinese government seemed outraged by Albright's comments. Most of its delegation wouldn't even listen to it, walking out en masse. Agence France-Presse reported this reaction:

> "Today the US Secretary of State Madeleine Albright has made some groundless charges and slanders against China's human rights situation," ambassador Qiao Zonghuai told the commission. Mr. Qiao denied there was persecution in China and referred to the banned Falun Gong as an "evil cult." He also claimed that China's position on Falun Gong had been embraced by other countries but did not name them. "The outlawing of the Falun Gong by the Chinese government has won the support of the majority of countries and their governments. We appreciate this," he said, regurgitating the claims that China makes in its own internal propaganda.

Albright's full remarks did not appear in the *New York Times* report on her visit, which only rated one paragraph on page A9. The *Washington Post* praised the Administration for sending her but opined that her visit may have been merely symbolic. "Direct presidential contact with European leaders would signal powerfully that the United States is committed to the resolution, and not just going through the motions to mollify his domestic critics," an editorial stated.

Human Rights Watch's Washington director Michael Jendrzejczyk said at a Senate press conference that Clinton, Vice President Al Gore, and then–National Security Adviser Anthony Lake had all worked on the issue in 1995, when the United States came within one vote of getting a resolution passed. "If the [UN human rights] commission fails to act, it will raise serious questions about the credibility of the commission itself," said Senator Tim Hutchinson (R-Arkansas).

But President Clinton did not mention China during his subsequent March 26 stopover in Switzerland, where he unsuccessfully sought to influence Syrian President Assad in a one-on-one meeting.

* * *

The debate in Geneva, unfortunately, was more of a side show to the debate about trade policy towards China. With $155 billion in foreign reserves, China's economy is strong enough to resist Western pressure; Western countries have become dependent on China's exports and manufactured goods. As Falun Gong practitioners have learned repeatedly, human rights concerns tend to take a back seat, in most countries, to economics and trade-driven foreign policy. Getting policymakers to issue resolutions is not the same as getting them to act. In Geneva, the Chinese made it clear that they believe that US policymakers were making show for domestic consumption, especially to influence critics of US trade policy and opponents of China's admission to the World Trade Organization in Congress. They may have been right.

Falun Gong practitioners showed up in Geneva and were permitted to make a very short statement to the Human Rights Commission. Chinese journalists invaded their press conference, hectoring speakers and trying to debate them. Their interference was blatant, promoting Swiss newspaper stories to ridicule their arguments and behavior. Practitioners from all over Europe did exercises in front of the UN headquarters. But it was all for nought. In the end, China prevailed, defeating an attempt to even consider the charges against its practices. It was the tenth straight year that a resolution against China's human rights practices had failed to pass.

Human Rights Watch placed the blame for this lack of support for the resolution on President Clinton's unwillingness to get personally involved. Director Ken Roth told me:

> China has become expert at using a combination of threats and bribes to get its way with many governments around the world. We heard stories about governments who felt that their entire aid package from China, which was quite substantial, was at risk if they didn't go with China on the resolution in Geneva. So China pulled no punches when it came to drumming up support. Unfortunately, the US government, while it was willing to deploy Secretary of State Madeleine Albright to make her phone calls, was not even willing to put this on the presidential agenda. It was not important enough for either Clinton or Gore to pick up the phone and call their counterparts, to push for their own support for the China resolution.

The Administration may have raised the issue, but it did not make a full attempt to see it through.

Sadly, after eleven months, China has not moved one inch vis-à-vis Falun Gong, except to adopt a more hard-line position. Can Beijing be budged? China scholar James Seymour thinks that only a new leadership in China will bring about substantive change in policy. "There are a lot of people in the Party that think [the crackdown] was a bad idea; indeed, there were a lot of people in the Party in the Falun Gong movement," he told me. "So, it's not inconceivable that somebody from that element would someday rise to the top in the Chinese Communist Party and handle these issues differently." Indeed, China's policy toward Falun Gong could change after Jiang Zemin steps down, as he is expected to do in 2002.

Li Hongzhi wants a dialogue with China, but unless third parties help it happen, such a dialogue is unlikely. Adds Seymour: "Li Hongzhi says that he is willing to have dialogue with the Communists. The Communists are not willing to have dialogue with him, they want him in jail . . . They are just determined to suppress every element that they don't understand or have good communication with. And they don't have communication with Falun Gong. And Falun Gong doesn't have good communication with them, they're just always talking right past each other. They're in different worlds."

Opportunities for Western governments to actively encourage a peaceful resolution to the crackdown have been ignored. Conventional political lobbying is unlikely to make a change. We have seen how pressure from the White House has pushed the peace process forward in the Middle East and Northern Ireland. But why not China? It appears that money, not morality, remains the central concern of governments on both sides of the globe.

CHAPTER 9
DESPITE THE SHAMEFUL SILENCE, RESISTANCE MOUNTS

China may have won the first round of this campaign. Some adherents there have reportedly given up the practice because of the pressure and propaganda. But as a Congressional Research Service report concludes, "the size, diversity, and fervor of Falun Gong adherents makes them difficult to suppress. The large number of persons involved and the simplicity of their aims enable them to mount collective actions on a national scale . . . The Communist government has reduced the group's ability to organize protests but, in the process, further damaged the government's credibility among many Chinese citizens."

The larger world outside of Chinese authorities, foreign governments, and NGOs alike has for the most part remained shamefully silent. Falun Gong's initial efforts to meet with UN Secretary General Kofi Annan or UN Human Rights Commissioner Mary Robinson went nowhere. Falun Gong practitioners later confronted Robinson after a speech at the UN. She dismissed them, saying, "We're watching it." She told me the same thing. Their faxes and calls went unanswered. Writers and publishers around the world have not even condemned the widespread burning of books in China.

Western leaders welcomed and fraternized with China's President Jiang Zemin during his state visits, while arrests of non-violent practitioners of Falun Gong in China escalated in intensity.

What is behind this complicity and silence?

There seem to be several factors. America has turned inward with less coverage of the world, and fewer international solidarity movements. On the left, there is suspicion that Falun Gong may be backed by the CIA or some other covert agency still trying to roll back Communism. There is no evidence for this, but that does not allay suspicion. Once you are into conspiracy-mongering, the absence of evidence may be all the evidence you need.

In the middle of the political spectrum are human rights groups who seem to focus most of their energies on helping political dissidents, often steering clear of movements with religious overtones. (This, despite the fact that many movements for human rights have been led by spiritual leaders like Martin Luther King Jr., Archbishop Tutu of South Africa, and Bishop Belo of East Timor.)

And on the right, the demands for religious freedom in China tend to reflect the evangelical and political agendas of Christian fundamentalists, not concern for persecuted Tibetan Buddhists or Falun Gong practitioners.

As for the US government, throughout this period it has been engaged in trying to repair a trade relationship with China that was ruptured in April 1999 when President Clinton put off making a decision on China's entry into the World Trade Organization, embarrassing Premier Zhu Rongji and alienating President Jiang Zemin. In the midst of all of this high-stakes, big-money wheeling and dealing, Falun Gong has been treated as a mere annoyance.

The governments of China and America want the problem to "go away." Yet China may be creating the very political force that it fears, predicts Human Rights Watch Director Ken Roth. "The more the Chinese government pursues these ordinary people, who had no political aspiration other than to lead their own lives and band together with other people who shared their interests, the more it's going to push them to become an opposition movement. Because at first they were simply defending their right to do what they wanted to do in their own autonomous realm. But increasingly, if they feel that it's impossible to do that with this government in place, they may well be pushed to the logical next step, which is to say we have to change this government. We can't tolerate this degree of intrusion in our personal autonomy. So it may well become the government's worst nightmare, simply by virtue of the government's strategy in dealing with it."

It would be far more productive for Western governments to try to facilitate the type of peaceful dialogue with China that Li Hongzhi has called for. China's "friends" in the West have to summon the courage to reach out and try to convince Beijing that it is in its own interest to change its policy. This is a point made by one China expert, Minzin Pei of the Institute for International Peace, writing in Singapore's *Straits Times*:

> China's inflexibility on human-rights issues violates its late leader Deng Xiaoping's precept about politics. Politics, Mr. Deng once said, "is to make as many friends and as few enemies as you can." To build some stability in US ties, Beijing must do its part to break this unholy Right-Left alliance. Because the Right's antipathy to China is fundamental and unappeasable, Beijing must re-orient its strategy and start building bridges to the Left. Most needed would be an abandonment of the traditional crude methods of repression—arrests, show trials, and long jail terms. Such practices have proven ineffective and harmful to China's international image.

But will China listen to these counsels from the West—or even those from its own people?

Despite the ongoing abuse in China, in the face of physical threats and worse, many dizi, or disciples, as some practitioners refer to themselves, continue their practice, exercises, spiritual study, and rather heroic resistance, with less media attention than they deserve. For them, the "fa" is their life. As Kenneth Qiu, a China-born Falun Gong practitioner from the United States put it, China's brutal suppression of the movement was "a mere test, not for the movement itself but for oneself. In Falun Gong, the personal and the political have merged."

Practitioners may be peaceful, but they are not passive. In this way, their campaign has aspects in common with Gandhi's civil disobedience movement in India and the non-violent civil rights activism led by Martin Luther King Jr. in the American South.

In New York, my friend Gail Rachlin and her practitioner colleagues continue their efforts by mail, fax, and e-mail to get the word out, to arouse solidarity, and to stimulate press interest and government concern. After ten months, they are reassessing how to sustain their own communications efforts as it is becoming clear that Chinese policy will not be reversed quickly. Within their movement, many practitioners are more concerned with their spiritual growth than any political activism. Some don't think there is any value in reaching out to the media, believing that the focus should be on spreading the practice itself.

At the same time, Falun Gong is no longer just a China-based movement. It has adherents in thirty countries, who have, if anything, been further mobilized to oppose China's persecution of their fellow practitioners. Nearly a thousand adherents from all over Europe turned out in Geneva to "appeal" to the UN Human Rights Commission in March 2000. (As discussed in the new introduction to this book, many practitioners again turned out for the April 2001 UN meeting in Geneva—only to be snubbed once more.) Demonstrations have continued in Tiananmen Square. Even some officials of the government have been quoted as having second thoughts, recognizing that many innocent people are being hurt. An article in the *Far Eastern Economic Review* suggests that a "hard core" has taken over Falun Gong, but it is more likely that the mass of practitioners have become harder themselves, and more determined.

There is always a danger that Falun Gong may become a "flavor of the week" among China-bashers or human rights groups; it is far easier for organizations and politicians to issue resolutions of support than actively work to defend practitioners over an extended period. If the movement is to grow and sustain the international support it has received, it may have to continue shedding some of its anti-political skin and educate its practitioners about two imperatives: building coalitions and doing further outreach into both the Asian-American community and the human rights world. As China becomes more brutal, it may be tempting for Falun Gong to escalate the anti-Communist rhetoric, or to build alliances with the American right and conservative groups like Freedom House and the Religious Freedom Coalition (led by figures such as former State Department official Elliot Abrams, whose bacground as a supporter of the military in El Salvador—which is infamous for having slaughtered Catholic nuns—is probably unknown to many Falun Gong practitioners).

Alas, some of these organizations have been more supportive of Falun Gong than the more Democratic-oriented human rights community. For instance, on March 14, 2001, Freedom House honored Li Hongzhi and Falun Gong with an International Religious Freedom Award. Even so, it would be in the interest of Falun Gong to avoid political alliances that would compromise bi-partisan support for their just demands. Otherwise, much of the international sympathy Falun Gong has drawn could be a flash in the pan, with the group retreating into the cocoon of its isolated spiritual practice.

* * *

Beijing, like many other repressive governments throughout history, has succeeded in politicizing the non-political and triggering an international movement.

Falun Gong may represent as many as 100 million people, but apparently for many Western governments and much of the media, they are still the wrong people.

Nevertheless, Falun Gong's voice is slowly percolating into world consciousness. While the cycle of protest and repression surges on, Falun Gong's hopes for peace and a dialogue with China were enunciated in a special report recently compiled by practitioners. These are their last words, and mine:

> We fear that the current crackdown on Falun Gong might, if unchecked, escalate into a tragedy comparable with some of history's most haunting nightmares. At present the livelihood and security, not to mention dignity, of millions of innocent people are at stake. On behalf of Falun Gong practitioners around the world whose voices cannot be heard, we hearby repeat our call for help in resolving the crisis.

Anyone listening?

In the documents that follow, readers will have a chance to evaluate this complex issue from a variety of perspectives, and hopefully come up with their own conclusions.

CODA
THE VANGUARD OF CHANGE

Modern Chinese history is organized around dates that mark moments of resistance and triumph. The government annually commemorates May 4, the anniversary of a 1919 nationalist student movement promoting "science and democracy," and October 1, the day on which the People's Republic was officially founded in 1949. Ever since 1989, pro-democracy activists inside and outside China have observed June 4 as the day on which the Tiananmen Square uprising was crushed. Each year, in advance of that date, the Chinese government detains dissidents to insure against commemorative protests.

Falun Gong is a relative newcomer to this world of anniversaries. But as the first anniversary of the April 25, 1999 protest approached, practitioners in China became increasingly active and the police mobilized, bracing for more protests.

In New York, on April 24, 2000, several hundred practitioners gathered at the United Nations, appealing once again to the international community to facilitate dialogue with Beijing. Their appeal was not reported by the US press, and neither the UN nor the Chinese government issued a response. But Falun Gong is persisting, keeping its faith in the potential of a resolution. "We reiterate our call for a peaceful dialogue with the Chinese Government, and ask for the support of all good people and institutions around the world . . . A peaceful resolution would benefit not only practitioners, but also the entire people of China and their government," said one appeal from Chinese practitioners.

On the night before, two practitioners, Gail Rachlin and Erping Zhang, were invited to a political fundraiser for the Democratic Party at the Sheraton Center, where a day earlier 1,500 practitioners had gathered to exchange experiences. Both Rachlin and Zhang stood in line to meet President Clinton, introducing themselves as Falun Gong representatives and thanking him for speaking out on their behalf. He smiled and told them to keep up their fight.

The next morning, April 25, Tiananmen Square was packed with more plainclothes and uniformed police than usual, waiting for Falun Gong practitioners to assert themselves. They didn't have to wait long, reported Jasper Becker, who has been following the story for the *South China Morning Post*:

In the corners of the plaza, one could see police officers haranguing some old woman or another, suspected of being a member. Occasionally, there would be a flurry of activity as police converged on anyone taking out a banner or lifting their arms above their head in a qigong meditation stance. There would be some vicious blows and then they would be shoved into a waiting van . . . It is a little like watching the Christians being thrown to the lions. Resistance does not last long. Then everything would return to normal—or what passes as such.

By day's end, more than 100 men, women, and one small child had been arrested. Some practitioners had unfurled banners with simple statements like "Falun Gong is good." Many were punched and kicked by police. Reported Reuters: "The protests, apparently coordinated because small groups popped up in different parts of the square, lasted the whole day. Around lunchtime, two groups of five men in their thirties sprinted across a main road into the square and tried to unfurl their yellow banners but were wrestled to the ground by police and taken away, the witnesses said." Associated Press described the protests in more detail:

Adding to the chaos were throngs of Chinese tourists who excitedly ran across the square to glimpse the rare acts of civil disobedience. Police, sometimes using bullhorns on their vans, shouted at bystanders to disperse. Foreign tourists also watched, mouths agape in surprise. Police made an American woman rip the film out of her camera because they suspected her of photographing an arrest. A tour guide told one group of American tourists not to photograph anyone in uniform. "China is still a comparatively strict country," the guide explained. Plainclothes police tried to separate Falun Gong followers from the tourists, asking people: "Do you practice Falun Gong?"

Most of these accounts of the protests have come from journalists, but some practitioners have made reports as well. One of them, Tracy Zhao, an airline stewardess, was arrested while taking a picture in Tiananmen Square, watching police brutalize a number of people. According to her account in *China Rights Forum*, she was hauled off to the police station next to the Museum of Revolutionary History.

The police were constantly yelling and cursing at us. When we were standing in orderly formation, some practitioners started to lead the rest in reciting poems from Master Li Hongzhi's *Hongyin*. In unison, everyone recited aloud:

Non-existence
To live with no pursuit

To die with no regret;
With all wild thoughts extinguished
Budda whose cultivation is not difficult.

"After a while," Zhao adds, "[the police] could only stand there and listen to us."

A world away in Washington, on the same day, several dozen Falun Gong practitioners gathered outside the Chinese embassy in solidarity with their colleagues in China. Some passersby in cars honked horns in support. At the State Department, James Rubin spoke out against China's violation of international human rights standards. "We call on the Chinese government to cease its crackdown on the Falun Gong," he said, urging Beijing to release all those placed in custody for the "peaceful expression of their beliefs," and to guarantee the rights of citizens to freedom of speech, conscience, association, and peaceful assembly. "We continue to see the arrest and detention of persons peacefully expressing spiritual or other beliefs as a matter that profoundly disturbs us. Such detentions are in direct contravention of internationally recognized standards of human rights that are enshrined in international human rights instruments to which China has acceded."

On the morning after the April 25 anniversary, the *Asian Wall Street Journal* tipped its editorial hat to Falun Gong. "Chinese society is changing quickly," noted the editorial, "and more and more people will follow the example of the Falun Dafa practitioners and demand their rights. Even if one finds their religion hard to fathom, they are the vanguard of change. This was the true import of yesterday's anniversary, carrying with it a bright light of hope."

* * *

Falun Gong resistance continued as this book originally went to press in July 2000, with three new anniversaries spurring practitioners into battle with police in Tiananmen Square. On May 13, 2000, the date recognized by practitioners as the birthday of Li Hongzhi (and Buddha), hundreds went to the square to "appeal" and were hauled away, often by the hair, along with some tourists taking pictures. Earlier in the week, China's state media had proclaimed yet another pyrrhic victory in its campaign against the practice.

Then, on the eighth anniversary of Falun Gong's founding, practitioners worldwide celebrated "World Falun Dafa Day." In New York, hundreds gathered in a balloon-festooned Bryant Park behind the Public Library. A block away in glitzy Times Square, news of the Beijing arrests were flashed on the famous news zipper that chronicles the biggest stories, although a similar gathering down the street was underway but not noted. The *New York Times*, which is based in the same neighborhood as the park, did not cover the gathering there—nor did any of the local New York news stations. Associated Press was there, however, and 300 miles away the *Boston Globe*, a *New York Times*–owned company, reported:

> Founder Li Hongzhi, who reportedly lives in New York, did not attend the Manhattan celebration. The crowd of about 300 practitioners lauded the perseverance of movement members in China, where Falun Gong is illegal, before performing the practice's meditative routine.
>
> "Chinese society has been torn apart this past year as 70 million people have been denied their basic human rights," Adam Montanaro said in a speech during the opening ceremony. "We look to them for inspiration."
>
> A feeling of serenity pervaded Bryant Park as the ethnically mixed group of practitioners performed the routine, which consists of traditional slow-motion exercises reminiscent of Tai-Chi, to the strains of simple, placid, Chinese music.

One unreported development was the presence of both Chinese government agents with cameras and of illegal Chinese immigrants who flocked to the event to learn some exercises and have their pictures taken doing them. The reason? They will now apply for political asylum claiming to be Falun Gong practitioners. What a final irony—a movement that is no longer free in China is being used by non-adherents as a pretext for winning freedom in America.

After World Falun Dafa Day, there was a lull. Still in hiding, Li Hongzhi issued several vague, mystical communiqués, while the Chinese government turned its attention to pressing economic issues. But as the first year anniversary of the July 22, 1999, banning of Falun Gong neared, the Chinese media dipped back into its well of invective, denouncing Li as a "running dog" and likening Falun Gong to a "rat crossing the road." Arrests followed in an almost routine manner. On July 19, 2000, the Chinese police, who had virtually sealed off Tiananmen Square, were startled when scores of practitioners raced into the square with banners aloft. AP reported: "All told, police detained more than 100 group members in a ten-minute explosion of seemingly coordinated protests across the vast plaza in central Beijing. Police immediately cleared the square, slightly earlier than scheduled, for a mid-morning visit by Russian President Vladimir Putin." I recalled how the 1989 student protests had followed a historic visit by Mikhail Gorbachev. Now, another Russian leader was to be treated to a new wave of protests, intended in part to capture the attention of the world press. It had been a year of repression and resistance with no end to the struggle in sight.

PART II
FALUN GONG READINGS

I've compiled a group of readings to facilitate an informed understanding of Falun Gong and the crisis surrounding the Chinese government crackdown. The reader will find a variety of testimonials from practitoners—inside and outside of China—and an excerpt from a new translation of Li Hongzhi's book, *Falun Gong*. I have also included a timeline of major events in the crisis, an analysis of the Chinese state-controlled media, excerpts from the Chinese constitution, reports from the US State Department and other world governments, as well as several articles and reports from independent voices and an Internet Resource Guide.

CHAPTER 10
TIMELINE OF MAJOR EVENTS IN THE FALUN GONG CRISIS

October 1, 1949—People's Republic of China founded.

May 13, 1951—Li Hongzhi born in Manchuria (Chinese government contests this date, claiming that Li's real date of birth is July 7, 1952).

1966-1976—Chinese Cultural Revolution led by Chairman Mao Zedong. Mao Zedong dies September 9, 1976.

October 6, 1976—"Gang of Four" arrested and blamed for excesses of the Cultural Revolution.

November 1978–April 1979—Democracy Wall Movement: the first democracy movement since the founding of the CCP.

January 1, 1979—China and the US establish full diplomatic relations.

June 4, 1989—Government troops carry out violent crackdown on students and citizens demanding democracy and an end to corruption around Tiananmen Square. Many killed and thousands arrested.

1992—Li Hongzhi introduces Falun Gong to the Chinese public; publishes his first book of teachings, *China Falun Gong* (title later changed to *Falun Gong*). Falun Gong registered with the China Qigong Research Society.

May 1992–December 1994—Li Hongzhi travels on a national tour, offering fifty week-long lectures on Falun Gong.

1993—Falun Gong awarded "Start Qigong School" award at the Beijing Oriental Health Fair.

1994—Li Hongzhi publishes his second book of teachings, *Zhuan Falun*.

1995—Falun Dafa Research Society dissolved.

1996—Li Hongzhi moves to the United States.

April 11, 1999—Derogatory article about Falun Gong appears in a magazine for teenagers in Tianjin.

April 20-23, 1999—Several thousand Falun Gong practitioners gather around the editorial offices of the periodical in Tianjin to protest derogatory article. Riot police beat protesters, arrest forty-five.

April 25, 1999—10,000-15,000 Falun Gong members gather in peaceful "appeal" around Zhongnanhai, the leadership compound in Beijing.

July 20, 1999—Mass arrests of practitioners nationwide; some taken from their homes in the middle of the night, materials confiscated. Thousands of US practitioners gather on the Mall in Washington, DC and in front of the Chinese embassy to protest the crackdown and appeal for support.

July 22, 1999—Chinese government officially bans Falun Gong, branding it an "evil cult."

July 23, 1999—Li Hongzhi appeals to world governments and human rights groups to support the rights of Chinese citizens to practice Falun Gong, and calls for a peaceful dialogue with China.

August 1999—Chinese government cites 307 "sieges" by Falun Gong practitioners since April.

October 1999—Execution of Liu Jiaguo, accused of leading the "Master of God" cult and raping eleven women.

October 1, 1999—People's Republic of China celebrates fiftieth anniversary of founding.

October 21, 1999—Chinese government reportedly seizes 7.8 million Falun Gong books and 4.9 million videotapes in the cities of Wuhan and Jinan.

October 30, 1999—Chinese government issues new legislative resolution banning cults.

November 1999—US Senate and House of Representatives pass concurrent Resolutions 217 and 218 urging China to stem the crackdown on Falun Gong.

December 1999—An estimated 35,000 Falun Gong practitioners arrested in China since July.

Feburary 2000—Zhong Gong spiritual practice declared a cult and banned.

March 2000—Annual session of the UN Human Rights Commission in Geneva. US Secretary of State Madeleine Albright criticizes China for pervasive human rights violations, including the crackdown on Falun Gong. China succeeds in blocking consideration of the US-sponsored resolution calling for a debate on the issue.

April 20, 2000—Chinese government concedes that it has been unsuccessful in stamping out Falun Gong; reports 2,591 Falun Gong–related cases being processed in courts; announces that students practicing Falun Gong will not be permitted to take their national exams.

April 20, 2000—*Wall Street Journal* runs exposé on the torture and death of fifty-eight-year-old practitioner Chen Zixiu while in a Chinese prison. Foreign media and human rights groups report at least fifteen deaths of Falun Gong practitioners while in government custody; more than 5,000 practitioners held in re-education camps.

April 24, 2000—Several hundred practitioners gather at the United Nations in New York, appealing to the international community to facilitate dialogue with Beijing. Appeal not reported by the mainstream US press; UN issues no response.

April 25, 2000—Falun Gong practitioners around the world mark the first anniversary of the Zhongnanhai protest; at least 100 protesters arrested in Beijing.

June 26, 2000—Associated Press reports that Falun Gong has "stepped up public demonstrations," leading to the arrests of more than 1,200 practitioners in one week.

September 2000—Nearly 3,000 practitioners gather to appeal to Chinese president Jiang Zemin during his visit to the UN in New York.

January 2001—Publication of the controversial *Tiananmen Papers* by Liang Zhang et al. (Public Affairs).

January 23, 2001—Five people, alleged by the Chinese government to be Falun Gong practitioners, set themselves on fire in Tiananmen Square.

CNN videotapes of the incident are confiscated, never aired. Falun Gong denies involvment. China's charges are unsubstantiated by outside parties.

February 2001—Meeting of 2,000 Communist Party officials; unanimous denunciation of Falun Gong and ongoing commitment to the crackdown.

February 2001—Li Hongzhi nominated for the Nobel Peace Prize for the second year in a row.

February 2001—US State Department issues annual human rights report declaring that the situation in China is deteriorating.

February 17, 2001—Over 1,000 Falun Gong practitioners stage human rights protest in Los Angeles; demonstration ignored by mainstream US media.

February 28, 2001—Chinese government holds rare press conference explicitly to denounce Falun Gong.

March 2001—New Li Hongzhi article circulates on the Internet: "Coercion Cannot Change People's Hearts."

March 14, 2001—Freedom House honors Li Hongzhi and Falun Gong with an International Religious Freedom Award for the advancement of fundamental principles of religious and spiritual freedom at a ceremony in the US Senate.

March 20, 2001—Amnesty International issues report alleging that an average of forty people per week have been executed by the Chinese government through the 1990s (totalling 18,194 executions from 1990 to 1999).

March 22, 2001—China's Vice Premier Qian Qichen visits the US to discuss trade agreements and Taiwan with President Bush.

March 25, 2001—*New York Times* estimates 3,000 Falun Gong practitioners kept in psychiatric facilities, tortured with nerve-damaging drugs.

April 1, 2001—US Navy spy plane collides with Chinese fighter jet off China's coast, sparking political crisis.

April 9, 2001—China issues human rights report celebrating its "progress."

April 18, 2001—UN Human Rights Commission annual meeting in Geneva. China again blocks US-sponsored resolution for a debate on human rights. Falun Gong practitioners stage candle-light vigils in cities around the world.

April 25, 2001—Second anniversary of the Zhongnanhai protest; at least twenty-four practitioners arrested in Beijing. Falun Dafa InfoCenter releases "April 25th Papers," condemning Jiang Zemin's policies.

May 2001—Hong Kong admits using blacklist to deny practitioners entry during Jiang's visit. Tourism from mainland China suspended during visit.

May 2001—Chinese government hosts restricted visit to Masanjia Re-education Labor Camp for foreign media. Journalists note fresh paint, scripted interviews. Prisoners seen watching anti–Falun Gong videos.

May 13, 2001—Second annual World Falun Dafa Day celebrated in over forty countries around the world.

May 24, 2001—*Asiaweek* magazine names Li Hongzhi "communicator of the year," based on Falun Gong's effective use of modern technology.

June 2, 2001—CCP publishes unprecedented 308-page report criticizing corruption and failed policies within its own ranks, "China Investigation Report 2000-2001: Studies of Contradictions Among the People Under New Conditions." Report appears the same week that US President Bush endorses renewal of normal trade status for China.

June 14, 2001—China passes new law permitting the execution of Falun Gong practitioners.

June 20, 2001—Fifteen female practitioners die at Wanija Labor Camp. Falun Gong alleges murder; China alleges suicide.

July 2001—Falun Gong holds worldwide appeal in Washington, DC on two-year anniversary of the crackdown. Thousands join in rally to advocate freedom for those illegally detained in Chinese labor camps.

September 2001—Daily arrests of practitioners in Beijing and around China continue as we go to press. Appeals in Tiananmen Square ongoing. Death toll of Falun Gong practitioners in Chinese government custody reported to be at 270.

CHAPTER 11
EXPERIENCES OF FALUN GONG
PRACTITIONERS IN CHINA UNDER THE CRACKDOWN

The following testimonials from Falun Gong practitioners inside China have been made available through Falun Gong websites. The Internet has allowed these voices to be heard, although as we go to press, many of the websites that have provided a forum for these postings have been hacked—particularly inside of China—presumably by the Chinese government or forces aligned with it. These translated testimonials are being reprinted exactly as they were posted on the web, with occasional minor editing for language clarity. Due to the nature of the government's assault on Falun Gong, we have no way to independently verify the authenticity of these postings.

* * *

My Experience Inside the Detention Center
Zhang Chunqing, Nanshan #13, 2-101,
Dalian Engineering University, Liaoning Province

(Note: The author of this article is a Falun Gong practitioner. On September 3, 1999, she was arrested because she was practicing the Falun Gong exercises in a park with her granddaughter; she was subsequently detained for fifteen days in the Dalian Nanguan Yaojia Detention Center for "disturbing social order.")

I was born in 1941. I lived through the war period and was happy for the new Communist China. I was brought up by the Communist Party, so as far back as I can remember, I have loved my country and the Communist Party. I cannot be labeled as an anti-Party, anti-government, or anti-social criminal.

On September 5, I told my cell leader that I wanted to practice the Falun Gong exercises and asked her to inform the guard. When I went to the office and told the guards of my request, the section chief heard me. She shouted: "Who wants to practice?"

"Me."

"You are too bold. You are not even allowed to practice outside. You want to practice here? What kind of place is this? Do you know? Who is feeding you meals to practice? Did Li Hongzhi feed you? . . . He fled to America. . . You still want to practice? You don't even know how you want to die. You dare not even listen to the Party!"

"Who else would I listen to if not the Party? I wanted to be a good member of the Party, a good citizen."

"Then why do you still want to practice?"

"Some leaders of our government do not know the truth. Our Central Party Committee does not know the facts. I am a lawful citizen of our country. I have the right to help the country to know what is real and what is fake. The changes I have experienced are the truth. I am a cultivator."

"Fine. You listen to him, right? Go ahead and practice it here. Do you dare? Go ahead."

I thought to myself: "I am a cultivator of the righteous Great Law. Why should I be afraid? Master Li told us to cultivate with honor and dignity. We ourselves should position the Great Law in the right place." So I started with the "conjoin hands" of the first exercise. As soon as I started, she struck me hard on the right side of my face with a letter-sized hard binder, and then struck the left side. Then she used all her force to strike me on my hands until I separated them. At the same time, she was shouting. Her voice kept up with the sound of the beating: "You filthy shameless xxx. I'll let you practice. Let you practice. Let you practice. Practice. Practice. Practice." A policeman who was about fifty years old also shouted, "I will see who is harder, you or the Communist Party!"

No matter how much she hit me and shouted, I was very calm and peaceful, with not a single complaint in my heart, because I knew she was an ordinary person, while I am a cultivator. She did not cultivate and did not know how precious Falun Dafa is. But I knew that Falun Dafa gave me a second life. I was actually thankful to her because she provided a chance for my cultivation.

After a while, they brought over a steel frame that I had never seen before. Obviously it had not been used for many years because there was a big stain all over it and it even had cobwebs on it. It was about twenty feet high and fifteen feet wide, and they chained my hands and feet to it. I learned afterwards that it was called the Di Lao (translated literally as "prison in hell") device, used for the most severe criminals. I could not walk with it, even though a policeman told me to walk in a certain way. But the chief ordered me to walk back to my own cell, which was about 200 feet away. I could only move an inch at a time. The chief was after me twice, shouting hysterically: "Faster! Why don't you move faster? Where is your Gong (cultivation energy)? Move faster!"

At some point, I could not move anymore, so I stopped and thought to seek help from the prisoners. But then I thought: "No. I should walk by myself, because it is my own tribulation. I have to cultivate on my own. No one can do it for me. I have to walk." So I started to crawl inch-by-inch. I became happy in my heart when I thought, "The Master is waiting for me. All the Buddhas and Gods in the universe are watching me. They are expecting me to return home. They will respect me because I had such an opportunity here to earn my divine virtues." It took me over forty minutes to move across the 200 feet from cell #1 to cell #7. At the gate of cell #7, there was a one-inch-tall hurdle that I just could not pass. Then Master Li's voice sounded in my ears: "If you want to pass, you can overcome it, unless you don't want to." I calmed down and made another effort. I passed it! I sat on the ground and cried. "Oh, my Master, you are so great." When I was walking, they ordered two prisoners to watch me, and they were all moved to tears. When I got back to my cell, all the fellow practitioners cried. I knew it was a manifestation of the power of the Great Law and the great virtues of the Master.

I had the Di Lao device on me until about 7 p.m. on September 7. At that time, the chief started to pressure other prisoners (prostitutes) that if anyone in the cell had to get handcuffed again, none of them would be allowed to see their relatives, and their jail terms would be increased. So some of them started to curse me. About ten of them kneeled down on the floor to ask me not to practice again. Seeing their suffering, I unwillingly agreed not to practice in the cell again. That was how the Di Lao device was taken off me.

A practitioner who was in the Di Lao device happened to have her menstrual period. The blood stained her pants and wet the floor. Many guards saw it but did not even allow her to change. Instead, she was told to exercise forbearance.

An elderly practitioner of age sixty-two was too tired after standing for many hours, and started to move her legs. A prisoner saw it and kicked her three times, shouting: "Stand properly! How did you practice Falun Gong? Where is your cultivation power?"

A practitioner asked to use the toilet. The chief said, "Aren't you able to endure? Just endure." The practitioner asked again later, and the chief said: "Didn't Li Hongzhi ask you to endure? Go ahead and endure. Where is your Gong?" So the practitioner was forced to have her stool in her pants.

Another practitioner could not endure any longer and said, "I will not practice. Please open my handcuffs." The chief pointed at her nose and shouted: "You practice when you want to, and quit when you don't want to? Do you have the right to decide? Keep it on." She just walked away.

At about 6 p.m. on September 10, practitioners started to recite "Lunyu (On Buddha Law)" from Master Li's book. Five or six guards started to beat the group of about thirty of us, until they were too tired to continue beating. Some ordinary prisoners wanted to show their cooperation with the police to shorten their jail terms, and also started to beat us.

They shouted as they were beating: "We'll let you recite. We'll let you recite." The guards ordered: "Slap them on the face, on the mouth. Slap them hard and make them swollen so they cannot speak." The practitioners kept on reciting until they finished the article.

One of the practitioners was quite loud when she recited, so they got tape to seal her mouth. She could still speak, so they put on another layer. Then another layer, and another layer, until she could no longer make any sound.

On September 9, the chief gave the order not to give us regular meals of bread and porridge. She said: "They are not humans. They are dogs. Not even as good as dogs. Don't give them any food." So we were given special treatment with rough corn bread and salted vegetables. On September 10, someone gave me some rice porridge with two pieces of pickles in it. The chief discovered it and started to shout: "Who let you give them vegetables? Are they human beings?" After her temper tantrum, she left. Actually we were not served with pickles. I smiled and said, "This is good. It is a chance that Master Li has given us to give up attachment of fighting and become extraordinary persons."

Once a policeman looked at my hands and feet and asked, "What happened?" I smiled and answered, "It is caused by this (the Di Lao device)." He said, "Look at yourself. Your skin is broken." He told me to say something "good" and he would take the Di Lao device off me. I told him, "This is the power of the Great Law. If it were not for the greatness and preciousness of the Great Law, I could not have endured this kind of torture even if you were to give me any amount of money. Why do I want to endure? For the past four years, the Master has given me so much, and sacrificed so much. I was dying with cancer. It was Master Li who gave me a second life for today. I am ready to protect the Master, to protect, promote, and perfect the Great Law, with my life. For my Master is the greatest. The power of the Great Law is infinite. I have absolutely no discontent."

During the days inside the detention center, the sound of beating and scolding was continuous. There were newly detained practitioners every day.

When I saw that the ordinary prisoners were ordered to work so hard to beat up practitioners, and the guards and police were so tired, I was very sad. Human beings, their lives are so miserable, so worthless, so tiring, and so difficult, yet they cannot be awakened from their deep delusion. This experience strengthened my confidence in the Great Law. I am more respectful and grateful to the Master. I am more determined to set aside all my human attachments.

I once told the police, "I have already been here for four days, but I have not seen the arrest permit yet. I still do not know what crime I have committed."

* * *

These first- and third-person postings offer brief accounts of the alleged terror experienced by various practitioners:

Cheng Zhong, Fifty-five years old
Menghe Town of Wujin City, Jiangsu Province, October 9, 1999
Local policemen asked me to give up the practice of Falun Gong but I didn't give in. On the afternoon of September 28, some policemen took me to the Third Hospital of Wujin city, which is a mental hospital. In the hospital, they forced me to take medicine and tortured me with an electric instrument five times. So far, it has been like this for more than ten days. I am feeling very cold as I only have a T-shirt on me. My family does not know my whereabouts. I do not have clothes to change, nor can I shave. In fact, the hospital, which is called a "humanitarian hospital," is detaining many people who appealed to the government for various injustices they suffered.

Zhang Lingde, Sixty-two years old
On September 13, 1999, I went to appeal to the City Committee and was put into a detention center. They said I would be detained for fifteen days. However, today is the thirty-first day and I am still here.

Li Wennan
Shanyujia Village, Jinling Town
At midnight of July 23, several people suddenly broke into his home and took him to the local government building. Five or six people surrounded him and viciously beat him until he fell down to the ground many times and could no longer stand up. Later an X-ray examination in the hospital showed that there was internal bleeding inside his chest. For many days he could not work after he went back home from the hospital.

Wang Cuiqin
Liujia Village, Jinling Town
The local government officials detained her in a room. Two people stood behind her and beat her with rubber clubs. Two people stood in front of her and beat her head and slapped her face. Her face was swollen because of the vicious beatings. After they tortured her like this for about half an hour, they forced her to stand with her legs bent and with a cement road-pile on her shoulders. As soon as she moved, they brutally beat her for another half hour.

Yu Aiyun
Yujia Village, Jinling Town
On the evening of July 21, she and four other Falun Gong practitioners were dragged to the residential area of the local government officials.

Local officials and their family members first verbally abused practitioners and then started to punch and kick them. The brutal beatings lasted for twenty minutes.

Yang Tongwu, Seventy-eight years old, retired
Big Chenjia Village
He was forced to stand barefoot on the asphalt road, which was 103 degrees hot, until his two feet were burned.

Fu Yingxia
Big Qingjia Town
She was forced to kneel on bricks holding bricks in her armpits and with a wooden stick in her legs until she lost consciousness.

Gao Yan
Gaojialin, Nanyuan Town
She was hung up with a rope and tortured and lost consciousness three times. After she lost consciousness, they would pour cold water on her face to make her regain consciousness so that they could continue the torture.

Lu Chunna
Wanjia, Daqingjia Town
On October 5, she came back from Beijing and was seriously injured from being beaten up by the local government officials. She was then sent to hospital for emergency treatment.

Wu Jianming, Zhang Shuxiang, Wang Meifeng,
Liu Yuejun, and Du Wangquan
Employees of a gold-smelting factory
Because they refused to denounce Falun Gong, they were first detained in the factory's security office for seven days and then detained in the city detention center for about ten to fifteen days. They were all fired the day after they were released.

Wang Shaohua
Employee in the sales department of Jinling Town
Wang Shaohua was seriously injured from torture on the evening of October 8. At one o'clock the next morning he was sent home half-dead and was warned not to disclose what he had suffered to other people.

Cao Zhiying
Cao Zhiying and her niece were tortured for a whole night by the local government officials after they were taken back from Beijing. They almost died of the torture. Those who beat them also confiscated 3,900 yuan.

Yu Yingbin
Zhaoyuan Gold Smeltery
Yu Yingbin and his brother of Zhaoyuan Gold Smeltery were fined 10,000 yuan. Liu Dianjun and Zhou Jinling each paid a deposit of 5,000 yuan. Yang Xiuying paid 2,000. Illegally confiscated properties include Yang Xiuying's computer, Liu Dianjun's tape recorder, etc.

Zhao Jinhua, Wang Haohong, Wang Fengnan,
Zhan Keyun, and other practitioners
Zhangxing Town
They were taken to the local government and then to the local detention center. The police beat them brutally with rubber clubs and electric clubs . . . On October 7, Ms. Zhao was tortured to death at the age of forty-two. To cover up the truth, the police sent her body to the city hospital without informing her family . . . They also threatened her family-members and forced them to write a statement to claim that she did not die of torture. When fellow practitioners went to the hospital to see Ms. Zhao, they were arrested and detained without any reason.

Wang Zhihui
Jinzhou, October 15, 1999
He was arrested in Beijing in his attempt to appeal to central authorities on September 27 and was then sent back to Jinzhou detention center. He fasted for seven days there. He was beaten up terribly. His gums became loose due to the brutal beatings. His whereabouts since then are unknown.

Deng Shaosong
Maoming, October 15, 1999
He was arrested in Beijing when he was there to appeal and sent back to Maoming detention center. He was beaten by the police until he lost consciousness, and was sent to the hospital for emergency treatment. The diagnosis was "broken skull and bleeding in the outer retina." His left eye rim was black and swollen. He could not have any food. Currently, many Falun Dafa practitioners in Maoming are still being detained.

Wang Wei, Hu Shuzhi, and Ning Guiying
Liaoning Province, October 15, 1999
In An-Shan City, Falun Gong practitioners Wang Wei, Hu Shuzhi, and Ning Guiying were arrested at home on September 24, only because they were contact people of Falun Dafa, and detained in the local Yuemingshan Detention Center. They were hung up to a heating pipe and were beaten for a whole night because they all declared to continue practicing Falun Dafa. Wang Wei has not been released yet.

* * *

Three Experiences at the Beijing Zhoukoudian Mental Hospital

1. Seven Falun Gong Practitioners (names omitted)

It was reported that on December 3, the Beijing Middle-Level People's Court was going to hold an open trial of members of the former Falun Dafa Research Society and that the public was allowed to observe.

On the morning of December 3, we went to the court and requested to observe the trial. We were told that the trial was not on that day. We were about to go home when we found that police were everywhere on the street. Without allowing any argument from us, they forced us into a transit bus. Along with several hundred Falun Gong practitioners from others places, we were taken to Shi-Jing-Shan Sports Stadium.

After some interrogation, the Public Security Bureau officers took us to Fang Shan Detention Center. We were all given a sentence of ten or fifteen days of detention for the charge of "disturbing the social order." We thought we'd be released after the ten or fifteen days of detention. Yet four days later, the police put us into a bus without any explanation. They then drove us to Beijing Zhoukoudian Hospital for Mental Patients and locked us up in a room that looks very much like a jail cell. Soon the director of the hospital summoned us and said, "The reason you are kept in the hospital is because the return of Macau and New Year are approaching and they are afraid that you Falun Gong practitioners would go to Beijing to appeal. Don't you even think about escaping from here because we have facilities similar to prisons." That was when we knew why we were sent there.

There are few necessities for us. We have nothing but one bed, one thin quilt, two bowls, and a pair of chopsticks. We do not have any other articles of everyday use such as washing utensils, let alone a change of clothes or a bath. At night, the attendants come to check us like they do to other mental patients. They turn on and off the lights many times to count the heads. The footsteps never stop.

Our cell is close to a karaoke bar. Every night, we have to bear the loud noises and can hardly sleep for more than half a night.

Our daily breakfast and supper is a bowl of porridge, a steamed bun, and a few slices of pickles. The lunch is just a half-bowl of rice and a few pieces of boiled cabbage. Few feel they have enough food.

We've been kept indoors for over forty days now. We are absolutely isolated and don't know what has happened outside. We are neither criminals nor patients. All we have been doing is practice Falun Gong to become good people, yet we are so unfairly and illegally treated. Where is justice and where are human rights?

2. Xu Jian-guan

I am forty-one years old. On December 6, 1999, I came home from work very late. My neighbor told me that my wife was taken away by the District police and the Village Public Security officers for a re-education class. I went to the village office. There I was told that they were afraid that my wife and others would go to Beijing to appeal and that my wife would be released after Macau's return and New Year's Day, provided she paid a penalty of 800 yuan (about the monthly income of an average Chinese worker). I was further told that our village was not alone; Falun Gong practitioners from the whole District were gathered to attend the re-education class.

I hurried back to see how Zhang Wen-Long's family were doing. I went there. The yard was empty. All the rooms were dark except for one. I went in and found two little girls there—one fourteen years old, cooking dinner, and another twelve-year-old in sixth grade. "My dad was arrested for practicing Falun Gong and I don't know where my mom went," said one girl with tears in her eyes. I felt very sad. As a Falun Gong practitioner I felt the responsibility and took the two little girls to my home. The next day I took off from work to take care of them as well as my own two kids.

At 8:00 that night, the District police came and asked me, along with another Falun Gong practitioner in my village, to go to the police station. I was taken to the station by police car. There I also saw the spouse of the other practitioner. The District police said that they would detain us two. The spouse of the other practitioner was scared and begged the police with kind words. The police then said, "OK, you two can go home; but you must come back tomorrow morning at 8:00 and ask your village officers and families to come to bail you out."

The next morning, I and the other practitioner went to the Police Station, along with the village head. The District police asked the other practitioner to write a promise "to abandon Falun Gong, not to get in touch in any way with so and so, and never practice Falun Gong again." If he did not sign it his kid wouldn't be allowed to take the middle school entrance exam next year. Facing the pressure from his family, the practitioner signed the paper, with tears in his eyes. The village head and the person's spouse also had to sign the paper in order for that person to go home.

"Xu Jian-guan, you must also write the same." I began to shed tears. How can I do this to my Master who deserves more respect than my parents? How can I stop practicing Falun Gong that teaches people to be good? I refused him right away.

Seeing my strong attitude, the police softened. "You should also think about your two kids. Don't ruin their future. If you continue the practice, your kids will not be allowed to join the army or the Communist Party. It will be difficult even for them to find a job." I said, "What can I do? I must practice Falun Gong." The police got angry, "Alright! Alright! I'll get you to a place to practice Falun Gong. You'll be released only when you tell me you won't practice it anymore."

I was thus taken to the Hospital for Mental Patients. I have been here for over forty days now.

I've lost all freedom. I have to stay in the room, with surveillance by the attendants. Over the forty days, I have only been allowed to go out twice—to shovel the snow under the surveillance of attendants.

Breakfast was just a steamed bun (now there is also a bowl of porridge). Lunch is a steamed bun, half a bowl of rice, and a little bit of vegetables. No one feels full.

What law have I violated to deserve being kept in a hospital for mental patients? Don't you know how much mental pressure a normal person suffers in this kind of place?! I don't know how much longer my respectable District officers will keep me here.

3. Su Xiu-rong from Rao-Le-Fu Village, Fang Shan District (Beijing)

I'm forty-five years old. On the morning of December 1, 1999, a few of our friends dropped by while my husband and I were having breakfast. Soon the village security officer came. Seeing the strangers in my home, the officer asked, "Are you all Falun Gong practitioners?" He took down the names of our visitors and warned them not to come again. Our guests left.

In the evening, the District police came to ask my husband and me to have a chat at the police station. From there they took us to the Fang Shan Detention center, claiming that we were to be detained for fifteen days. Six days later, we were sent to the Zhoukoudian Hospital for Mental Patients. The director of the hospital said to us, "The District Police sent you here and asked us to keep you until Macau is returned."

We don't have any mental illnesses, yet we are kept here, with no freedom, little food, and are treated like criminals. We've been kept for over forty days, without any paperwork. No one has ever come to talk to us.

Keeping us in the hospital also hurts our kids. Our eighteen-year-old and thirteen-year-old kids are under great pressure at home. The electric power supply at our home has been cut off for over a month now. They are also threatened to be thrown into the hospital for mental patients. Our oldest daughter had to quit her job to take care of her young brother and sister. We are not only suffering economically, our kids are also unable to bear the stress.

We are citizens of the People's Republic of China. We did not violate any laws. Why can't we be given a legitimate environment for practicing Falun Gong and for leading a normal life?

There is another villager named Liu Shu-Xing. She was forced into the hospital while staying at a relative's home. She was kept for over twenty days before being bailed out by her family when they found out. Because of this, her husband keeps abusing her physically and mentally. She is devastated. Will the authorities show us justice?

We are kept in the hospital for mental patients simply because we've learned Falun Gong. We try to become good people. Since we started practicing Falun Gong, we've been healthy and kind. What's wrong with that?

* * *

Rare Encounter

A practitioner went to Beijing to visit a childhood friend whom she had not seen for dozens of years. He was an official in the Chinese Academy of Sciences, and also a member of the writing group headed by Mr. He Zuoxiu for "exposing and attacking" Falun Gong.

When they talked about Falun Gong, that person began to recite official propaganda against Falun Gong and Teacher Li. She quietly listened until he finished. Then she asked him, "Have you ever read *Zhuan Falun* by teacher Li Hongzhi?"

"No," he said.

"How could you write the critical articles, then?" she asked.

He could not answer.

"Let me tell you the truth," she said again. "I am a Falun Gong practitioner myself. What have been reported by TV and newspaper are all lies."

Then she told him about her own experience and what Falun Gong is all about. Finally, she said to him, "As an old classmate, I just told you the truth. I hope you can distance yourself from He Zuoxiu, who is doing harm to others and to himself, too. You will regret someday if you continue to do such things together with him."

"I am a materialist," he replied. "But I understand you and respect your beliefs."

Two months later, he called her, saying that he had decided to retire and will no longer do those things.

* * *

"Mom Will Go to Jail for the Truth"

Ms. Liu Can is over seventy years old. She was a former principal for a school affiliated with the Guoguang Electric Tube Factory in Chengdu, Sichuan Province. She had been a Party member for over thirty years. Recently, she was expelled from the Party and detained as a criminal for practicing Falun Gong and appealing for Falun Gong.

On the day when she was to be taken away by police, her son and her grandson rushed back from Singapore. They knelt down in front of her crying. "Just tell the police you won't practice Falun Gong, okay?" her son begged. "They told me that if you promise not to practice again, they won't take you away."

With tears in her eyes, she gazed at her son saying, "My son, Mom will go to jail for the truth. It is worthwhile! Mom will stick to the principles of Falun Dafa. Don't feel sad for me any more."

Then the police arrested her and detained her in the Lotus Village Detention Center.

* * *

Six Reports of Persecution in Zhao-Yuan City, where Ms. Zhao Jinhua Was Tortured to Death in October 1999

1. In two days, more than fifty practitioners (in Linglong Town of Zhaoyuan City, Shandong Province) were arrested and detained and were tortured afterwards. In the detention center where Youying Lu and Dewen Li were detained, fifteen people were allowed only one kilogram of water each day. Sometimes, no water was given for several days and nights. They were insulted and beaten every day. Once, in the police department, five or six people took turns beating practitioner Caimei Lu for more than two hours (using electric shock treatment) until she lost consciousness. On the same night, the chief of police, Mr. Ma, and another two people tied Ms. Dongfang Chang and then beat her for more than 4 four hours, and another four more hours on the following night. Her face was swollen and there was internal bleeding under her skin in many places.

She also had been given electrical shocks on both nights. On the night of September 22, 1999, Mr. Wende Li was hung up and beaten for the whole night. He was also put in handcuffs and shackles and electrically shocked. Practitioner Jinguo Li was beaten up and could not stand up for the whole night. Zifen Zhang, Jinwei Wen, etc. were beaten with pails covering their heads. Qihua Wei and Jinqin Wei, who were nearly sixty years old, were forced to stand in a position with their arms stretched out and legs bent from 7:00 p.m. to very late at night.

These practitioners were detained for more than forty days without any reason. At last, those who were arrested on September 22, 1999, were released after their relatives signed and left their thumbprints on the "pledge" of quitting Falun Gong, and paid 5000–6000 yuan (about a half year's income of an average Chinese worker) to the police department. Those who were arrested on September 23, 1999, were released after their relatives paid 2000 yuan.

2. On September 28, practitioners Weidian Qin, Meixin Li, Xibin Fu, and Xili Fu from the Daqinjia Village of Daqinjia Town in Zhaoyuan City were arrested at midnight by the local police station without any legal formalities. More than fifteen people were put into an "iron cage" which is less than 4.5 square meters. They were detained for twelve to eighteen days. The police station did not notify anyone to send them food. A secretary of the township government used a shoe brush to hit the head of the practitioner Ying-xia Fu, and the brush was broken from the beating. Later, that practitioner bought a new shoe brush for the police station.

After October 1, these practitioners were still in custody. Several Falun Gong practitioners from Nanyuan Town of Zhaoyuan City went to the Daqinjia Town government to request that they release the detained practitioners. However, these practitioners, including Zhigao Li, Shuying Li, Yunying Zhou, Defa Lu, Xirong Lu, and Aihong Yun, were detained by the Daqinjia Town government and tortured.

3. On October 1, Ms. Chunna Lu, a practitioner from Daqinjia Town of Zhao-yuan City, went to Beijing—to appeal—by walking and getting rides. She arrived in Beijing on October 4. She was sent to the police station immediately because she told the truth when asking for directions from a police officer. She was escorted back to the Daqinjia Town on the next afternoon. As soon as she got out of the car, some local officers surrounded her and beat her. She lost consciousness right away. These officers thought that she was pretending to be dead, and continued to torture her. Later, they even waved a lighter in front of her to see whether she had any response. When they found that she had no response, they poured cold water on her face. It still didn't work. They then sent her to Daqinjia hospital for emergency treatment. After her relatives came, the police officers lied and said that she looked like that because she had refused to eat anything for three days. Three days later, she was sent to the city police station for detention for half a month. After she came back home, the officers went to her home asking her to pay for the transportation fee, and threatened to confiscate the salaries of her elder sister and father.

4. On November 9, two practitioners from Daqinjia Town of Zhaoyuan City—Ms. Yu-hua Zhang, who was fifty-five years old, and Ms. Lianfang Wang, who was fifty-eight years old—went to Beijing to appeal for Falun Gong. They were intercepted by police in the Weifang Train Station. Some governmental officials of the Daqinjia Town came to pick them up. In public, these officials beat and kicked these two women as soon as they met them. After that, they robbed the only 330 yuan that these two women had. At 9:00 p.m., dozens of people from the Daqinjia town government beat these two women on the ground. Four people held the two women on the ground and others took turns beating them using police clubs and rubber

clubs until they lost consciousness. They had been beaten until they lost consciousness several times during one day and two nights. Later they were sent to the police department of Zhaoyuan City for a fifteen-day detention.

(Note: after being detained for nine days in the prison, their relatives went to visit them, and took pictures of the bruises on their bodies.)

5. On November 10, Caixia Fu, a practitioner from Wohu Village of Daqinjia Town of Zhaoyuan City, went to Beijing to appeal for Falun Gong. The next morning, at the entrance of the Appeals Office, when she was just handing over the appeal letter, some officers from the government of Daqinjia town rushed over and took away the letter by force. Then she was brought into a hotel where she suffered beatings until she lost consciousness. Right after she woke up, she was handcuffed in a closet for about forty hours. She was sent back to the Daqinjia Town on the night of November 12.

Some officers continued to torture her for more than two hours until they got tired. After that, they demanded that she pay 10,000 yuan and threatened that her tractor used for farming would be taken away if she refused to pay. An officer whose last name is Wang wrote a mortgage document and forced her to copy it by hand and leave her thumb-print on it (the mortgage document still exists). Then they sent her to the local police station. On November 15, she was transferred to the City Public Security Bureau for criminal detention.

6. On December 15, the Fushanzhen local police station of Zhaoyuan City arrested seven Falun Gong practitioners, including Xiang Liu, Shuqing Li, and Mingzhu Liu, who went to appeal. They were detained in an underground prison, with no light at all. And they were tortured. The punishments included being forced to squat down with both arms stretching out, heels lifted off the ground; being forced to hold clubs by bending legs; electric shock; etc.

* * *

My Trip to China—Days with Falun Dafa Practitioners in China (Author Unidentified)

On November 22, 1999, after I got two weeks of vacation, I said goodbye to my daughter and left my husband a letter, then I went to Denver Airport. I've thought about this China trip for a long time, but my final decision was made three days ago; I knew that maybe it would be more than two weeks, maybe several months or even several years before I would return.

Every day I followed the situation in China from the Internet. The Chinese government's persecution against Falun Gong has been escalating. Thousands of practitioners had risked their lives to appeal to the government. They were asking the government to reverse its wrong policy to avoid more suffering of people. Every day I could not help crying when reading these stories about the practitioners. I had that growing feeling that I should be with them, and I should tell their stories to more people—to let all of the kind-hearted people in the world learn about Falun Dafa.

The first time I read Master Li's *Zhuan Falun* was from the Internet at the beginning of 1997. I felt I had found the ultimate treasure. *Zhuan Falun* answered all of my questions regarding the universe and human life. I have studied philosophy and supernormal abilities; I have practiced qigong; and I've thought about different religions. I've been searching so hard, but could never find the key to solve all of my confusions. I seemed to have lost my destiny in this puzzling world. While practicing Dafa, the improvement in my mind and my body have strengthened my faith in Falun Dafa. I believe it is true cultivation to allow human beings to become unselfish and enlightened. It is the Universal Principles that had never been taught before.

Just as my plane landed in Beijing airport, heavy fog suddenly appeared, and my plane had to halt in the middle of the runway. The flight attendant told us if we had arrived three minutes later we would have been diverted to Shanghai. I thought it was not a coincidence, it's not easy for me to come here. A practitioner who came back to China three weeks ago was waiting for me. She told me that there would be an experience-sharing meeting in Guangzhou and many practitioners from all over China would be there. Therefore, we took the train to Guangzhou the next day.

It was in a suburban resident-home that I met over thirty practitioners. It's an apartment on the fifth floor with three bedrooms and a living room. There's no furniture. Practitioners sat on cotton quilts that covered the floor. As we entered the door, they all got up and greeted us. The serenity and modesty from the practitioners brought a special warm feeling upon me. From conversation I noticed that all of them had come here after overcoming many barriers. There were practitioners from Australia and Sweden as well.

They started to assemble in here on November 18. Everyone had written down their cultivation experience. They exchanged their experiences and helped each other to make progress. They have not stepped out of the door for several days to avoid outside attention and any disturbance to neighbors.

A practitioner from Shijiazhuang came to sit in front of me and started a conversation. Her voice was calm, and I could feel her heart was very pure. It seemed that she had cultivated herself quite well. She said the Master had suggested group practice and study, as well as experience-sharing meetings as the ways to spread Dafa . . . The Swedish practitioner had practiced for over five years. She told me that some Swedish practitioners have been visiting China once a year to exchange experiences with Chinese practitioners. They called that "return to mother's home." The Swedish practitioners went to Changchun particularly since it is the place where the Master started his teaching. There're more and more Swedish people practicing Dafa, and there are more Swedish practitioners than Chinese practitioners in Sweden.

After midnight, we turned off the lights and went to sleep. I slept with several girls in a bedroom. The room was tiny and could barely fit us. Men slept in the living room. Less than an hour after we laid down, we heard shouting and fierce knocking on the door. A practitioner said calmly, " Must be police." We didn't panic. We all came to the living room as the police rushed in, shouting, "Don't move! Sit down!" Practitioners asked, "Which law have we broken? How can you just break in?" The police gave no answer and showed no search or arrest warrant. They started to hit practitioners on their heads and bodies. A practitioner was beaten by four or five policemen at the same time. One practitioner was beaten to the ground; her body rolled up, and she was sweating from the pain. As the police started to beat on an Australian practitioner, two Chinese practitioners tried to protect her with their own bodies. Two practitioners were dragged downstairs by the police. From the beginning to the end, no one fought back, displaying great forbearance. I saw tears coming down several male practitioners' cheeks. They felt sorry for not finishing the meeting and not being able to warn practitioners in other locations.

The police handcuffed every two of us together and then took us downstairs. I happened to be handcuffed with a short old man from Sichuan. I told him I was also from Sichuan, and he said that it must be predestined. Police then started to search through our luggage. Anything related to Dafa was confiscated. Books brought by Australian practitioners were all taken away. They even took some of our personal belongings. When a policeman found two Dafa books in my bag, he took them away, too. I asked him to return them to me, and he said he'd talk to me about that later. When we were in the police car, he returned the books to me. I was so happy to see that he still had a kind heart. The Sichuan practitioner's books were taken away so I gave him my "Essentials for Further Advances." He smiled at me and hid it under his clothes. Practitioners all treasure Dafa books, and they know these books contain the Universal Principles. The Sichuan practitioner told me that his last name is Pan. He came from A Ba County of Sichuan and was sixty-two years old. His family consisted of five members and all of them were practitioners. His experience paper read: "Master told us to be good people. I have two grandchildren, one of them is six and the other is seven. They both conduct themselves to the standard of Dafa. They never fight with classmates, even if others take away their belongings. Dafa can change and temper people. Dafa is good!" Simple words, truly touching.

Police took us to the Tianhe Detention Center. They ordered us to sit on the floor of the dining hall, then took us one-by-one for questioning. From time to time, I heard beating noises. Later I was told that the noises were caused by the beating of the practitioners. There was one practitioner who got slapped on the face every time he was asked a question. He was also forced to squat half way down for one and a half hours. I was taken for questioning before dawn. Police asked me why I still practice Falun Gong after it was banned. I told him, "Falun Dafa helped millions of people become free of painful illnesses, this is a fact witnessed by the whole society; Falun Dafa taught people to be better, and helped millions to improve their morality—that is also witnessed by the whole society. For such a precious Dafa, no matter who bans it, I will still practice it." He asked why I came to China. I said because I saw the Chinese government couldn't tell right from wrong, and they are defaming Dafa; as a Chinese citizen, I have the obligation to come and clear the facts on Falun Gong; and I cared about practitioners in China; I came to see their situation. I told him that when a person sees the true meaning of life, he will not change no matter how you abuse him. The police sighed and told me that they had to do those things because they were ordered to do so. At last he asked me, "Can a person like me practice Falun Gong?" I said sure. Master Li is compassionate to everyone, and you should treasure this opportunity. I suggested that he should first read *Zhuan Falun*.

After all thirty-six of us were questioned, we were locked up in three rooms on a second floor. We decided to carry out a hunger strike. We also demanded that they return our books and release us since we hadn't broken any laws. I felt lucky that we were not locked up separately so we still had chances to exchange experiences. I heard many touching stories from fellow practitioners. They have been striving to improve their realm of mind and enlighten to the teaching of "Zhen-Shan-Ren" (Truthfulness-Benevolence-Forbearance). They treasure Dafa. When they saw Dafa was facing the current tribulation, Master Li was being slandered, and the practitioners were being arrested, they stood out and used their own experiences to tell the world the greatness of Dafa. They are using their own lives to safeguard Dafa.

A practitioner from Shangdong told us a story she heard in Beijing regarding a medical doctor from Anhui. The Anhui practitioner was in her forties. She planned to appeal to the government in Beijing. Right after she purchased her train ticket to Beijing, her luggage and ticket were stolen. She had no money with her and decided to walk to Beijing along the railway. It was over 1000 kilometers, and most of the area she crossed was deserted land. She drank from ponds, slept by railroad tracks, and ate almost nothing. When she saw a household, she would ask for some food.

After much tribulation she came to Beijing. She had walked for twenty-four days, about fifty kilometers a day. She met other practitioners in Beijing and told them about her travel experience. Then she was arrested along with the other practitioners.

A practitioner from Dalian told her story and it truly moved me. Once, without knowing what she looked like, the police came to her house to arrest her. As she heard the police ask her parents about her whereabouts, she calmly walked past the police and out of the house. Unfortunately, she was arrested in Beijing. The wardens used electric shock on her and other practitioners for over two hours. They didn't complain. There was only the sound of electric shocks and the smell of burnt flesh. Even though the practitioners were shocked by the wardens, they didn't hate the wardens at all. On the contrary, they helped the wardens with their laundry and also helped them to understand Dafa. Wardens said all Falun Gong practitioners are good people. She was on a hunger strike for nine days. Right after she was released she came to the experience-sharing in Guangzhou.

Most of us felt all right after two days of no food and no water. I heard from the Dalian practitioner that she knew someone who starved for thirteen days and walked out of the jail like nothing had happened. Someone even starved for nineteen days. Those extraordinary phenomena from true practitioners are enough to amaze the world. Only a slim girl in her twenties said she didn't feel well. She sat there with her eyes closed. By the afternoon, she already felt better. We all knew that we were in the process of eliminating karma.

The doctor in the detention center visited us once in a while. She could not believe Falun Gong's magical effects to treat illnesses. A practitioner from Henan told the doctor that three years ago she was famous for her bad health. She had heart problems, arthritis, and hepatitis B. She tried Western treatment, Chinese medicine, and many alternative treatments, but her condition only got worse. There was even a time that she took medical leave for half a year. After she practiced Falun Gong, all of her illnesses were gone. Many practitioners had different illnesses before, and now we are all healthy. That was our own personal experience. How can it be possible to ask us not to believe in Falun Gong?

In the afternoon, the guards ordered us to have our photos taken for their records. We told them that we were not criminals, so we would not take photos. Then they came over to drag us. A guard dragged that slim girl out and shouted, "I will beat you to death." The girl screamed. We then encircled the guard, and asked him to let her go. He then loosened his hands. In order not to let them deal with us separately, we sat together in one detention room. Later they had to give up the intention of taking our photos. At night, the guard told us that they would transfer us to another place and ordered us to get out. We knew that they were going to punish us. Then the practitioners from Australia requested to see the Australian consulate in Guangzhou, saying that they would not move before their request was granted because they felt that their personal safety was in danger. The officer who was responsible for foreign affairs came and after some negotiations he agreed to call the Australian consulate. But he never came back. Later the guards dragged all of us out while beating and kicking us madly. They dragged us to the yard downstairs and ordered us to squat down. Then they ordered us one-by-one into a room and conducted a thorough body search. Later we were separately detained in different cells with criminals.

I was assigned to the sixth cell. I found a practitioner from Jiangxi in that cell, plus six criminals. One of the criminals immediately came over with a bowl of cereal and persuaded me to eat. She said that this was the task assigned to them and they would be punished if they could not succeed in persuading us to eat. I said that I would tell the guards that it had nothing to do with them. After a short while, the officer in charge of female prisoners came over and asked whether I had eaten or not, and threatened to fill me with salt water if I refused to eat. The inmates all told me that it was a very terrible thing to be filled with salt water. Meanwhile, I heard someone screaming in another cell. They told me that it must be someone being filled with salt water. The officer then ordered four to five male criminals to come over. One of them carried a tool for filling salt water, which is a long glass tube attached with a soft and thin tube and some other stuff. I sat on the ground and was close to the wall. The officer approached me and asked whether I still refused to eat. I asked him why I was arrested since I had not committed any crime; and up to now I had not seen the arrest certificate. He became extremely angry and kicked my right breast heavily, yelling, "Who do you think you are?" He then said to the criminals, "Fill her with salt water."

Several male criminals came over and dragged me on the ground to the door, pushed me down, and put shackles on me. I felt somebody squeezing my nose and I could not breathe. Then something big was squeezed into my mouth. My mouth was immediately full of salt water. Since I could not breathe I had to swallow. It was high-density salt water. My throat felt like what I swallowed were all grains of salt, or a lot of salt plus a tiny bit of water. I wanted to struggle but my hands and feet were forcefully held. I could not move at all. After a long time, I still heard the officer order, "Fill more." I thought that I would suffocate to death if they continued to do that. After another three to four minutes, they let me go. But I could not breath freely for a long time. I felt like I would be suffocated to death. Then my stomach felt terrible. I wanted to drink water. I could not speak. My inmates held a bowl of cereal and fed me. But after a short while, all the cereals were thrown up. I had to constantly drink water and throw up. My clothes were full of water and dirty stuff. Ms. Ye could not help crying upon seeing me like that.

After throwing up for a long time, I started to feel a little better. My inmates took me to the water pool to clean my body. They tried to take off my pants. However, it was very difficult since I was in shackles. At last, they had to tear off my pants. After they washed me, one of them offered her skirt to me kindly. It was already three in the morning after they cleaned me. They told me that they had to work during the day. They went to sleep. I also went to sleep after throwing up a few more times.

At eight the next morning, everyone had to get up according to the prison's regulation. My stomach felt much better, but I had to drink water constantly. I could only speak in a low voice. Somebody sent in raw materials for the forced labor. We were forced to work to make plastic flowers. I then started to chat with my inmates. They said that they also would like to learn Falun Gong but they could not get a book. Some other Falun Gong practitioners had been detained together with them and had introduced them to Falun Gong. They felt very good about it. They have changed themselves after they got to know the teachings of Falun Gong. They used to beat and swear at each other; now they get along with each other very well because they know that they should be good people and should purify their hearts. On the previous night, I had felt their kind hearts when they took good care of me and lent me the skirt. They had practiced Falun Gong exercises secretly in the cell. One time, however, they were caught by the guards while practicing the exercises, and were beaten up. The head-criminal had a swollen bottom from the beating. These criminals said that the practitioners who had been detained with them often told them stories of Falun Gong practitioners, which moved them to tears. Anyone would be moved by Falun Dafa as long as he still has some kindness remaining in his heart.

It was dark when someone came to take off my shackles. I felt much more comfortable. After a short while, the guard ordered Ms. Ye and me out. We got in a police car, not knowing where the car was heading. Ms. Ye felt very calm. She is only twenty four years old and has practiced Falun Gong for three years. I had read about her experience. She had had many illnesses before practicing Falun Gong. At such a young age, she had a severe stomach illness and piles, which all disappeared after practicing Falun Gong. She had been arrested several times. One time she was arrested in Beijing. The police found out the place where she and other practitioners stayed. She thought that she should not be taken away like this and jumped out of the building without thinking about how high the building was. She said that she just felt that she had landed on the ground softly. Later someone told her that the building was about twelve feet (four meters) high. But she did not have any bruises. She was not talkative and she looked very quiet. But she had been so courageous. Facing those abusive police officers, she always had a serene countenance and a kind heart.

It turned out that they were going to question us again. We were taken to the Police Station in Yuexiu District. After a two- or three-hour interrogation, they finally convicted us of "participating in illegal Falun Gong activities," and we were given a fifteen-day detention. I asked to use a telephone, but was refused. They completely ignored citizens' rights and even deprived us of the rights to appeal. Afterwards we were sent to Yuexiu Detention Center. I was separated from Ms. Ye. I was put in a big barn where wind can blow inside from two directions. I was locked up with some thieves and drug users. I had been asking to use a telephone to at least inform my family members, but they did not allow me to do so. Other detainees could make phone calls; only Falun Gong practitioners could not.

On the tenth day in Yuexiu Detention Center, police from Chengdu (my hometown) came to take me to Chengdu. I was taken to a police office in western suburban Chengdu. They had me sit on a chair waiting for their verdict because they wanted to reinvestigate my case. I didn't know what other "evidence" they could collect. Did I violate the laws and deserve to be detained and to have heavier punishment simply because I'm a Falun Gong practitioner and visited other Falun Gong practitioners? After having sat on a chair for two days, finally the news came—they decided to release me. They said they really could not let me go back to the US, but they decided to release me due to other factors.

After I came back to the US, I learned that many friends had given me great help, and that even the senators from Colorado were involved. However, I'm concerned about the fate of other practitioners. If they were sent back to their hometowns, what's waiting for them would not be as easy as detention. That female practitioner from Shandong told me that if she were sent back to her hometown, she would be sentenced for at least a two-year labor camp (which had already happened to many practitioners in her hometown). On my way back to the US, I stopped by Beijing. I wanted to check whether the practitioner detained in the room next to mine was released or not. I knew his cellular phone number and his phone was confiscated. If he had been released, he would answer the phone. I dialed his number from a public phone; no one answered. The strange thing was that as soon as I hung up, someone called back and asked who I was. Less than half an hour later, from a distance, I saw a police car come to the place where I made the phone call. Obviously he was still under detention.

Although I've returned to the US, I'm still thinking of our fellow practitioners in China. Their spirit, their courage, and their tolerance can move everything. With their own conduct, they are showing to the world that Falun Dafa practitioners' faith is rock solid. They are showing Falun Dafa's sacredness and solemnity to all humankind.

* * *

Letter to UN Secretary General Kofi Annan from a Group of Falun Gong Practitioners in Beijing:

November 15, 1999

Dear Mr. Annan,

We are Falun Dafa practitioners in Beijing. As you may have already known, most of Falun Dafa practitioners are suffering persecutions of various degrees from the Chinese government simply because they are practicing Falun Dafa. A lot of kindhearted people have been thrown into prison just because they are faithful to their beliefs and are determined to practice Falun Dafa to become better people. Right now some are enduring cruel tortures, some have been tortured to death, and many have been sent to labor camps without trial.

Falun Dafa has brought health and morality to all practitioners, and this fact has been widely recognized. However, since July 20, the Chinese government has been viciously slandering Falun Dafa and brutally persecuting Falun Dafa practitioners. By doing this, it has violated the Chinese Constitution and the United Nations Universal Declaration of Human Rights that China has signed.

We have learned that you are going to visit China during November 14th to 17th. We appeal to you to urge the Chinese government to:

1. Rescind the arrest warrant for Mr. Li Hongzhi.
2. Release all arrested and detained Falun Dafa practitioners.
3. Stop persecutions against Falun Dafa practitoners.

Thank you for your kind help.

Sincerely yours,
Falun Dafa Practitioners in Beijing, China

CHAPTER 12
REPRESENTATION OF FALUN GONG
IN THE CHINESE STATE-CONTROLLED MEDIA

China has denied all of these accusations of human rights abuses and violations. The 270 deaths of practitioners in custody are all officially considered suicides or the results of natural causes.

In 1997, I visited China at the invitation of Beijing Television to speak at an international television conference. At the outset, the conference organizer brought all of the speakers into a room and told us that we could say anything we wanted, but that we shouldn't mention "human rights." Those words seemed *verboten*, in part because they had become equated with the club that China was continuously beaten with by Western governments and media outlets for refusing to embrace democratic ideas or a pluralist system.

To avoid creating trouble for my host, I respected her request; instead, I showed a portion of my own film, *Countdown to Freedom*, documenting South Africa's first democratic elections in 1994. The film addressed human rights, but in a country far from China. I made a point of praising China for supporting the South African liberation struggle. The audience got my point, even if the commissars did not—they were just pleased that I had not invoked the dirty words. At the time, I wondered if their Party-line had become a religious ritual, a dogma not unlike that adhered to by their detractors.

Over the years, China raged at critics, challenging their hypocrisy, selective standards, and unwillingness to acknowledge that ideas appropriate in an advanced country might not apply in a developing one—or one with a different political and economic system.

In considering China's response to Falun Gong, I realized that there is an internal logic to the government view, even if it expresses itself in wooden prose and political formula. What follows are eight themes that surface again and again in the official Chinese state-controlled media, which hews closely to the government line.

Theme #1: Delegitimizing Falun Gong as an "Evil Cult"

A partial transcript of a television show produced by CCTV, China's national state-run TV network, entitled *Falun Gong: Cult of Evil* (distributed widely on video and CD-rom) offers a representative example of this theme. The program begins with a highly visual guilt-by-association argument: other cults are bad, dangerous, and deadly . . . and so is Falun Gong. This approach is designed to validate the government's repressive role as protector of the people and savior of innocents at risk:

> Since the 1960s, a number of cults have appeared in countries around the world. The founders of these cults share one thing in common: They advocate their heresies with the aim of attracting followers, and then controlling their thoughts and actions. They do this despite the threat they pose to human civilization and development. The founder of Aum Shinrikyo, Shoko Asahara, claims to be the omnipotent god. He predicts that another world war will break out before the end of 1999 and that only his followers will survive to save the world from disaster. The founder of the People's Temple, Jim Jones, denied the existence of any god. He said he was the only being capable of understanding the past and foreseeing the future. The founder of the Branch Davidians, David Koresh, claimed to be the only god, and called on the whole of mankind to follow his teachings, and give themselves, even their lives, to his cult. The founder of the Solar Temple, Luc Jouret, told his followers that he had come from outer space from the star Cirius to save mankind from the earth's destruction. He told them that their only hope of survival was to reach Cirius, and that they could do so only by burning themselves to death.

> In 1992, a cult appeared in China, too, that shared much in common with the other cults. Before long it had attracted 2,100,000 people, with claims that it could cure illness with its advocacy of truthfulness, benevolence, and forebearance. The cult was Falun Gong, and its founder was Li Hongzhi. . .

Theme #2: Discrediting Li Hongzhi

Hundreds of one-sided attacks on Li Hongzhi appeared in the state-controlled media after July 22, 1999. Here is an excerpt from one article, "Life and Times of Li Hongzhi," published on July 22, 1999, the day that the government officially banned Falun Gong:

> Li Hongzhi, the founder of Falun Gong, is not the "highest Buddha" who brings salvation to suffering people, but an evil person who has had an extremely disastrous effect on society . . .

> In a resume he prepared in 1993, Li . . . claims that he has supernatural abilities like the ability to move objects, control thinking, and make himself invisible and that he understands the truth of the universe and has insights into life and can see the past and future.

On September 24, 1994, Li changed his date of birth from July 7, 1952 to May 13, 1951 and acquired a new ID card. On the Chinese lunar calendar, May 13 is the birthday of Sakyamuni, the founder of Buddhism, so by changing his birthday Li could pretend that he is a reincarnation of Sakyamuni. However, Li's family members, relatives, neighbors, former schoolmates, teachers, leaders, and fellow servicemen say that they believe Li is just an ordinary person and that his so-called qigong learning and miraculous abilities were "nonsense" or " impossible" or something they'd never seen. His only talent in childhood, many said, was the ability to play the trumpet . . .

Li's resume consists of nothing but fabrication and outrageous lies.

Theme #3: Ridiculing Li Hongzhi's Ideas

Li Hongzhi is presented in many media accounts as a "heretic"—an odd choice of term in a Marxist-Leninist society. The Chinese media has carried many articles from "intellectuals" deriding his "fallacies." Most of these quote selectively from his lectures in ways that Falun Gong practitioners insist distort his message. Here is an excerpt from a September 14, 1999, Chinese media report, "Li Hongzhi's Heretical Fallacies Deceive People, Ruin Lives":

> A newly published book claims that Li Hongzhi, founder of the Falun Gong cult, repeatedly preached his heretical ideas and fallacies to deceive his followers. The book, entitled *Li Hongzhi and His Falun Gong: Deceiving the Public and Ruining Lives*, disclosed that on many occasions Li Hongzhi had told his followers, "the human race has experienced many destructive catastrophes," and "the next complete destruction of the world will come soon."

> . . . He declared, "Mankind on this earth faces inexorable doom. Our planet should have been totally destroyed last year, according to my calculations." He said he was the one who had postponed the destruction of the Earth by thirty years.

> While hawking the "doomsday" theory, Li Hongzhi cursed the human race and regarded the Earth as a rubbish heap.

> . . . The book also exposed Li Hongzhi's absurd attitude towards modern science. Li proclaimed to practitioners of Falun Gong that "science today is not science in the real sense, because you can never use this science to probe into the profound mysteries of the universe."

The following excerpt from "Analysis of Falun Gong Leader's Malicious Fallacies," an article posted on the *China Daily* website, is another example of this theme:

> The Falun Dafa, or Falun Gong, an illegal organization headed by Li Hongzhi, has deceived a lot of people and harmed them in recent years and been involved in many illegal activities that have seriously disrupted public order, misguided people, and confused right and wrong.
>
> Falun Gong has a set of ridiculous ideas, a basic one of which claims that doomsday is coming, that human beings will be extinct soon, that modern science can do nothing to prevent the catastrophe, that only Falun Gong can save mankind, and that Li Hongzhi is the sole "savior."
>
> Because of this doomsday prediction, Li ordered his followers to concentrate on their Falun Gong and forbid them to hold any other belief. Human civilization has experienced at least eighty-one periodic changes, he says, and society is now deteriorating and if this trend continues, it will be exterminated.
>
> . . . Li's doomsday idea denies the truth of the existing world and it has created strong anti-government and anti-social sentiments. Its true purpose is to win public support for his wicked political ambitions.

Theme #4: Falun Gong Threatens Society

The Chinese government presents itself as the benevolent guardian of order in Chinese society, and consequently frames Falun Gong as jeopardizing the country's stability and threatening its social fabic. This theme is presented in the following excerpt from a news report, "Falun Gong Cult Endangers Society," dated November 4, 1999:

> The banned cult organization Falun Gong poses a grave threat to society, and the Chinese government can't just sit back and do nothing, a senior official said here today.
>
> Ye Xiaowen, director of the State Administration of Religious Affairs, briefed the press on the cult at a press conference held by the Information Office of the State Council.
>
> "Like every other cult in the world, the cult of Falun Gong poses a great danger to society," the official said, noting that its founder, Li Hongzhi, has spread heretical ideas just as other cult leaders have done.

... Li has ordered that Falun Gong practitioners not to take medicine, and he preaches that the power achieved by practicing Falun Gong cult can automatically kill disease and break away with the karmic chain— the cosmic principle that acts from previous lives are rewarded or punished in this life.

Should anyone overtly criticize or even make negative remarks about Falun Gong, Li Hongzhi and his Falun Gong organization would, under the pretext of "seeking a clarification" or "safeguarding Falun Dafa," mastermind large-scale illegal gatherings to besiege and harass government institutions, media and schools, for the sole purpose of taking revenge against society.

"These activities have seriously disrupted the public order, disturbed the normal life of the people *and infringed upon their freedom of speech and personal safety*," Ye stressed.

Theme #5: Unmasking Li Hongzhi as a Criminal

Chinese propaganda is filled with "evidence" of crimes committed by Falun Gong members—to disrupt society, steal secrets, and swindle money. No defense to any of these charges has been permitted or reported. Here is an excerpt from a December 29, 1999, Xinhua News Agency report, "Falun Gong Cult Crimes Exposed":

Four key members of the banned Falun Gong cult were tried and sentenced here on Sunday. The trial produced sufficient evidence of the Falun Gong crimes and the accused showed their remorse in the courtroom. The four—Li Chang, Wang Zhiwen, Ji Liewu and Yao Jie— were sentenced to eighteen, sixteen, twelve and seven years of imprisonment respectively on charges of organizing and using the cult organization to undermine the implementation of law, causing deaths by organizing and using the cult organization, and illegally obtaining state secrets.

The Falun Gong cult had evil intentions and endangered society and the country as a whole.

Among the examples was the April 25 siege of the central leadership compound Zhongnanhai by over 10,000 Falun Gong practitioners from Beijing, Tianjin, Hebei and elsewhere in the country. This incident seriously disrupted the work of government departments and the daily routine of the general public, threatened social stability and had negative political consequences.

> The accused employed various means to illegally obtain state secrets which were later made public by the accused . . .

Another example of this theme is found in an article entitled "Falun Gong Fined \$9.3m for Evading Tax," reporting that "tax authorities have discovered that branch organizations of Falun Gong and its US-based founder, Li Hongzhi, have been dodging taxes." The article charges that "Falun Gong organizations earned more than 22 million yuan from selling books, posters, and videos. Retailers earned more than 66.6 million yuan in profits from selling Falun Gong materials."

Theme #6: International Criticisms of China Are Hypocritical

When criticized for its treatment of Falun Gong, China's leaders avoid the specifics and lash out at the critics as hypocrites with double standards, who are meddling in China's internal affairs. This excerpt from a *People's Daily* article, "China Against US Double Standard on Falun Gong Cult," reveals the media's role in perpetuating this theme:

> China is indignant over the US government's double standard on the Falun Gong Sect. The US appears to be totally oblivious to the pernicious influence of the sect in China and continues to meddle in China's internal affairs, Chinese Foreign Ministry spokeswoman Zhang Qiyue said on December 7.
>
> In reply to a question that US President Bill Clinton expressed concern over China's stance on dealing with the Falun Gong cult yesterday, Zhang Qiyue said China urges the US government to take back comments made on the sect that might place new obstacles to Sino-US relations . . .

Theme #7: The Practice of Falun Gong Has Harmed Chinese Citizens

The Chinese press has carried many stories reporting on allegations of suicides and anti-social acts by Falun Gong practitioners; some even blame the practice for murders. None of these stories has been independently verified. Here is an excerpt of one report found on an anti–Falun Gong website, "Falun Gong Causes Another Tragedy," which first appeared on the national TV network, CCTV:

> Zhu Changjiu is a farmer from Cangzhou in Hebei Province. He had a happy family with a nice wife and two lovely kids. He used to do some extra work in his spare time to increase the family's income. But ever since he started following the Falun Gong cult in 1996, he

stopped caring for his family. Falun Gong was banned in July and pronounced illegal by the Chinese government. The local cadre asked Zhu's father, a veteran of the Anti-Japanese War, to help Zhu get out of the cult.

Local Party Committee Secretary said: "When I asked Zhu's father for help in the matter, he promised me he'd solve it. He said it will be OK, don't worry about it, leave it to me."

Zhu did not stop practicing Falun Gong. Instead, he hated his father for not letting him believe in the cult. For some time, he did not even speak to his father. He continued doing Falun Gong in bed, avoiding his family. On the morning of November 26th, Zhu allegedly knocked his seventy-three-year-old father on the head with an iron hammer and stabbed his mother with a scissors, killing them both.

Even after the police arrested him for the crime, Zhu still asserted that his behavior would bring his parents to paradise and end their sufferings. He explained that by dying, they could leave the hell of living in the world. He also said his parents were due to die that day. Zhu Changjiu (murder suspect) said: "According to the theory of Falun Gong, it is the right time. I can tell through my mind it is the time. That is why I killed them. In fact, I killed them to send them to the paradise. I don't think I did anything wrong, absolutely not" . . .

Zhu was a nice simple farmer before he followed the cult. Now he's a suspected murderer. The case proves that Falun Gong is undoubtedly an evil cult and will only cause more hardship and tragedy.

Theme #8: Falun Gong's Organization Threatens China

China has insisted that Falun Gong is a highly structured organization. It never explains how such an organization could have been created in a country dominated by security police and party organs. One article posted on a Chinese website, "Falun Gong Revealed As Structured Cult," sources a commentary published in *People's Daily* to buttress allegations that "Falun Gong is also a tightly organized cult . . . Li tricked the practitioners of Falun Gong into joining his 'kingdom,' and gradually separated them from mainstream society, eventually convincing them to fight against it . . ."

Another online report on November 1, 1999, "Falun Gong Has Irrefutable Cult Features," details the events from a symposium sponsored by the Chinese Academy of Social Sciences (the country's "top think-tank"), with the explicit purpose of criticizing Falun Gong. A researcher from the Institute of History is quoted as saying, "Under the pretext of religion, the cult persuaded its believers to depart from mainstream society. Therefore, it is a kind of spiritual opium."

* * *

Most of the news reports excerpted above can be read in their entirety at Chinese media websites (see Chapter 19: Internet Resource Guide, for the URLs of websites with anti–Falun Gong postings and news reports). Unfortunately, it has become increasingly difficult for people within China to use the web as a tool for researching the other side of the story, as many of the pro–Falun Gong websites have been blocked, filtered, or crippled through sophisticated electronic hacking.

CHAPTER 13
STATEMENTS FROM PRACTITIONERS AROUND THE WORLD

An American Practitioner's Story
by Gail Rachlin, Public Relations/Media Volunteer and Spokesperson
November 1999

Nearly two years ago, a friend introduced me to a Chinese spiritual practice that she said had helped her transform her life. I'd never heard of it, but as one of many corporate executives seeking meaning in their lives, I agreed to check it out. As a media person with over twenty years of experience in the business for many large companies, I was certain that I would be able to spot inflated claims or marketers of phony miracles.

I am still doing PR, but today I am also a practitioner of Falun Gong or Falun Dafa, a system for personal self-improvement that combines ancient Chinese qigong exercises with ideas about strengthening the mind, body, and spirit. Until recently, only a relatively small number of people in America had heard about Falun Gong because it was not marketed or sold as the next great thing.

Falun Gong quietly spread among millions of people interested in improving their health and deepening their spiritual awareness. Practitioners do exercises in parks and public spaces. Since its introduction in China in 1992, it has grown to between 70 and 100 million practitioners, amazing in light of the lack of media attention it received.

I am one of many Americans who have found the practice meaningful. It has helped me feel better about myself, more confident, even physically stronger.

Falun Gong's relative anonymity changed overnight last April, when 10,000 practitioners spontaneously turned up at the compound housing Chinese top leaders to call their attention to increasing local harassment. They wanted to talk with the leadership and explain that they were non-political and good people who just wanted to be left alone. They were not activists or advocates, just a cross-section of the Chinese population, including many members of the Communist Party, ordinary people who have found Falun Dafa to be helpful in their own lives.

Instead of dialoguing with its own people, the Chinese government decided that Falun Gong and its founder Li Hongzhi, who now lives in New York, were a threat. In late July, the Chinese authorities charged practitioners with trying to overthrow the government, and launched a hysterical campaign of intimidation. Thousands were rounded up. Over a million books and videos were burned and destroyed. An arrest warrant was issued for Li, and rumors surfaced in the Japanese press of assassination squads being dispatched to get him. Now, the Chinese are planning show trials for the detained Falun Gong practitioners, and have forbid them from having lawyers. It all seems like a throwback to the dark days of the Cultural Revolution.

Because of my media background, I was asked to be a spokesperson and volunteered to try to get this story out. There has been considerable press interest although the story has not received the kind of play it deserves, considering the number of people involved, the seriousness of the human rights abuses, and the implications for the future of China.

I have been distressed to see many American press outlets just echoing Chinese propaganda claims without doing any investigations of their own. For example, Beijing has branded Falun Gong a "cult," a pejorative term that just does not apply. Cults dominate all aspects of their member's lives, controlling their minds and bodies. Members surrender material goods to cults, to enrich the cult and its leaders. This is not true of Falun Gong. All of our activities are free and entirely voluntary. People practice Falun Gong or not according to whether they believe it to be a good thing.

Like the Chinese media which keeps projecting Falun Gong as a nefarious conspiracy, some in the American media won't accept us as we are, without any structured organization, hierarchy, or charismatic leader. They prefer stereotypes to hard information. This is troubling because it misinforms the American people.

Ironically, sometimes it seems easier to publicize products, with all of their self-serving claims, than a growing spiritual practice with many benefits for humanity. Why is that? Has skepticism in the media become so engrained that you have to be a celebrity to get attention? Shouldn't what is happening to 70 million people be of concern to us all? Or am I just naïve?

Gail Rachlin runs a media management firm in Manhattan.

* * *

Falun Gong practitioners hold regular "experience-sharing" conferences in which individuals tesitify to their own experiences. I attended one at Columbia University in New York in October 1999. I was struck by how personal and individual they were, as well as by the similarities in their vocabulary. Here are some statements from practitioners from different countries:

Moscow, Russia
The Truth Is in Dafa
by Eager Anochin

I am a Falun Dafa cultivator in a Moscow practicing site. I work in a security company now. My original career was sports teaching. In the past, I have been engaged in all kinds of martial-arts techniques and also practiced various forms of qigong. Last August after coming back from a qigong conference in Southeast Asia, I was looking for qigong websites on the Internet when I found Master Li Hongzhi's books unexpectedly. Thus I got to read the books *Zhuan Falun*, "The Great Perfection Way," and "Law Lecturing in Sydney." After that, I ceased trying any more qigong and realized that even the combination of all the existing qigongs could not compare with even half a truth. So I wholeheartedly threw myself into Falun Dafa from then on.

At the beginning I was practicing by myself. Later I got in touch with practitioners in St. Petersburg through Canada. From St. Petersburg, I got to know Dafa practitioners in Moscow. Then we established our own practicing site in Moscow. If there hadn't been Master Li's books, I would have been still wandering in the maze of various qigong schools. However, this predestined relationship has enabled everything of mine to eventually find its own position.

I had been an irascible person before. Now having practiced Falun Gong for one year, my family members and friends can see that I have become so calm and kind. I drive quite often. I find that there are many good opportunities to upgrade my Xinxing on the roads, especially when the traffic is crowded. If I had not had the firm mind that I am a cultivator and should behave myself according to the Great Law of "Truth-Compassion-Forbearance," I would not have passed those ordeals. After all, I am very glad I can often maintain myself in the state of Xinxing cultivation.

My right hand and forearm have been fractured a couple of times. And I could not open my palm completely because of the pain. However, after constantly practicing Falun Dafa, I do not have the problem of hand pain anymore. I can open my palm freely now and do not need an operation any more. I have also been able to keep free from catching a cold. Coldness and warmness do not have much influence on me now. A short sleep is enough for me every day. In the beginning of my Falun Gong practice, I did not feel like going to sleep at all, because my body energy could last for several days and nights.

I accepted Master Li's Dafa as soon as I saw it. And I will go on with my practice firmly by making full use of all my time. Many things that I experienced have enabled me to understand that the truth is here, in the Dafa.

I am hereby showing my deepest respect to Master Li, because he gives us Falun Dafa.

Riga, Russia
My Heart Is Brighter for Cultivating Dafa
by Andlie

My name is Andlie. I am thirty years old, and come from Riga. I have cultivated Falun Dafa for about one and a half years. Through studying Dafa, I have discovered the answers to many questions that nobody was able to explain to me before. In the past, I thought that nobody could tell me the answers just because these questions of mine were very childish, since there is a difference between adults and children, and the latter always have many questions about the world. As they grow up, they would form concepts for themselves about the world, the universe, and other things with conventional mentality. What kind of role should we play in this world? I understand the Buddha's Fa more and more deeply as I study Fa more and more frequently. I would like to give you several examples in my cultivation. I had been suffering from allergies during a certain time every year, and I also often caught colds. I had to take medicines, but I had subconsciously known that medicines could only reduce suffering temporarily, because the root of illnesses exist inside the body, and it would be worse and worse as time went by. Of course I had not known the real principles, since I had never heard about the miraculous book *Zhuan Falun*, written by Master Li. I instantly understood what I used to do when I finished reading Dafa for the first time. As Master Li said, by taking medicines I had actually pressed the diseases deep into my body. My allergy disappeared instantly when I began to cultivate Falun Dafa, but after a certain period of time, the symptoms appeared again. It seemed to refresh my memory. At that moment, I remembered at once what Master Li said about why this kind of phenomenon always recurs periodically. Master Li said: "Cultivation means that you will be cleaned up from the origin of your life. The human body is like a tree with annual rings, and disease-karma exists in each layer of your body. So your body has to be cleaned up from the very center." Then what I had encountered was just to eliminate karma and upgrade my enlightenment quality by means of this tribulation. Master Li had been testing whether I could believe in Dafa solidly and how well I could comprehend Dafa, as well as what attachments of mine should be given up.

All of us want to attain a perfect completion. I think that it is impossible for us to accomplish cultivation practice if we can not reach the state of non-leakage. If I had still worried about my illnesses or other tribulations in my life, and cared for losses of my personal fame . . . could I say that I had given up the attachments? Of course not. Master Li said: "Cultivation itself is not so painful, but the key is to let go of the attachments of ordinary people." We just have to forbear when we feel painful. In order to eliminate the pain, we should let go of our fame, gain, and emotions. I am working for a privately owned furniture factory. The leader of factory decided to rebuild the machinery workshop in order to enlarge the production area. When we hung up the roof, we would reinforce the crooked roof-beam. Otherwise the ceiling would probably collapse. When I hung up the ceiling using the crane for straightening the crooked beam (to then install the trestle), the crown block of the crane suddenly flew to my head and "Bang!" fell by my side. In the meantime, the ceiling fell down quickly but did not collapse. I was very calm at that time and I was not scared at all. I understood at once, it was the teacher who had protected me. I did my work continuously and finished it very quickly. Another time, our workshop was cutting MDF plates for producing furniture. Two workers carried a plate onto a cutting machine. I was standing by the machine while one worker accidentally dropped the plate onto my feet. It would have injured me seriously because of the heaviness of the plate. Workers were all astonished, but I remembered at once: "I am a practitioner, I am all right, and it might be that I owed him before." So I told them: "Never mind. I am OK." If I had been an ordinary person, I would probably not have said anything like this, and I would probably have thought with anger: "It is so painful and you are so stupid." My skin did not even show a purplish sign of injury. From now on I will upgrade my Xinxing and eliminate various attachments unceasingly until I have achieved the consummation. Now I often remember Master Li's words: "Giving is a manifestation of one's abandonment of attachments of an ordinary person. If one can really give willingly with his heart unmoved, he is actually at that level already."

Heidelberg, Germany
The Enormous Power of Dafa
by Marius Herb

My name is Marius Herb, and I started practicing Falun Gong a year ago. Before I met Falun Gong, my life was controlled by bad deeds, and I was taking drugs. My body conditions were terrible, and people around me disliked my behavior. Though all these told me that what I was doing was wrong, none of them had any actual effect on me. One night, I reached the judgment of life or death. I couldn't see anything with my flesh eyes, but I did see lots of things, which I don't wish to make any further explanations of here. I then understood that those lives known by us are not limited within this dimension only. I wish that I could change myself. After some time I got Master Li Hongzhi's book *Zhuan Falun*. While reading it, I understood what great power this book possesses, and how true its contents actually are. I could feel the boundless benevolence, and I returned to truthfulness from mistakes. I started taking actions once I realized this. But soon I was aware that those concepts and customs that I was trying to get rid of were much stronger than I had expected. At the beginning I couldn't resist the temptations, though I knew that some of the things were quite bad indeed. However, through my firm confidence and understanding, I became aware that Master Li would help us cultivators, as long as we change our concepts and wish to cultivate from the bottom of our hearts. I have been cultivating very firmly all the time. I quit drinking and smoking, as well as other drugs. I now feel lighter than any time before. Because of this understanding, many barriers that seemed impossible to overcome at the beginning can now be overcome. Before I started cultivation, my working environment wasn't very comfortable at all. On each Monday, I was thinking about the following weekend. None of the things I did were of my own free will. However, through reading *Zhuan Falun* over and over again, as well as practicing the movements, my wisdom grew day after day. I keep discovering that the understanding which I thought was correct will soon be replaced by another one. When I tried to seek externally for reasons for my mistakes, the resisting force would become stronger. This told me that I should look inward for reasons from time to time. My work hasn't changed, but my concepts have. I understood that a complicated environment is good for one's cultivation. Now I help others whenever possible and I can also keep calm when my colleagues get cross with me. I keep trying hard to rectify myself according to Zhen-Shan-Ren (Truth-Compassion-Forbearance). All my family thinks that I have made positive changes. Others think so as well, and even my girlfriend believes firmly about the deep meanings in this book. She can be a mirror for me, because through her I see the power of the Great Law. Until now, all the problems that I have come across through my cultivation were answered through reading the book *Zhuan Falun*, and other articles by the Master. I also believe that the problems I will meet later on can also be answered in this way. I hope that more people can obtain the Law, and return to their original true selves.

Sweden

What Falun Dafa Has Given Me
by Magdalena Savic

My name is Magdalena Savic. I live in Sweden. I have practiced Falun Dafa since 1995. I want to share with you what Falun Dafa has given me. I shall give a short account of how my life was before I started practicing Falun Dafa. I was a very sick person. Since birth I had weak physical health. Nobody really knew what was wrong with me. I was just weak, had no immunity to sickness, could faint anytime, and was susceptible to all kinds of illnesses. My parents carried me to many doctors to seek help. The doctors never found the cause of my weakness and sick physical body. So the doctors recommended strong tablets, change of environment, varying food, and so on. At one time my life was hanging on a straw and the doctors could not help me. In desperation, my father who had faith in God promised to donate his whole month's salary to the church if I could recover. I survived that time and my father kept the promise and paid the amount to the church. I survived the crisis. I felt better periodically, but no significant change had taken place. There were not many days when I could go without treatment. So I tried my whole life to take great care of my body through physical training, strong tablets, and many visits to doctors.

Despite all these efforts, and the fact that I have never smoked or drunk alcohol, I suffered from muscular problems at the age of twenty-six—my body twitched and I could not control my movements. The doctors suspected epilepsy, so it could not be cured. There was something wrong with my brain. I had to take medicine for the rest of my life. The next shocking message came at the age of thirty-six. I had cancer in my lungs. I was treated with radiotherapy but instead of becoming better, the cancer spread to my whole body. Then I was treated with chemotherapy. I got worse and worse. I did not know what to do. The doctors could only give me painkillers. I nearly gave up my life but for some reason I struggled to survive. The doctors did not give me much hope. I started to look for alternative methods. I thought that they could help me. For several years I tried all sorts of physical and spiritual treatments and qigong. I paid an enormous sum of money in my endeavor to become healthy, but I did not succeed. When one symptom disappeared, a few others appeared. It never ended. Nothing helped and I continued to search.

In 1995 I came in touch with Falun Dafa through an acquaintance. Just a short while after I began practicing Falun Dafa, my physical body became indeed purified from all illness. Today at the age of forty-nine, I am free from all illnesses. I do not need any tablets, any therapy, or any ordinary physical training. Like a miracle, my body feels fantastic and it is healthy. To obtain Fa, and the feeling of having a body free from illnesses, is difficult to describe with words—it has to be experienced. Yet getting a healthy body is just a side effect of practicing Falun Dafa. That is the very first thing a Falun Dafa practitioner experiences. In the book *Zhuan Falun*, Master Li Hongzhi said, "I do not talk about healing illnesses here, nor will we heal illnesses. However as a genuine cultivator, you cannot practice cultivation with an ill body. I shall purify your body. The body purification will be done only to those who come to genuinely study the practice and Dafa. We emphasize one point that if you cannot give up the attachment or that illness, we cannot do anything and will be helpless to you. Why can it be done to a practitioner, then? It is because a practitioner is most precious, and he wants to practice cultivation. Therefore, having this thought is most precious. When his Buddha nature comes out, the enlightened people will be able to help him."

I understand that the orthodox Fa provides salvation unconditionally to people who want to cultivate genuinely. Apart from the fact that my physical body is free from diseases, I know the reason why I am here on earth as a human being. Falun Dafa has given me a new life with a clear and conscious mind. It also gives me the ability to differentiate between right and wrong, good and bad, a possibility to cultivate my Xinxing, assimilate to the characteristics of the Universe—Zhen-Shan-Ren, become enlightened, return to my original true self, and attain perfection. Falun Dafa has given all this to me. I thank deeply Falun Dafa and the teacher of Falun Dafa, Mr. Li Hongzhi. Thank you, Mr. Li Hongzhi!!

Toronto, Canada
by Susan Mitchel

I'm a Canadian of English/Scottish ancestry in my mid-fifties, who started practicing Falun Dafa January 17, 1999—a date I shall cherish for the rest of my life. For the last thirty years, I have been interested in spirituality and have read widely and practiced various forms of meditation. As soon as I read the first page of *Zhuan Falun*, its Truth resonated through my whole being. After working my way through the first two or three chapters, I felt as if I was waking up from a very long dream and knew from the depths of my being that my life was finally coming back into focus. Over the past ten years, I had major health problems and was spending over two hundred dollars a month on Chinese herbal medicines and other dietary supplements. Within a week and a half of starting to read *Zhuan Falun* and beginning to learn the Falun Gong exercises, my digestive system and other body functions normalized and I was able to stop taking all of those things. Another important benefit has been an upgrading of my moral and ethical nature. Because of illness, I've had to rely on Unemployment Insurance and support from other government agencies, friends, and family for much of the last five years. It has taken less than six months of practicing Falun Dafa to be able to really "stand on my own two feet" in every way. You can't imagine the feelings of self-worth and peace this brings. I can highly recommend this practice to everyone who sincerely wants to become the best person they can possibly be.

Melbourne, Australia
Why Do People Choose Falun Dafa?
by Kati Turcu

I studied for years: languages, Eastern and Western philosophy, religion, and other subjects. So armed with two university degrees and all this knowledge, I had more questions than ever. Nothing I had studied ever brought me any closer to the truth. One day I was given the book *Zhuan Falun* to read. I read day and night for two days as if my life depended on it, and found it hard to put down the book. Finally I was introduced to the exercises. As I moved my arms and legs, I felt them stretching to infinity.

All my doubts and pains fell off my body like an old and rusty armor. I felt myself growing large and my head filled with stillness and peace. I knew then that I had finally found my way back.

Sunshine Coast, Australia
Glenda McNiece

Twenty-two years ago I was involved in a motor-bike accident which left me with a broken collarbone and back injuries including bruising around the vertebrae and a misaligned pelvis. From this, I suffered severe neck and sciatic pain. Over the years, I have managed and to a degree overcome these injuries by practicing yoga and meditation and visualization techniques. Though my mobility improved, I still suffered some neck and shoulder and sciatic pain. I also had numbness and pain in my left foot due to a breakage ten years ago, as well as an ongoing intermittent pain in the abdominal region from menstrual and intestinal spasming. When I first started practicing Falun Gong almost a year ago I felt immediate relief from the neck and shoulder tension, as if a great weight had been lifted from me! As I continued I found my overall strength greatly improved, especially through the arms and legs.

Brisbane, Australia
Leisa Griffiths-Park

Knowing that the major responsibility is internal for my mind, thought, actions, and reactions, I consequently sought to find extensive spiritual, metaphysical ways to contribute to world healing . . . peace. Along the way I became increasingly ill, including a diagnosis of an incurable genetic brain disease. On receiving Falun Dafa I came to recognize amidst so much, the knowledge that practicing multiple metaphysical healing systems in turn creates physical and spiritual turmoil. In immediate and total respect for Master Li, and with increasing discipline, my illnesses and disease have rapidly disappeared. I now celebrate pregnancy and a life of ever-growing well-being.

* * *

Statement by American Practitioner William Woodton
August 1999, New York City

I live in the Bronx. I was diagnosed about two or three weeks ago with . . . I had clogged arteries. So I went to the hospital. Well, first I didn't even know this. I was having trouble with my circulation when I went to sleep at night. I just couldn't sleep. Every time I lay down I would have pain. So

I had a series of tests when I went to the hospital and after the tests the doctor told me that I had some clogged arteries.

Usually, I live a pretty straight life. I don't smoke, I don't drink, I don't do this. I was playing by the rules. I don't eat this, I don't eat that. He tells me my arteries are clogged. He tells me, "I want to do a bypass on you." Now I'm really scared. So, I come to work and I'm a little depressed and one of my co-workers tells me, well look, we're doing something here in the park on circulation. When I went back to the doctor he said we can't do the bypass because the arteries are clogged in too many different spots. But, he said, we have a laser surgery that we could do—go in through the capillaries and laser these spots, so you know, I'm just saying to myself— because I really don't like doctors, I mean, I guess nobody really likes doctors. I hadn't been to a doctor in so many years. I just had that fear of going to a doctor and letting him cut into me. So my co-worker said come down here and just try this out and see how you like it. You know your circulation will be increased . . . like twofold, man.

So last Sunday I came down here. Now, before I came down here, I could walk like maybe three blocks and get a little slight tightness in my chest. "Man, I gotta stop. I'm fifty-five, gotta stop." I came down here and took one exercise last week with the movements. I got the book, I read the book, you know, followed the exercise. I wasn't doing them perfectly, but I was opening up some channels. Then I go outside, I start walking—three blocks, four blocks, five—and I am not getting tightness in my chest at all. I'm like hey, there is something to this!

Now I don't have to go back to my doctor, my cardiologist, until the end of next month. He gave me some [medication] to bring the cholesterol down. With the medicine he gave me, I still felt some tightness after a few blocks. I don't know if I was getting better from the medication or what but I know this much: the one day I was here, doing this exercise, when I walked away, I just felt like something—the congestion was gone. And I'm walking down here, down the hill, up here, not one time did I feel any tightness. By the time I got back to the train to go back to the Bronx, I felt a tiny bit of tightness. But it had never been cut back that much.

So, I got up this morning, looked out the window, and said, "Oh, it's raining. . . I'm gonna come down here anyway. I don't know if they are out here." But I saw everybody out here and I was like, WHOA!, let me get some more of this. That's what I would say. And I'm telling you, I don't know what it is but something changed inside. The circulation done changed. And I'm saying that the medicine that the doctor gave me, it may be good and it may be working, but it doesn't have me walking as far as I did with the three hours that I got last week. In the nighttime, before last week, I would get up around two times in the nighttime. You know, to go to the bathroom. Before I go to sleep at night I go through what the book is showing me and I sleep right through. I get up five o'clock every morning . . . I sleep right through the night. I look, and it's five. I usually get up around three, four, something like that. I lay down to go to sleep and I'm out cold. I wake up just before the alarm goes off at five o'clock. I look and I'm like . . . "Yo, I slept all through the night." And every night when I go to sleep, I try to use the exercises and it helps me sleep. I don't know if this is going to cure what my problem is, but I do know that it makes me feel better.

Like I said, I only had one demonstration last week, then at lunchtime my co-worker took me to the park and went through it a little bit, and then today. This is the third time I've done this, but I'm telling you when I do this . . . maybe it's the flow. I wanted better circulation, but the flow is real. There is something there that is real. It's no joke—I wouldn't be back here today.

* * *

Conversation with Practitioners Noah Parker, Adam Montanaro, and Levi Browde, Software Engineers
August 1999, New York City

Levi Browde: A friend of mine was practicing and I noticed it. I had done some meditation like this before, and was heavy into athletics and sports. So I asked him about it, and he gave me one of the books and showed me some of the exercises and I just sort of dived into it from that point there.

Adam Montanaro: I knew someone who had been practicing it for a while, about six months. I watched his progress and watched him seem to be healthier every day. He seemed to have a better state of mind every day. I would always ask him, "What is this you're doing?" He would tell me a little bit about it. Slowly I got into it and eventually I asked him, "Well, do you have this book, can I borrow this book, *Zhuan Falun*?" He gave it to me and I read through the book and shortly after that I learned the exercises and I've pretty much been doing it every day since then. I've done a lot of martial arts. I've even taken Tai Chi. So the slow movements that we do in Falun Gong weren't alien to me. But it's very different than the martial arts that I've been familiar with in the past.

Actually, the way we got into it is the way people commonly get into it. There's no advertisement with Falun Gong. They put their websites up there and you have a bunch of people that are in a certain area that practice. Maybe one person would like to share the information—they are very open about what they do and they want people to see that they can try it if they are interested. That is why you practice publicly in the park, and you put up a sign that says, "Hey, we're doing Falun Gong. If you're interested come on by, it's free and you can stop by any time and learn it."

Noah Parker: I went and tried it out and I was pretty turned off. I didn't find it that interesting, but I kept doing it and now I totally love it. It makes me feel very relaxed and very calm.

It hadn't shown up in the news when we first started. I don't have any political background and I don't have any political interest at all in it whatsoever. I don't feel politically involved in my practice. I just feel concerned for people who aren't allowed to practice. That's the extent of my political involvement. It's not a political movement at all.

After I do the movements, I feel very relaxed and very calm, almost like when I used to go jogging a lot. I used to go jogging once or twice a day and afterwards, I just felt very peaceful and relaxed. This does that for me but on a larger scale—this sort of stays with me throughout the day. I feel very peaceful and relaxed. If a stressful situation arises, I just take it in stride, which is a new thing for me. I wasn't really like that before.

It's not a workout like Americans think of a workout, but the sensation is, at least for me, very similar, in that afterwards I feel very healthy. I feel healthier than I've ever felt before. I feel relaxed, just sort of mentally balanced.

Levi Browde: I'd like to say something—Noah touched upon a key point which really attracted me to this. When I first started doing this, I was doing heavy athletics. I would work out for several hours a day and I did that for a number of years. And in addition to that I got into Buddhism, which is pretty much the opposite, because it deals with sitting meditation and stuff like that. But in both cases I failed to realize the calmness or cleaner state of mind that should come to you from whatever that practice is, whether it be athletics or a form of spiritual practice.

Adam Montanaro: It's a little bit like when you asked me the difference between this and martial arts. There's a whole other aspect to Falun Gong. It's not just the physical exercises, but there's also the book. And it does help, when you read the book. It teaches you about certain things, like virtues, which may be considered a dirty word in modern-day America, but it has always seemed important to me. I always thought it made sense to be a good person and to put other people before you. It's very hard to find examples of that in the modern world. If you work in New York City, you can go the whole day and not see anybody doing much of anything nice for anybody else. But it always seemed to me that just because everything is like that doesn't mean that's the right way to be. So the book, *Zhuan Falun*, talks a lot about the three principle ideas behind Falun Gong, which are Truthfulness, Compassion, and Forbearance, and it actually talks a lot about how to implement these in your life so you have tools to go about with during the day and work with. When I actually get to a place where I feel compassion for the people around me, it feels stronger and deeper than love, or love that I've experienced in the past.

Levi Browde: One of the things—and Adam touched on that a little bit—is that we're still in the learning phase so we're on a certain level, we have a certain kind of understanding. But what I've come to see from reading the book and doing the exercises, is that this compassion, it seems like such a simple thing. You open the book, it teaches about compassion, and this changes your life? Wait a second. But when I look at all the other practices I've tried in my life, it is the first practice that breaks things down to a very simple exercise and a very simple idea of Truth, Compassion, and Forbearance. And just because it's simple doesn't necessarily mean that it's not powerful. In fact, it might just mean that it's more powerful than all these other systems that may have a lot more to keep in mind.

Adam Montanaro: I guess I can speak to the morality issue. I think everybody knows how to be a better person, but it's not an easy thing to do anymore. Most religions talk about truth, compassion, and forbearance. They're not new ideas, and I know everybody was raised with those principles in mind, but there's always this sense that you have to force yourself to be that way. When I first got into Falun Gong, I was shying away from those principles, because I thought I would have to force myself to behave a certain way. But it didn't turn out that way. To my surprise and pleasure, I just ended up behaving better and I don't necessarily ever have to force myself or remind myself to do that. And I'm grateful for that.

Question: What about Master Li?

Adam Montanaro: Well, I'm just really appreciative that he made this book. I was lucky enough to see him when they did a conference in Chicago— he stopped by and answered some questions there and it was nice to see him . . . As for cults, what I see with these people and what they are doing—they seem very normal people. They're from all walks of life, all different ages. And then on the other side, you have this picture that the Chinese government is painting, and the two just don't match. So people are saying, "What is going on here—what's the real story?"

Noah Parker: At first glance, to an American this just looks like some weird practice: it's strange, it comes from China, what is it? I felt the same way, but I tried the exercises, I read the book, and that's it . . . and I felt better. I felt more relaxed, I felt calmer. Before the practice started to work, my life was so complex—just to get through the day and keep track of everything was a serious task, let alone any personal self-inter-est or any other kind of exploration. And like I said, I tried the exercises and I read the book. I didn't force myself to behave a certain way. I didn't subscribe to any foreign belief system, I just did the exercises and read the book, and I feel better. So just from that point of view, I would recommend it to anybody. If you're curious, check it out. It's really a deceptively simple thing. Other people have other experiences in the practice. This is mine, and it's making me feel better, so it seems to be doing a good job for me.

Adam Montanaro: People are out there and they're watching this. They may decide that it's something that's not for them. But there's a whole other side to this issue and that's the human rights issue. And I think as Americans we can all agree that if you have something you want to believe in, you should have the right to believe that. You should have the right to get together with other people who believe that. So there are two issues here: There is Falun Gong, and then there's just these basic human rights.

Levi Browde: I'd like to say one more thing. It's hard, at least from the American point of view, to really get a sense of what's going on in China right now. The best analogy I've heard is to imagine if the United States government were to outlaw baseball. So suddenly anybody who's practicing baseball or even has baseball paraphernalia in their house gets arrested, gets fired from their job, and their family is suspected as well. That's what's going on in China right now. You have to wonder why something that innocent, something that doesn't hurt anybody, is being persecuted in China right now. That's the issue.

* * *

Falun Dafa—A Science of Body, Mind, and Spirit
by Jingduan Yang, M.D.

Health Benefits—By-product of the Practice

In March 1999, Mrs. Song, a sixty five-year-old Chinese woman, came to the United States to visit her son and his wife. For ten years she had hesitated to leave China, where she was under close care of physicians of both Chinese medicine and modern Western medicine. She had a longstanding history of coronary artery disease with angina, which she had to take nitrates every day to prevent. She also had severe rheumatoid arthritis and she took a number of medications and Chinese herbal remedies. Despite such complementary treatment, she had very low energy, shortness of breath with mild exertion, and swollen legs, ankles in particular. She could foretell weather changes according to the severity of her joint pain. She had eye surgery thirty-five years before, which left her with a pair of glasses and uneven vision. In addition, she suffered tobacco addiction and smoked a pack of Chinese cigarettes every day for thirty-five years. Of course it did not help her poor lung and heart function at all. She had tried every possible way to quit, with no luck, before she arrived in Minnesota.

With the promise that she could have a physician with knowledge of both traditions of medicine, and being secured with a three-month supply of all her medications and herbal formulas, and, believe it not, twenty cartons of Chinese cigarettes, she came with her husband (a smoker, too!) for a three-month visit. As you can imagine, very soon the whole apartment building smelled pretty smoky.

Both her son and daughter-in-law practice Falun Gong. They began to read aloud to their parents *Zhuan Falun*, essentially a transcript of Li Hongzhi's lectures in China, one chapter every day. Mrs. Song found the book very interesting and liked the reading very much. It reminded her of traditional moral teaching she received from her mother when she was young. One day, when they read chapter seven, in which there are two paragraphs about how smoking negatively affects the practice of cultivation, it says, "I advise everyone that if you truly want to practice cultivation you should quit smoking from now on, and it is guaranteed that you can quit. When you smoke a cigarette again, it will not taste right. If you read this lecture in the book, it will also have this effect."

Mrs. Song was very excited about it and really wanted to practice it. However, she did not expect this effect could happen so soon. That day after lunch, she habitually lit her cigarette, totally forgetting what she had read. Her son and daughter noticed, but said nothing. After several deep drags, she suddenly dropped the cigarette and rushed to the bathroom. She almost vomited. Apparently, it was more than just "not taste right." She did not give up her skepticism and kept testing herself by putting the unlit cigarette under her nose and just smelling it. Every time she did that, it made her sick. She has not smoked ever since.

After reading the whole book and also watching the video lecture, Mrs. Song began to understand a lot of things she had never known, such as why people have to go through life stages like birth, old age, illness, and death. She learned that people should cultivate and practice in order to assimilate into the nature of the universe, to be mentally enlightened to the truth of the universe, and to be physically purified and transformed. She embraced the teaching and learned and practices the five exercises every day, too.

One day after a group exercise practice, she suddenly had chest pain, which was new to her; medication she took should have prevented it. Feeling puzzled, she began to remember the Teacher's words she had read: "I do not talk about healing illness here, nor will we heal illness. As a genuine practitioner, however, you cannot practice cultivation with an ill body. I will purify your body. The body purification will be done only for those who come to truly learn the practice and the Fa." "We must dig it out and eliminate it completely from its root. With this, you may feel that your illness has recurred. This is to remove your karma fundamentally, thus you will have reactions."

She continued her reading and exercising despite her episodic chest pain. In about one week, all the symptoms disappeared, together with her joint pain and edema in her ankles. She had to, with happiness this time, buy herself a new pair of shoes at the size she used to have twenty years ago. She was amazed at the power of Falun Gong, and began striving to live every moment of her life following the principles of "Truthfulness, Compassion, and Forbearance." One morning in June 1999, she woke up and found her glasses broken under her, a kind of accident that had not happened to her before. She immediately discovered she did not need them to see clearly any more. On June 25, Mrs. Song gave a speech to share her experiences at a conference held in Chicago. On stage in front of a large audience, she read her paper wearing no glasses.

Such health benefits are common to practitioners of Falun Gong. In 1997, a group of scientists and physicians from top hospitals and medical research institutions in Beijing surveyed 12,731 Falun Gong practitioners about the health benefits obtained from practicing Falun Gong. According to the survey, out of 12,731 participants, 93.4 percent had medical conditions, and 49.8 percent had suffered from at least three diseases before they began practicing Falun Gong. Through practicing Falun Gong, the total healing effectiveness reached 99.1 percent, among which the complete recovery rate was 58.5 percent. The fraction of "very energetic" people increased to 55.3 percent after practicing from 3.5 percent before practicing. 96.5 percent of the people also felt mentally healthier. Each one of them saved the state an average of 3215 yuan of medical expenses.

However, if you ask Falun Gong practitioners if health is the goal of their practice, the answer may surprise you: "No, health benefits are only the by-products of our practice."

How could they obtain these by-products almost for free while, using the best that modern medicine has to offer, it costs lifetimes and enormous amounts of dollars and talent even to try to obtain such effect? Can we make sense of it from the perspective of modern medicine or even traditional Chinese medicine?

Medical Perspectives—Scratching the Surface of Body/Mind Relationship

What benefit people could obtain from practicing Falun Gong? Following are some common answers: Become more relaxed, clear-headed, and free of stress; raise the quantity and quality of your personal energy; give up smoking or other undesired habits; improve relationships with people around you, especially through learning how to handle interpersonal conflicts beneficially; improve your health and increase your physical fitness; Understand more about what constitutes your "true self"; learn about fundamental natural laws and principles; understand why tribulations enter our lives and how they can be useful; learn about the relationship between mind and matter; work on self-improvement while spending time with a group of compassionate, accepting, and likewise-committed people.

It is obvious that Falun Gong practitioners are free of stress and free of bad habits.

Modern medicine is embracing a biopsychosocial model. After investigating 170 sudden deaths over about six years in 1971, George Engel observed that serious illness or even deaths might be associated with psychological stress or trauma.

Emotional stress can contribute to a wide range of health problems, such as coronary artery disease, asthma, ulcerative colitis, rheumatoid arthritis, flare-ups of virus infection, likelihood of contracting infectious mononucleosis, cancer, AIDS, and even Alzheimer's disease.

Bad lifestyle causes seventy to eighty percent of all illness. For instance, in the United States, about ten percent of woman and twenty percent of men have met the diagnostic criteria for alcohol abuse. About 200,000 deaths each year are directly related to alcohol-related disorders such as suicide, cancer, heart disease, and hepatic disease. Alcohol abuse reduces life expectancy by about ten years. The direct and indirect social costs of these disorders are estimated at more than $150 billion, about $600 per capita.

In this country, an estimated 61 million people were current smokers in 1995, 4.5 million adolescents. Every year, there are 170,000 new cases of lung cancer diagnosed, with about 150,000 deaths occurring each year. eighty to ninety percent of all lung cancers occur among smokers. In China, there are 300 million smokers today.

Poor diet and lack of exercise and depression also lead to a higher risk of heart disease. Despite the modern technology and health education, 400,000–500,000 people die from coronary artery disease each year.

While modern medicine looks primarily to mechanical or biophysical problems as causes of illness, in traditional Chinese medicine, body and mind have never been separated.

The organs are seen not only in terms of anatomical existence of the particular organ, but also in terms of the concepts of energetic networking and commanding sites of mental function.

For example, when the heart receives emotional stimuli such as joy, anger, sadness, fear, and worry, these emotions then affect the energy of heart, liver, lung, spleen, and kidney, respectively. As a result, the physiological function of these organs will also be affected, and a number of somatic dysfunctions may manifest. Vice versa, if these organs are assaulted by other pathogenic factors, such as infection, vascular event, toxicity, trauma, etc., they tend to generate corresponding emotional changes.

For example, anger, either toward others (irritability) or toward oneself (depression) will affect the liver. In traditional Chinese medicine, liver regulates energy flow smoothly, helps digestion, nourishes sinews and ligaments, stores blood, and regulates women's menstruation, is in charge of the ethereal soul that relates to dreams, and is responsible for vision and eyes. Its meridian is connected, through its partner, gallbladder, with the shoulder and neck, temple area of the head. When liver energy is disturbed, as in conditions of stress, one may have several illnesses, as explained by modern medicine, going on at same time. Chronic pain syndrome, fibromyalgia, migraine, PMS, irritable bowel syndrome, depression, nightmare or sleep disorders, dizziness and vertigo, abnormal menstruation and breast fibroids, etc. In traditional Chinese medicine it is all primarily caused by or secondary to a single condition called Liver Qi Stagnation. It may not be just coincidental that when Prozac was widely used for treating depression, people also found it very useful in treating PMS and migraine.

All these interactions are realized through an energetic networking system called meridians. Meridians have their representative points on the surface of the body, which you can stimulate with different tools such as needles, pressure, moxa, etc., to modulate energy dysfunction of the internal organs. For thousands of years, traditional physicians have been helping people with their Qi by using acupuncture, herbal formula, Dao Ying (like qigong today), and in particular by telling people to stay emotionally peaceful.

However, the secret to optimal health is to have a "clean heart and few desires." In the Yellow Emperor's *Internal Classics of Medicine,* "Heart is the organ of Emperor, when Emperor is not wise, the other twelve organs will be in danger." But how can one come to have a clean heart and few desires?

Cultivation Practice—Spiritual Renewal

When you see our demonstration, you may find the movements are very graceful and soothing. However, you may not find it particularly different from other forms of qigong, yoga, and Tai Chi. How come this practice has attracted such a large population within such a short time; how come its practitioners acclaim such wonderful, sometimes miraculous healing effects?

While the term Qi, life force or energy, is becoming popular to many everyday Americans, Falun Gong practitioners are trying to get rid of the Qi and replace it with what is called Gong. Described in Mr. Li's book *Zhuan Falun,* Gong is a higher energy from the universe. While Qi is subject to all kinds of dysfunctions (what are described in traditional Chinese medicine as qi deficiency, rebellious qi, sinking qi, stagnant qi, collapsed qi, etc.), Gong is seen as a higher level of energy from the universe that is resistant to any kind of pathogen. However, Falun Gong holds that the only way to obtain this higher form of energy, or Gong, is to cultivate one's spirit and mind to assimilate to the nature of universe; Zhen, Shan, and Ren. Practicing the five sets of Falun Gong exercises is said to enhance and accelerate the process of Gong development, but only if one accompanies the exercises with cultivation of one's heart and mind in daily life.

So, is this belief true? And what exactly happens if Gong is in fact developed? Professor Lili Feng and her assistants at the Scripps Research Institute in California are studying seventeen Falun Gong practitioners' lymphocytes' efficacy against HIV in vitro, and the preliminary results have been very impressive. Some of these cells have been proven to be resistant to HIV infection. Accidentally, another scientist in the group found the practitioners' neutrophils—white blood cells that have a key role in fighting against bacterial infection—to live thirty times longer than average cells, and to also remain in high function during their extended lifespan. Currently, this molecular biologist is expanding her study samples to include more practitioner data. She could not explain her findings using science's current understanding of such things. She told me, "it can only be explained by the teachings in *Zhuan Falun*."

According to the Buddha school, bad karma accumulates from wrong-doing in this and past lifetimes, causing suffering. Falun Gong holds that the suffering of illness results from karma, and that through self-cultivation this karma may be eliminated, bringing one to an illness-free and ulti-mately enlightened state. In *Zhuan Falun*, Mr. Li states, however, that "cul-tivation depends on one's self, and a cultivation system depends on one's teacher." So it is understood that through obtaining the right teachings and through self-cultivation, one may not only reach an illness-free state, but enlightenment.

When a practitioner follows the right teachings, miracles can hap-pen. This is the way I understand what happens in Falun Gong practice. They begin to be fully aware of their personal, ethical shortcomings, and make improvements. They begin to understand how to live a truly mean-ingful life, and for this they are rewarded. It becomes very clear to them that without the health of one's spirit, one's mind and body can never be healthy.

Starting in 1949, when the Communists took power in China, any belief in enlightened beings, divine beings, demons, or gods were totally regarded as backward and superstitious. The people who dared to hold onto their beliefs were severely punished; many were even executed. In the last seven years, over 100 million people in China and abroad have become spiritually renewed through practicing Falun Gong. For them, though, it hasn't been simply faith that has led them in this direction, but incredible personal experiences, including healing of chronic, and some-times so-called incurable illnesses, and enlightenment to the truth of the universe. Because of the power of such experiences, upon facing severe punishment and even threats of death, practitioners have not given up, but instead have become more persistent. They return the government's fabrications with stories of truth; they return the persecution with compassion and tolerance.

CHAPTER 14
WHO IS LI HONGZHI?

The following Li Hongzhi biography was assembled by Falun Gong practitioners:

In May 1992, Mr. Li Hongzhi, the founder of Falun Dafa, began teaching his cultivation system to the general public in China. Ever since then, Falun Dafa (or Falun Gong) has attracted more than 100 million people worldwide.

Mr. Li was born in the city of Gongzhuling in Jilin Province, China, on May 13, 1951. Li Hongzhi began his cultivation practice from childhood. Being gifted and compassionate, he differed from other children his age and voluntarily undertook the major household tasks and the care of his younger siblings to assist his mother, who worked long hours.

When he was four years old, Mr. Li received personal instruction from Master Quan Jue, the tenth heir to the cultivation system of the supreme order—the school of "Truthfulness, Benevolence, Forbearance," which was handed down to a single disciple in each generation. At the age of eight, Mr. Li achieved a high level in cultivation and was given three special words, "Zhen, Shan, Ren"—Truthfulness, Benevolence, Forbearance. "Zhen": truthfulness; requiring one to be honest, not cheat, and never lie. "Shan": compassion; showing sympathy for the weak and helping the poor and less fortunate. "Ren": forbearance; remaining optimistic and bright in the face of adversity, enduring hardship, having tolerance, and enduring all without resentment.

At the age of twelve, another superior master imparted to Mr. Li the Taoist cultivation system. Through his teacher, Mr. Li mastered boxing, sword-and-spear play, and internal (meditation) exercises. After his second teacher left him, Mr. Li continued to practice diligently and became quite advanced in his cultivation practice while still a teenager.

In 1970, Mr. Li attained the profound mystic law of the cultivation practice transmitted by Superior Master Li Jiang from the Changbai mountains. From 1974 onwards, he was instructed in succession by more than twenty masters from both the Buddha and Taoist Schools. He arrived at an immeasurably advanced stage of cultivation with an awakening and enlightenment to the truth of the universe, and profound insight into human life.

After his Enlightenment in 1984, he was saddened by the condition of mankind. With their demoralized spirits and physical suffering, people's living standards were growing, but their spiritual qualities were not keeping up with their material improvement. He made up his mind to devote himself to mankind's well-being and to create a cultivation practice suitable for ordinary people. Under the guidance of all of his masters, and taking into account what he had painstakingly practiced for so many years, through many setbacks, much deliberation, creation, and modification, he established Falun Dafa (Falun Gong). Since its establishment, substantial evidence has shown that the practice of Falun Dafa is outstanding for its mental and physical benefits.

Mr. Li introduced the public to his teachings of Falun Dafa through participation at the 1992 and 1993 sessions of the Oriental Health Fair held in Beijing. Falun Dafa and its founder, Mr. Li Hongzhi, received much praise and quickly won international recognition.

Mr. Li Hongzhi lectures all over the world on the principles of Falun Dafa. Mr. Li does not take any remuneration nor does he allow his students to collect any fees for teaching the exercises. He maintains that the teaching of Falun Dafa should be for the salvation of all sentient beings with no distinction made based on nationality, race, or religious belief, and that all are equal in the matter of obtaining the wisdom of Falun Dafa.

* * *

Interview with Li Hongzhi by Danny Schechter
July 23, 1999 (the day after Falun Gong was officially banned)

On the Crackdown

"Practitioners of Falun Gong would like to express to the government all the indignities that they have suffered, but they have encountered obstruction and they have no recourse to express their views to the government. As such, many people have been detained, beaten up, and even incarcerated, causing great harm to practitioners of Falun Gong and to the Chinese people. There are reports saying that our Falun Gong is a tightly-knit and secretive organization. When I heard this, I was really shocked. It is ridiculous, because Falun Gong doesn't have an organizational structure at all . . . I do not oppose the government, nor will I get involved in politics."

On the Size of Falun Gong

"A reporter told me that the number of people practicing Falun Gong has already exceeded the number of Communist Party members, so the government feels nervous about it. Actually, I don't think they should feel that way. Falun Gong does not participate in politics; it simply teaches people to be good people. So if they truly understood Falun Gong, they wouldn't think that way."

On Dialogue with China

"I would very much like to have a dialogue with the Chinese government. If they had done this earlier, I don't think these problems would have appeared. Regardless of what consequences they will have on Falun Gong, it is certain that they will ultimately have serious negative consequences for the Chinese government and the Chinese people."

On Human Rights

"I think, judging from the current situation, the human rights of the more than 100 million of our practitioners have been violated. And the attacks on myself and the fabricated videotapes can only be seen as a serious human rights issue.

"I hope that all these kind-hearted people and the various governments will be able to stand forward and help resolve this issue. In actuality, each and every one of the over 100 million Falun Gong practitioners have families, wives, children, and friends, so it's very likely that it's really an issue of several hundred million people. That's why I hope that this will arouse the concern of the international community."

On Falun Gong Being Portrayed as an "Evil Cult"

"I think that in the beginning, many of the operational departments of the Chinese government, and in particular the Public Security Bureau, called us an evil religion or a cult. But I am only teaching people to practice qigong for healing and fitness, and, at the same time, to be more noble people. So it cannot really be called an evil religion . . . As for us propagating superstition, are all of the religions, including Catholicism, Protestantism, and Buddhism, superstitions? The issues I address have not really gone beyond the scope of what [other religions] discuss. Moreover, I also incorporate scientific knowledge with regard to many issues in an effort to have everyone understand.

"I hope the Chinese government will truly be able to handle this situation well, keeping the interests of the people in mind, and not make this so confrontational. I would like to do this through a dialogue. The practitioners as a whole are reasonable and they definitely won't create trouble for the government. Is it possible to use other methods to reach a better resolution? I hope that I will be able to have the kind of contact with the Chinese government that will allow this situation to calm down.

"If the situation cannot be resolved in the manner in which I hope, and it continues to develop, human lives could be at risk. There could be beatings, killings . . . another Tiananmen incident. The way I see it, that would be of no benefit to the Chinese government either. But I'm worried that that's what is going to happen.

"I hope that the various governments and peoples of different nations will show concern for this situation and will give it a just resolution."

On Resolution to the Crisis

"With respect to the present situation in China, I feel that it will bring no favorable outcome to either the Chinese government or the people of China. I hope that the Chinese government will justly, fairly, and promptly act on the matter and not put up an opposition.

"I believe that the people involved in this mass protest would never give trouble to the government. The government began labeling them as a cult and as an illegal sect, and wanted to control them. They felt that this was unjustified and so engaged in the protest.

"It is possible to come up with another solution to better solve this problem.

"I hope that I can reach an agreement with the Chinese government to enable the situation to be peacefully resolved. At the same time, I believe that if this ideal state cannot be achieved and that if events escalate for the worse, in which lives are endangered, it could result in the imprisonment and killing of people, becoming a second mass massacre.

"I feel that this, too, does not have any benefit for the Chinese government. But as I am worried that such a scenario may occur, I hope that international governments and human rights groups can help keep the situation guarded and under control, and that it will be given a fair treatment."

CHAPTER 15
HUMAN RIGHTS REPORTS AND
OTHER THIRD-PARTY PERSPECTIVES

Amnesty International Report (excerpts)
The Crackdown on Falun Gong and Other So-Called "Heretical Organizations"

March 23, 2000

> *"Our struggle against Falun Gong is protracted, acute, and complicated."*
> —LUO GAN, member of the Political Bureau of the Chinese
> Communist Party Central Committee, addressing a national conference
> of directors of justice departments, December 28, 1999.

1. Introduction

Amnesty International is calling on the Chinese government to stop the
mass arbitrary detentions, unfair trials, and other human rights violations
resulting from the crackdown on the Falun Gong and other groups branded
by the government as "heretical organizations." All the information available indicates that the crackdown is politically motivated, with legislation
being used retroactively to convict people on politically driven charges, and
new regulations introduced to further restrict fundamental freedoms.

In its New Year editorial on January 1, 2000, the official newspaper
People's Daily listed the "serious handling" of the "heretical organization
Falun Gong" as one of the Chinese government's major achievements of
1999. The government claims that the Falun Gong, which teaches a practice of meditation and exercises, represents a serious "threat to social and
political stability" in China. It banned the Falun Gong on July 22, 1999.
A legislative decision on the banning of all "heretical organizations" was
subsequently adopted by China's parliament, the National People's
Congress, in October 1999. Since the ban, the Chinese authorities, at
national and provincial level, have carried out a severe crackdown on Falun
Gong practitioners and members of other organizations deemed to be
"heretical organizations."

Tens of thousands of Falun Gong practitioners have been arbitrarily
detained by police, some of them repeatedly for short periods, and put under
pressure to renounce their beliefs. Many of them are reported to have been

tortured or ill-treated in detention. Some practitioners have been detained in psychiatric hospitals. Those who have spoken out publicly about the persecution of practitioners since the ban have suffered harsh reprisals.

While it is difficult to estimate accurately the number of Falun Gong practitioners currently detained or imprisoned—notably due to the continuous succession of arrests and releases—the information available indicates that the number is likely to be in the thousands. Some have been charged with crimes and tried, while others have been sent to labor camps without trial. According to Chinese official sources, by late November 1999, at least 150 people, officially described as "key" members of the Falun Gong, had been charged with crimes. The number of those by now charged or prosecuted under the Criminal Law is believed to be much higher. By early February 2000, at least forty of those charged under the Criminal Law had been tried and sentenced to prison terms after unfair trials. In addition, hundreds, possibly thousands, of other practitioners have been assigned, without charge or trial, to serve terms of "administrative" detention in forced-labor camps for up to three years. Unfair trials have continued, and arrests and detentions of practitioners continue to be reported every day.

Amnesty International is concerned that the detention and prosecution of members of Falun Gong are politically motivated, and that many of those held in police custody, sent to labor camps without trial, or sentenced to prison terms under the Criminal Law are being held arbitrarily for the peaceful exercise of fundamental human rights. Most have been accused of offenses such as organizing or taking part in "illegal" gatherings or peaceful demonstrations, or printing, selling, or circulating books and other material about the Falun Gong. In the case of those prosecuted, the authorities have widely publicized the trials and harsh sentences passed in a few "key" cases, but they have not provided any evidence that the defendants were involved in activities which would legitimately be regarded as "crimes" under international standards. Most trials have been closed to the public and some have been held in secret. The reports available indicate that these trials have been grossly unfair. In addition, there are many reports that detained Falun Gong practitioners have been subjected to torture or ill-treatment, and at least ten people have died in police custody in circumstances that remain unclear, some reportedly due to torture.

Amnesty International is also concerned that similar human rights violations are resulting from a nationwide crackdown on other groups branded as "heretical organizations." This crackdown has been going on—largely unreported outside China—since 1998 in the context of an "anti-superstition" campaign. As of July 1999, this campaign had already resulted in over 20,000 arrests. It is now being extended to a number of qigong organizations that promote meditation and breathing exercises similar to Falun Gong. Examples of the variety of groups and individuals targeted in this campaign are cited in this report. The information available indicates that at least some of those held are being arbitrarily detained in violation of international standards.

In addition, Amnesty International is concerned that the government directives, regulations, and judicial interpretations issued in the course of the campaign against the Falun Gong and other groups may have a broader impact on freedom of expression, association, and belief in China. Some of these official documents are examined in this report. The government has promoted the campaign as an example of its new emphasis on rule by law. However, the official directives and legal documents issued for this campaign undermine rights set out in the Chinese constitution as well as international standards.

International standards permit some restrictions on freedom of expression, association, and belief, but they do not grant discretion to states to define for themselves the circumstances in which these freedoms can be restricted. Under international standards, such restrictions must be "provided by law," must be "necessary" and must be in pursuance of a "legitimate" objective, such as the protection of national security, public order, or public health or morals. These fundamental principles are interpreted narrowly, and the principle of "proportionality" is associated to that of "necessity" and "legitimacy." For example, the requirement that the restrictions must be "necessary" to meet a "legitimate" objective—such as to protect public security from a particular threat—means that the restrictions imposed must be in direct proportion to this specific threat, and not beyond. Indeed, restrictions must not have the effect of entirely undermining the exercise of fundamental rights. Furthermore, restrictions may not be applied simply to suppress an opinion or belief. In the case of Falun Gong and other groups, the Chinese government's crackdown and the legislation on "heretical organizations" are being used precisely for this purpose.

The obligation clearly lies with the government to demonstrate why particular restrictions are necessary and why punishing members of Falun Gong and other groups is warranted. It has so far failed to do so.

Amnesty International has records of nearly 1600 cases of detention, arrest, or sentencing of Falun Gong practitioners since June 1999. Around 740 of these cases concern individuals or groups of people reported to have been detained around the ban on the group in July or soon after, who may have been released since then—no further information became available about them. The other cases include around 200 more recent cases of people detained in police custody, and around 640 cases of people either held without trial in "re-education through labor" camps or sentenced to prison terms under the Criminal Law. Some of these reports concern identified individuals, others refer to unnamed groups of people. A list of these reports and the names of identified detainees and prisoners will be published shortly in a separate document (ASA 17/12/00).

2. The Crackdown on "Heretical Organizations"

2.1. The Government's Campaign and Accusations Against the Falun Gong:

The Chinese government has stated in recent months that there are around 2 million Falun Gong practitioners in China. According to Falun Gong sources, previous government estimates put the figure at between 70 and 100 million. The Falun Gong was founded in 1992 by Li Hongzhi, who now resides in the USA. It is described by its adherents as a spiritual practice of body, spirit, and mind, based on various schools of Buddhism and traditional forms of self-cultivation that center around a practice of meditation and qigong exercises. These exercise sessions are often held by groups in public places. Before it was banned, the Falun Gong had training stations, practice sites and "contact persons" across China, with practitioners coming from all sectors of Chinese society and almost all provinces. Among the thousands detained over the past few months, the majority were ordinary workers or farmers, but they also included teachers and academics, university students, publishers, accountants, police officers, engineers, and people from a variety of other professions. Those detained also include officials, notably a Railways Ministry official, a former official at the Ministry of Public Security (police), a recently retired major from the People's Armed Police, and a seventy-four-year-old retired air force lieutenant general . . .

Another important part of the government's propaganda campaign has been to publicize statements from people identified as former Falun Gong practitioners who denounce the Falun Gong movement and its leader, speak of the damage that the movement has brought to Chinese society, and praise the government for its firm action against the movement. Such denunciations, whose authenticity cannot be verified, are a typical feature of the political campaigns periodically launched by the authorities in China. These denunciations are encouraged by the authorities with promises that those who leave the "heretical organization" and perform "meritorious service" will not be punished.

Throughout China, local government authorities have also been carrying out "study and education" programs to purge their provinces of Falun Gong practice. This can take the form of reading newspapers and listening to radio programs, as well as having office cadres visit villagers and farmers at home to explain "in simple terms the harm of Falun Gong to them." "Study and education" can also be a euphemism for detention for "re-education." Numerous reports indicate that the authorities have used detention, fines, threats, and other means to "persuade" followers to renounce their Falun Gong beliefs and practice.

The government's accusations against Falun Gong followers range from "organizing illegal gatherings" to "threatening political stability."

These accusations include "forcefully occupying parks," organizing or taking part in "illegal" sit-ins, assemblies, or demonstrations, obstructing "normal religious activities," having "illegally" published and distributed books, "leaking state secrets," "harming people's health," or "causing deaths" through the philosophy it promoted.

This latter accusation in particular has been used widely by the government to justify its crackdown on the group. According to information published by the government, Falun Gong "caused over 1400 deaths," most of which concerned people who died from illnesses allegedly because they refused medical treatment due to their Falun Gong beliefs. In the current climate of censorship and repression in China, this allegation cannot be independently verified. In view of the government's political crackdown and massive propaganda campaign against Falun Gong, the impartiality of the government's information is questionable. Furthermore, the information published by the government leaves many essential questions unanswered. It fails for example to demonstrate any direct connection between the alleged deaths and Falun Gong leaders or organizers. Under international law, criminal responsibility is determined case by case, on an individual basis. In the case of leaders or local organizers of Falun Gong who have been prosecuted on charges of "causing deaths," the government has not presented evidence of a direct link between the alleged deaths and the defendants. Nor has the government presented evidence that the defendants had full knowledge that the philosophy they were promoting might cause deaths. Evidence of this direct link and of "knowledge" is essential to determine criminal responsibility, but such evidence is lacking in these cases . . .

2.2. Other Groups—The Ongoing "Anti-Superstition" Campaign:

Even before the crackdown on the Falun Gong, the authorities had targeted a wide range of other groups and individuals in the ongoing "anti-superstition" campaign. Alleged leaders or "core members" of such groups were detained, assigned without trial to re-education–through–labor, or tried under a variety of criminal charges. The scale of the campaign is demonstrated by police reports that in the seventeen months before Falun Gong was banned, they had "cracked" 11,870 cases of "using feudal superstition to disrupt social order or defraud property," arresting 21,400 suspects.

In 1998, in one county alone (Lingbi, Anhui Province) authorities boasted that a crackdown on "illegal heretical organizations who, in the name of 'promoting the heretical organization' engaged in illegal incitement, sowing discord between the party and the masses," had resulted in the closure of 292 illegal religious venues and 23 "heretical organizations" venues, and the arrest of 87 heretical organizations" members and fifteen illegal evangelists (chuanjiao ren).

Since at least the mid-1990s there have been repeated calls by provincial governments, and sometimes the state Religious Affairs Bureau, to crack down on a number of named groups that are deemed illegal and a threat to stability, and labelled "heretical" (xiejiao). These include the Huhan Pai (Shouters Faction—previously outlawed as "counter-revolutionary"), the Mentu Hui (Disciples Association), the Lingling Jiao (Spirit Church), and the Quanfanmian Jiao (the Holistic Church). Alleged members of these and other groups labelled "heretical" have also been targeted in the most recent crackdown. At the beginning of 1999, President Jiang Zemin himself gave impetus to the campaign, stressing: "We must suppress cults and the use of religion to engage in illegal activities to maintain social stability in farming villages . . . "

3. Legislating to Legitimize the Crackdown

Since July 1999, a whole series of "decisions," "notices," "regulations," "judicial interpretations," and other official documents have been issued by the government and judiciary to orchestrate the crackdown on Falun Gong and other "heretical organizations." In October 1999, China's legislature, the National People's Congress, also adopted a "decision" to legitimize the government's crackdown. Many of these official documents contain specific instructions on how to conduct the crackdown, how to use the law to charge those detained, and how to conduct trials. Some also introduce further restrictions on freedom of expression, association, and belief in China. These documents are cited or examined below.

—On July 22, 1999, the Ministry of Civil Affairs issued a Decision banning "the Research Society of Falun Dafa and the Falun Gong organization under its control" as "illegal organizations."

—On July 22, 1999, the Ministry of Public Security also issued a Notice based on the above Decision by the Ministry of Civil Affairs. The notice announced sweeping new prohibitions related to the ban on Falun Gong, including prohibition of the right to "petition," which is guaranteed by the Chinese Constitution. These prohibitions were:

1. Everyone is prohibited from displaying in any public place scrolls, pictures, and other marks or symbols promoting Falun Gong;
2. Everyone is prohibited from distributing in any public place books, cassettes, and other materials promoting Falun Gong;
3. Everyone is prohibited from gathering a crowd to perform "group exercises" and other activities promoting Falun Gong;
4. It is prohibited to use sit-ins, petitions, and other means to hold assemblies, marches, or demonstrations in defense and promotion of Falun Gong;

5. It is prohibited to fabricate or distort facts, to spread rumors on purpose or use other means to incite [people] and disturb social order;

6. Everyone is prohibited from organizing or taking part in activities opposing the government's relevant decision, or from establishing contacts [with other people] for this purpose.

The same month, the Ministry of Personnel also issued a circular, stipulating that government civil servants were prohibited from practicing Falun Gong. In a further circular issued by the General Office of the State Council (central government), local governments and departments under the State Council were asked to "properly deal with civil servants who have practiced Falun Gong."

—On August 28, 1999, the General office of the State Council (government) also issued a Notice on the implementation of "opinions" issued by three government bodies "concerning certain problems in strengthening the management of healthy qigong activities." This Notice (No.77/1999) introduces restrictions for all qigong groups . . .

—On October 30, 1999, the Standing Committee of the National People's Congress (NPC) passed a "Decision on Banning Heretical Organizations and Preventing and Punishing Heretical Activities."

This Decision was said to be based on existing legislation, but it effectively called for a political crackdown against "heretical organizations . . . qigong or other illicit forms." It states: "All corners of society shall be mobilized in preventing and fighting heretical organizations activities, and a comprehensive management system shall be put in place." An official from the NPC commented in December 1999 that the Decision provided "a legal system to ensure the efforts of banning heretical organizations, preventing and punishing heretical activities, safeguarding social stability, protecting people's interests and guaranteeing the smooth progress of reform, opening up and socialist modernization . . . "

—At the same time as the NPC Decision, the Supreme People's Court (SPC) and the Supreme People's Procuratorate (SPP) issued on October 30, 1999, a judicial interpretation entitled "Explanation on Questions Concerning the Concrete Application of Laws in Handling Criminal Cases of Organizing and Making Use of Heretical Organizations" (hereafter cited as SPC/SPP Explanation).

In a commentary on the SPC/SPP Explanation cited by the official Xinhua news agency on November 19, 1999, the "person in charge of the Beijing Municipal High People's Court" said that this judicial interpretation will help courts to "distinguish more accurately whether or not an offense has constituted a crime and whether or not a crime is serious. Consequently, the people's courts will be able to integrate severe punishment with lenient treatment, severely punish an extremely small number of criminal elements . . . and educate and save hoodwinked people and criminal elements who have repented and rendered meritorious services."

The SPC/SPP Explanation defines the specific activities which will be considered crimes and punished under the Chinese Criminal Law (1997), notably Article 300 of the law (see below). It shows that many activities that involve the peaceful exercise of fundamental human rights, such as peaceful assemblies and demonstrations, are treated as crimes . . .

—On November 5, 1999, the Supreme People's Court issued a Notice giving instructions to local courts on how to handle the cases of people charged with crimes for "organizing or using heretical organizations, particularly Falun Gong." [hereafter cited as SPC Notice.] . . .

This Notice was issued shortly before the trials of Falun Gong leaders and organizers started. It gave an unambiguous political message, making clear to all courts that it was their "political duty" to punish those charged with crimes for their role in "heretical organizations," "particularly Falun Gong . . . "

—On November 24, 1999, the Ministry of Public Security also issued some "Regulations on Managing Mass Cultural and Sports Activities," which are intended to control and restrict certain types of public gatherings, including those by qigong groups. They specifically ban gatherings that "threaten national security and public order," without further defining what this "threat" might be.

Under the regulations, holding concerts, sports meetings, qigong or other body exercises, and other mass congregations involving more than 200 participants in public places "shall be subject to approval by public security (police) departments above the county level." Events which may involve more than 3,000 participants require approval by the public security body at or above the prefecture level, and events involving two or more localities shall get the go-ahead from a higher public security department responsible for these areas . . .

4. Politically Motivated Charges

The charges brought against most members of Falun Gong who have been prosecuted under the Criminal Law are essentially political in nature. They include "disturbing social order," "assembling to disrupt public order," "stealing or leaking state secrets," and "using a heretical organization to undermine the implementation of the law." This latter charge is in fact a catch-all phrase for a variety of other accusations that range from organizing demonstrations to using the Internet to disseminate information about Falun Gong. Some people have also been charged with "taking part in illegal businesses" or "illegal trading" because they printed, published, or sold

Falun Gong publications, videos, or cassettes—in most cases this referred to publishing or selling such publications before the group was banned, when such activities were not illegal . . . [See full report on the Amnesty International website for detailed cases of politically motivated charges.]

5. Unfair Trials and Harsh Sentences

The information available from many sources, including Chinese official sources, shows that the trials of those prosecuted for their role in Falun Gong were grossly unfair—the judicial process was biased against the defendants at the outset and the trials were a mere formality. In most of the cases, legislation was used retroactively to secure convictions and defense lawyers were prevented from entering pleas of "not guilty" on behalf of their clients. This in itself breaches fundamental principles of international law.

In addition, before the trials started, it was made clear to the courts that they should "fully understand" the political importance of these cases and treat them accordingly. This usually means finding the defendants guilty, whatever the charges or the evidence against them. A Notice issued by the Supreme People's Court on November 5, 1999, for example, gave clear political messages to all local courts, instructing them notably to do their "political duty" in bringing to trial and punishing "severely" those charged with "heretical organizations crimes," "particularly Falun Gong," and to handle these cases "under the leadership of the Party committees."

At least forty members of Falun Gong are known to have been tried in various places in China since November 1999. The total number of those tried is believed to be higher, with some trials being held secretly or without being publicly reported. Chinese official sources have publicized the trials and sentences passed against some alleged leaders or key members of Falun Gong, most of whom have received harsh sentences. Most of these trials have been closed to the public, though selected information on the cases has been widely publicized by the state media. In one particularly significant trial held in Beijing in late December 1999, part of the court hearing was shown on Chinese central television. Despite the high profile given to these cases, the Chinese authorities have not provided evidence that the defendants were involved in activities that would legitimately be regarded as "crimes" under international standards. In other cases, trials have been held behind closed doors and, in some cases, even the relatives of the defendants were denied access to the court.

The information available on a number of cases shows that these trials have been grossly unfair. Some of these cases are described below. Amnesty International believes that the prisoners have been arbitrarily detained, convicted, and sentenced for the peaceful exercise of fundamental human rights, in violation of international human rights standards.

LI XIAOBING AND LI XIAOMEI

Li Xiaobing and Li Xiaomei, two sisters from Beijing, were among twenty-two Falun Gong practitioners who were tried in secret in Beijing on January 28, 2000, in three separate sessions of the Dongcheng District Court. Li Xiaobing and Li Xiaomei were tried in one of the court sessions and sentenced to seven and six years' imprisonment, respectively. Their case illustrates in several respects the arbitrariness of the judicial process against members of Falun Gong.

The two sisters were charged with and convicted of "illegal trading." This charge referred to the sale of Falun Gong publications by the two sisters, who were running a bookstore in Beijing before their arrest. Both, however, had been arrested on July 20, 1999—two days before Falun Gong was banned—and the sale of Falun Gong publications was not illegal before the ban. Following their detention by police, they were held for over three months without charge, in violation of the provisions governing the time limits for detention without charge in the Chinese Criminal Procedure Law. They were denied contact with their family throughout their detention and their relatives were not allowed to attend their trial.

On August 15, 1999, before formal charges were even issued against them, the official Xinhua news agency published accusations against them, showing clearly that they were already considered guilty. The Xinhua report described them as "key members" of the "outlawed" Falun Dafa Research Society in Beijing and accused them of earning large sums of money from the sale of Falun Gong publications and audio-visual material since 1997, with most of the money being given to another "leading" member of the Falun Gong, Yao Jie (f), who was tried and sentenced in Beijing in December. Xinhua also said that the two sisters had contracted and registered a bookstore in Dongcheng district in 1998 "in the name of others," "using it as a base to spread the fallacies of Falun Gong." According to unofficial sources, the Ditan bookstore and audio-video shop, which the sisters run, was a legal business. It belonged to the Wenhua Publication Corporation, itself subordinated to the Ministry of Culture. Furthermore, the sale of Falun Gong books and other material was not illegal until the group was banned on July 22. This fact, however, appears to have been ignored, and legislation was used retroactively to convict them. According to unofficial sources, their lawyer was put under pressure not to present a plea of "not guilty" at their trial.

It is clear that several fundamental principles of international law were violated in these cases, and that some standards of Chinese law itself were ignored or bent in order to convict Li Xiaobing and Li Xiaomei. They were illegally detained for three months without charge; legislation was used retroactively in order to charge and convict them; they were presumed guilty long before they were tried; they were tried in secret and their right to defense was severely restricted.

LI CHANG, WANG ZHIWEN, JI LIEWU, AND YAO JIE

The most high-profile trial to have taken place to date is that of Li Chang, Wang Zhiwen, Ji Liewu, and Yao Jie (female). They were described by Qian Xiaoqian, Director General of the State Council Information Office, as "four former senior government officials." All four were members of the Chinese Communist Party (CCP). Li Chang, aged fifty-nine, is a former departmental deputy director at the Ministry for Public Security; Wang Zhiwen, aged fifty, is a former official with a company under the Ministry of Railways; Ji Liewu, aged thirty-six, was the manager of a Hong Kong subsidiary of a government metals company; and Yao Jie, forty, was the Communist Party secretary of a large real estate company in Beijing.

All were accused of holding leadership positions within the Falun Gong movement. They were charged on October 19, 1999, with "organizing and using a heretical organization to undermine the implementation of the law," "causing deaths by organizing and using a heretical organization" and "illegally obtaining and leaking state secrets." These charges referred to their activities before Falun Gong was banned. Li Chang was detained on July 20—two days before the ban—and it is believed that the others were detained around the same date.

On December 26, 1999, after a hearing at the Beijing No.1 Intermediate People's Court, the defendants were found guilty as charged and sentenced. Li Chang was sentenced to eighteen years' imprisonment, Wang Zhiwen to sixteen years' imprisonment, Ji Liewu to twelve years' imprisonment, and Yao Jie to seven years' imprisonment.

Part of the trial was "open" to a selected audience of government cadres and reporters from the official media. The hearing of the "state secrets" charges was held behind closed doors. Only one family member per defendant was permitted to attend the "open" part of the trial, and, according to Falun Gong sources, relatives of the four defendants were detained ahead of the court hearing "as a warning." Foreign reporters were excluded. They were told that "their presence was a violation of regulations controlling news gathering" and were ordered to leave.

The official news agency Xinhua reported on December 26 that "during the trial, some of the defendants argued that they had no idea which laws they had broken." According to official reports, the main accusations against the defendants related to their alleged role in setting up the structure of Falun Gong and in organizing a number of protests, including the peaceful demonstration by 10,000 people in front of the Zhongnanhai CCP leadership compound in Beijing on April 25, 1999. The defendants were accused of having set up "thirty-nine command posts, more than 1,900 training centers and more than 280,000 contact posts" of Falun Gong across the country, and of having "plotted and directed" seventy-eight protests, including the April 25 demonstration. They were also accused of "stealing thirty-seven state secrets" and of disseminating them or including them in protest letters. No detail was published about the nature of the alleged "state secrets." According to Falun Gong sources, this referred to the contents of official documents about the crackdown on Falun Gong. Official reports also indicate that the charge of "causing deaths" was not substantiated beyond the general accusation that Falun Gong activities "caused deaths," as previously alleged by official sources, and that no evidence was presented of a direct link between the alleged deaths and specific actions of the defendants. The Xinhua report of December 26 said that some of the defendants had "claimed" that they were in no way responsible for these deaths. Xinhua cited a Chinese legal expert's comment that the deaths "were the result of cult activities which the defendants helped to organize" and that "if the defendants had directly caused or forced the deaths or suicides, they would have been charged with homicide and received more severe punishment."

According to official sources, Li Chang, who received an eighteen years' prison sentence, and Yao Jie, who received seven years, had been treated "leniently" because they had made "confessions." There are grounds to be concerned about the way in which these "confessions" were obtained—according to unofficial sources, the defendants were held incommunicado for several months after their arrest.

The trial and verdict against the defendants received wide coverage by the state media. Part of the trial was subsequently shown on Chinese central television news. The four defendants were shown admitting to having organized group activities, including the April 25, 1999, demonstration in front of Zhongnanhai. Yao Jie was said to be in tears and to have expressed regrets for having "caused trouble for the Party." Commenting on the trial on December 28, a Foreign Ministry spokeswoman described the four defendants as "backbone elements" of the group, and said that their sentencing was "an embodiment of China's principle of ruling the country by law."

This trial—described above as an embodiment of China's "rule by law"—was grossly unfair. It was clearly staged by the authorities as a show trial for which the verdict was determined in advance. [See full report on the Amnesty International website for more detailed cases of unfair trials and harsh sentences.]

6. Administrative Sentences

In addition to the high-profile trials at which heavy terms of imprisonment have been passed on alleged leaders of Falun Gong, thousands of practitioners have been detained "administratively." Ye Xiaowen, Director of the State Council Bureau for Religious Affairs, was cited as saying in November after one demonstration by Falun Gong practitioners that the mostly elderly protesters were being "re-educated" and treated "in a humanitarian spirit" and that most had already been sent back to their provincial hometowns. In practice, however, "re-education" has meant detention for many people.

Since the beginning of the crackdown in 1999, many people have been detained for up to fifteen days of administrative detention, under detention orders issued by the police. Some have been detained repeatedly in this fashion. Many others have been assigned to periods of up to three years' detention for "re-education through labor." This is a punishment imposed by local government committees or by the police alone, without charge or trial, which is usually served in a forced-labor camp. Practitioners who do not "reform" after a short period of detention may face a lengthier period of "re-education" in police custody or be sent to a labor camp . . .

7. Reprisals and Sentences for Speaking Out About the Repression

The repression of Falun Gong has been unusually well reported outside China due to the high number of practitioners living around the world and the use of the Internet by some practitioners in China. However, a number of people have received prison sentences or long terms of administrative detention for speaking out about the repression or giving information over the Internet. Others have been punished for communicating with the foreign press or for organizing press conferences . . . [See full report on the Amnesty International website for detailed cases of reprisals and sentences.]

8. Detention in Psychiatric Hospitals

Several cases have been reported in which Falun Gong practitioners, alone or in groups, were taken by police to mental hospitals where they were detained for periods varying from a few days to several weeks, and often forced to take drugs against their will. [See full report on the Amnesty International website for detailed cases of these detentions.]

9. Other Punishments

A number of Falun Gong practitioners are known to have been heavily fined, dismissed from their jobs, or expelled from the Communist Party because of their Falun Gong beliefs. Some of those unable to pay the heavy fines have been detained. In cities like Beijing, police have reportedly raided suburban hotels and guest houses and fined landlords for housing followers of Falun Gong. In some places, practitioners have been subjected to public humiliation to force them to renounce their beliefs and warn others. In Shandong Province, for example, a police official from Guangrao county reportedly stated in January that in late December 1999 six Falun Gong members were forced "to parade in public with signs round their necks and their hands cuffed behind their backs." The signs reportedly condemned their actions. The police official reportedly added that the punishment had been very successful in reducing the number of Falun Gong followers in the county.

Civil servants and members of the Communist Party who were followers of Falun Gong have been disciplined and punished if they did not "correct their mistakes." On July 22, 1999, the Central Committee of the Chinese Communist Party of China (CCP) issued a circular prohibiting Party members from any Falun Gong activities and saying that Party members' participation in Falun Gong activities has "tarnished the image of the Party and made very bad impression in society." Party members were told to make a "clean ideological break" from Falun Gong. The circular warned that those who were "key members . . . and have committed serious mistakes will be given disciplinary punishment" and those "who refuse to correct their mistakes after repeated education will be asked to give up their Party membership, and those who refuse to give up their Party membership will be expelled from the Party."

Civil servants were prohibited from practicing Falun Gong in a circular issued in July 1999 by the Ministry of Personnel. A further circular issued by the General Office of the State Council, requested that local governments and departments under the State Council "properly deal with civil servants who have practiced Falun Gong," stating that those "who have been politically motivated and have organized illegal gatherings with a result of disturbing social order and causing social instability should be sacked . . . " [See full report on the Amnesty International website for more details.]

10. Torture, Ill-Treatment, and Deaths in Custody

Amnesty International is deeply concerned by the numerous reports alleging that detained followers of Falun Gong have been tortured or subjected to cruel, inhuman, and degrading treatment in detention. While it is difficult to verify these reports, many of them contain specific and detailed information about the circumstances in which torture is reported to have occurred, and the testimonies of individuals who were held in the same place often corroborate each other. These reports describe patterns of torture which are known to be common in China. Amnesty International believes that the serious allegations made in these reports should be impartially investigated, in line with China's obligation as a state party to the UN Convention Against Torture and Other Cruel, Inhuman, or Degrading Treatment or Punishment, which China ratified in 1988.

In October 1999, Amnesty International published a document entitled "Reports of Torture and Ill-treatment of Followers of the Falun Gong" [AI Index: ASA 17/54/99, October 22, 1999]. Since then there have been many new reports of detained practitioners being tortured or otherwise ill-treated, in some cases resulting in death. A few of these reports are cited below.

Liu Juhua, from Tangshan city, Hebei Province, who is currently serving a three-year term of "re-education through labor," was reportedly tortured in police custody. Liu Juhua and another practitioner, Yang Xuezhen, were detained in Beijing on September 22, 1999 after resisting a police officer who tried to take away some Falun Gong books they had with them. Both were reportedly ill-treated, including by having their hands roped behind their backs to their feet and being burned with cigarettes on their hands. According to unofficial sources, they were taken the same day to the Beijing Qinghe Detention Centre and interrogated until 2 o'clock in the morning. They were deprived of sleep and were not allowed to talk to anybody. After three days they were sent to the Kaiping Detention Centre in Tangshan City. At the detention center they met another practitioner, Zhang Shuzhen, who had also just been escorted back from Beijing by the police. She too had reportedly been tortured with electric shock batons, beaten with a large club, and forced to stuff dirty underwear and socks into her mouth.

Among other cases, it was reported in January 2000 that practitioners from Shunyi County near Beijing were brutally tortured after attempting to attend the trial of Li Chang, Wang Zhiwen, Ji Liewu, and Yao Jie in Beijing in late December 1999. One of those detained by the Shunyi police was Cheng Fengrong (f), aged forty-two. According to the reports, police slapped Cheng Fengrong while handcuffing her to a tree and later beat her with a broom which eventually snapped into two pieces. She was then reportedly forced to stand barefoot in the snow, punched and kicked, and had two basins of cold water poured onto the back of her neck, which froze under her feet.

Deaths in Custody:

Since September 1999, at least ten Falun Gong practitioners are reported to have died in police custody in circumstances which remain unclear, some reportedly as a result of torture. Two of these deaths were previously documented by Amnesty International in the report cited above. They concern the cases of Zhao Jinhua (f), a farmer from Zhaoyuan county in Shandong Province, who was reportedly beaten to death in police custody on October 7, 1999, and Zhao Shulan (f), fifty, from Jinzhou City in Liaoning Province, who reportedly died in early October 1999 after being on hunger strike in detention for several days.

Official sources have confirmed that at least three Falun Gong practitioners died in police custody. On November 8, 1999, Li Bing, deputy head of the information office of the State Council, confirmed that three female Falun Gong practitioners had died after being detained for their

Falun Gong activities, but he denied they had been tortured. Citing police reports, Li Bing said that Zhao Jinhua of Shandong Province and Li Ruhua of Chongqing, Sichuan Province, "had previous heart conditions and died of heart failure." Zhao Jinhua "had collapsed during questioning and died in the lavatory," while Li had died in hospital, he said.

The third death in custody confirmed by Li Bing was that of Chen Ying (f), an eighteen-year-old student at Shuren High School in Jiamusi, Heilongjiang Province. Li Bing stated that she had "died after jumping from a train while being sent back to her home town . . . accompanied by local officials." Chen Ying had travelled to Beijing to join fellow practitioners in petitioning the authorities about the ban on Falun Gong. She was detained by police in Beijing and was being escorted home by train. A police officer interviewed by Reuters on October 27, 1999, said that Chen Ying "was not abused . . . She was a stubborn element and jumped on her own to give her life for Falun Gong . . . When the train reached Hebei Province one hour after leaving Beijing, she went to the toilet and jumped from the train, catching police off-guard." According to the Reuters report, the police officer declined to comment on another case, that of Zhao Dong, thirty-eight, from Jixi City in Heilongjiang Province, who reportedly also jumped from a moving train and died from injuries sustained in the fall. A Falun Gong representative cited by Reuters said that Zhao had jumped after being tortured by police and that his "body was found with handcuffs still on his wrists."

Other cases of deaths in custody which have been reported since then include the following:

Dong Buyun (f), thirty-six, a Falun Gong practitioner and school teacher from Lanshan district, Linyi city, Shandong Province, reportedly died on September 21, 1999, while being held in custody in her school. She had been arrested earlier in Beijing and sent back to Lanshan under police escort. According to Falun Gong sources, following her death, local officials in Langshan claimed that Dong Buyun was killed when she jumped out of a building in the middle of the night, but gave no further explanations. Her body was reportedly cremated the same day. There has been no official report on her case.

Gao Xianming, forty-one, a practitioner from Guangzhou in Guangdong Province, reportedly died in police custody on January 17, 2000. According to unofficial sources, Gao Xianming was detained in Tianhe park in Guangzhou city on December 31, 1999, where he and ten other practitioners were having lunch. He was later sent to the Tangxia detention center in Tianhe district. On the afternoon of January 18, Gao Xianming's family received notification of his death from the public security section of Jinan University. The police claimed that Gao Xianming had lost consciousness suddenly after being on hunger strike at the detention center for several days. They said he had been sent to a hospital for emergency treatment but had not recovered. According to unofficial sources, while detained, Gao Xianming had been force-fed with highly salted water while he was tied up and his nose was covered with wet towels. It is suspected he may have suffocated due to this treatment. Another practitioner who had been detained in November 1999 subsequently claimed that he and others held at the Tangxia and Tianhe detention centers had received to same treatment when they went on hunger strike; he stated that he had nearly suffocated to death when his nose was squeezed and salted water was poured into his mouth.

Liu Zhinan (f), a practitioner from Fangshan district, Beijing, is reported to have died from gas poisoning in a police station on January 17, 2000. Liu Zhinan, who was over forty years old, was detained on January 10, 2000, with two other female practitioners, Pu Shunan, aged in her forties, and Li Fuhua, aged thirty. All were from the Changgougu coal mine in the Fangshan district of Beijing. They were detained for appealing for other Falun Gong practitioners and taken to the Zhoukoudian police station, where they were reportedly required to work at shovelling snow and undertaking cleaning. On January 14, after having their lunch in the boiler room of the police station, the three women became unconscious and were taken to a hospital in the Yanshan district for emergency treatment. Pu Shunan and Li Fuhua recovered, but Liu Zhinan never regained consciousness. Family members were allowed to see her in the mortuary but were told by the police that they should not disclose the news of Liu Zhinan's death to other practitioners. Liu Xuguo, a twenty-nine-year-old engineer, allegedly died in a labor camp on February 11, 2000, due to injuries sustained when he was force-fed by police. According to the report, Liu Xuguo had been arrested in October 1999 for protesting against the ban on Falun Gong, given a sentence of three years of "re-education through labor," and sent in early February to a labor camp in Jining, Shandong Province. He reportedly started a hunger strike at the camp just before February 5, but was taken to a hospital the following week and brutally force-fed with a tube pushed down his throat, which caused injuries to his lungs. According to an AFP report, this was denied by the detaining authorities, and the hospital refused to comment on the case.

Chen Zixiu (f), a sixty-year-old practitioner from Weifang in Shandong Province, reportedly died under torture on or before February 21, 2000, while held by police in Weifang. She had been detained for only four days when she died. According to her daughter, the family was asked to come and fetch her body on February 21 and found it covered with bruises, with her teeth broken and blood coming out of her ears. Chen Zixiu has been arrested on February 17 on suspicion she was planning to go to Beijing to petition the authorities against the ban on Falun Gong. Police then reportedly requested her family to pay a fine of 1,000 yuan for her release, but the family could not raise the money.

As far as is known, there have been no impartial investigations into any of the reported cases of death in custody that are cited above.

11. Detention of Practitioners Around the Macau Handover

Some Falun Gong practitioners were detained in Macau and some deported in the days running up to the handover of sovereignty of Macau to China, at midnight on December 19, 1999. One practitioner from Macau has also been detained in south China . . . [See full report on the Amnesty International website for more details.]

12. Harassment of Foreign Journalists

On November 10, 1999, the Foreign Correspondents Club (FCC) of China sent a letter of protest to the Chinese Foreign Ministry about official "intimidation and harassment" of foreign correspondents in relation to news reporting of the crackdown on Falun Gong. The letter said that "members have been followed, detained, interrogated, and threatened."

Many foreign journalists attended a news conference organized covertly in Beijing on October 28 by members of the Falun Gong. The Foreign Ministry claimed that foreign journalists who attended and covered the event had engaged in "illegal reporting." Later on, journalists from a number of news organizations, including Reuters, the *New York Times,* and the Associated Press, were questioned at length by police, obliged to sign a "confession of wrongdoing," and had their work and residence papers temporarily confiscated. Several of the reporters were put under police surveillance. Foreign correspondents also complained that television satellite transmissions had been interfered with while being routed through China Central Television.

* * *

Statement By Human Rights In China
July 22, 1999

Human Rights in China (HRIC) strongly condemns the current crackdown on Falun Gong practitioners, including the detention of more than 100 group leaders and thousands of followers, apparently solely for engaging in peaceful protests and exercising their rights to freedom of association and freedom of thought, conscience, and religion. In some of China's major cities, large numbers of followers have been detained in stadiums and other locations, and in certain cases police have been seen to use excessive force in arresting people engaging in non-violent demonstrations. HRIC believes that the order to ban the group is a violation of the right to freedom of association, which is enshrined in China's constitution, as well as in international human rights instruments.

The moves against the spiritual group are the largest in a series of actions to restrict the efforts of Chinese people to organize independently of the Party-state, demonstrating a pattern of systematic violations of the freedoms of association and assembly and expression by the Chinese government. Immediately following China's signature of the International Covenant on Civil and Political Rights in late 1998, government authorities intensified their ongoing campaign of persecution against individuals associated with unofficial Christian groups, independent labor organizing, and the human rights and democracy movement. In October 1998 the Chinese government also enacted a series of regulations that further curtailed the already-limited right of association available to people in China.

These regulations, which require that all non-profit entities be sponsored and managed by government agencies and mandate no association without registration, were cited in the banning order on Falun Gong issued yesterday by the Ministry of Civil Affairs. The order labeled the Falun Gong group "an illegal organization." The Ministry of Public Security followed with a decree prohibiting the posting and distribution of Falun Gong materials, as well as gatherings of its members, whether for spiritual practice or demonstrations, threatening those who disobey with criminal penalties. The Ministry of Public Security's decree also bars Falun Gong supporters from exercising their constitutional right to petition against the actions of the authorities, and bans all opposition to the government's crackdown.

The Chinese government has routinely employed the pretext of criminal charges to dissolve religious and spiritual groups and to punish their leading members. Over the last twenty years, among the harshest sentences for "counterrevolutionary crimes" have been imposed on those accused of "organizing and using reactionary sects or secret societies for counterrevolutionary purposes." To our knowledge, almost all of the "counterrevolutionaries" sentenced to death in this period have been in this category. Although the revisions to China's criminal code enacted in 1997 abolished counterrevolutionary crimes, the government's attitude toward such issues evidently has not changed. Involvement in so-called "secret societies and heretical religious organizations" is now categorized under "Crimes of Disturbing Social Order." Serious offenses carry sentences of seven years or above.

In addition, the Chinese Communist Party (CCP) has launched a nationwide "education" campaign among its Party members, who are required to cease all practice of Falun Gong exercises, as well as cutting themselves off from the organization. If they fail to do so, a Party notice issued on the same day as the ban said, they would be expelled from the CCP.

HRIC urges the Chinese government to respect international human rights standards and to abide by the provisions of the Chinese constitution. HRIC believes the ban on the Falun Gong group should be lifted, and demands the release of all practitioners detained. HRIC will be raising this case with the office of the UN High Commissioner for Human Rights and will be asking the UN Special Rapporteur on Religious Intolerance, who visited China in 1994, to take up this issue with the Chinese authorities as a matter of urgency.

We also urge the Chinese government to take note of the Special Rapporteur's recommendations following his visit. As well as asking the Chinese government to eliminate the categorization of certain types of spiritual practices as "abnormal"—a category which is completely arbitrary and undefined, and which now certainly includes Falun Gong —and thus proscribed, the Special Rapporteur encouraged the government to show more tolerance toward practice of religion by Party members. His report (E/CN.4/1995/91) said that he recommended "the adoption of the text recognizing the right to freedom of belief and freedom to manifest one's belief for all, including members of the Communist Party and other socio-political organizations." He reminded the government that according to international law, freedom to manifest one's religion or belief may only be subject to such limitations as "are prescribed by law and are necessary to protect public safety, order, health or morals, or the fundamental rights and freedoms of others."

* * *

The Wheel of Law and the Rule of Law
by James D. Seymour

Should the human rights community rush to the defense of China's newly visible sect, Falun Gong? After all, there is much that is unattractive about this phenomenon. Although the creed of the group is part Buddhism, part Taoism, part physical training in the qigong tradition (breathing exercises which move the practitioner's non-physical energy or qi), there are some other, rather troubling, features of the belief system. Falun Gong materials preach medical practices which most would consider bogus, thus in effect tending to deny sick people proper medical attention. It is also a rather narrow, inward-looking philosophy. Members are expected to adhere rigorously to the teachings of their bible, the *Falun Dafa,* and may be ostracized if they violate "the principle of practicing only one way of cultivation." Other belief systems are seen as promoting immorality, excessive material and sexual desire, and homosexual behavior. For all their talk of "tolerance," the Falun Gong leaders' homophobia is disturbing.

Should we be concerned about these people, who seem a bit insensitive to the rights of others? Indeed we should. Human rights protections do not depend on whether people are right or wrong. It is precisely when people are "wrong" that our human rights principles are put to the test, and it is we human rights activists who are being tested.

For one thing, it is not because of what has been actually said or done that the Chinese authorities are campaigning against Falun Gong. Rather, they are cracking down because of fears of where they imagine the movement might be heading. According to *People's Daily,* Falun Gong is "political in essence" and "a force contending with our party and government." Such assessments become almost self-fulfilling, as the ban is more likely to drive the movement underground, resulting in it becoming a sort of secret society, than to eliminate it. Nationalism- and mysticism-driven secret societies have a long, politically destabilizing history in China. Now, an organization hitherto concerned with mysticism and martial arts has been politicized as a result of the authorities' decision to "completely smash it."

The "smashing" began on July 22, 1999, when the Ministry of Civil Affairs (an agency some naïve foreigners think is helping to pluralize Chinese society) declared the group outlawed. Indeed, Chinese law does require that all organizations register and be sponsored and overseen by official agencies; Falun Gong had not met these requirements. But on this basis the government not only outlawed Falun Gong but forbade its practice even in private. Notices have gone up in the parks in Beijing declaring that no practice of Falun Gong is permitted; the capital's police will undoubtedly be having to get up extra early in the mornings to make sure that the mostly middle-aged and elderly crowds of exercisers are not doing the forbidden movements or meditations.

Actually, the crackdown is widely seen as having little basis in law at all. When Beijing asked Interpol to aid in the apprehension of New York-based leader Li Hongzhi, the international police agency scoffed at the request. "The General Secretariat has informed the National Central Bureau of Interpol in China it cannot use Interpol channels to ask member states to locate and arrest Li Hongzhi, in the absence of any information about ordinary-law crime he would have committed." And it is clear that the victims of the crackdown within China will not enjoy their legal rights. The Ministry of Justice issued a notice to all PRC lawyers that any attorney representing Falun Gong people would have to obtain the government's approval, and then must interpret the law in a manner consistent with the spirit of the government's decrees.

Rationale for Suppression

The government has made two general accusations against Falun Gong. First, it accuses it of "advocating superstition, spreading fallacies, and hoodwinking people." Second, it is accused of "inciting and creating disturbances, and jeopardizing social stability." Are such charges justified? Regarding the first charge, it must be acknowledged that Falun practitioners do make some bizarre claims such as miracle cures and defying death. The faithful are promised salvation and supernatural powers, including levitation (gravity supposedly being controlled by the deities). Everything depends on the "wheel of law," which practitioners are meant to visualize in their abdomens. (Falun Gong means "Wheel of Law Practice.") Li Hongzhi and his disciples insist that they have "supernormal capabilities to cure diseases." Li says that "many patients with cancer or other terminal diseases are still living because of this practice." Practitioners are not encouraged to enter Chinese hospitals (which often are institutions most would want to avoid anyway). But in general he and his colleagues try not to let such claims get out of hand or dominate the movement's ethos. They have sometimes not objected when the authorities crack down on quackery carried out in the name of qigong. "The government has always been trying to ban a small number of fake qigong practices that conduct superstitions, deceive and harm people to get money," observes the Falun website (http://www.falundafa.org). "This is right and absolutely necessary." It should be noted that in the 1950s qigong was very popular among, and promoted by, the Chinese Communist Party (CCP) itself, as well as by Chinese scientists. More recently, during the reform era, qigong, and investigation of its scientific validity, have been promoted by many high-ranking officials in the Party and the Army. Now, however, it is officially dismissed as quackery.

The authorities appear to be making far too much of the quackery issue. They prevailed upon Gao Qingyin, who had been deputy chief of the Falun Gong General Instruction Station in Anhui, to admit that after a Falun practitioner suffered a brain hemorrhage in 1994, "We called on the Falun Dafa Research Society four times and asked for the help of Li Hongzhi." However, complains the Xinhua News Agency, "Li, the founder of Falun Gong, did nothing," and the man died. The authorities cite rather few concrete cases of quackery, and this one falls on its face. Li did nothing to harm the man; rather, the government is attempting to deny the rights of Falun Gong followers.

What of the government's second charge, that Falun Gong jeopardized social stability? The Falun Gong website insists the group is apolitical, and only preaches healthy living and the three moral values of truthfulness, benevolence, and forbearance. "We are not against the government and we do not get involved in politics," it says. But the government fears otherwise, and, with little substantiation, accuses Falun Gong of "using illegal organizations to engage in political activities."

The main sin of the organization is the same as that of the Tiananmen demonstrators of 1989: they are popular. But is that a legitimate reason to outlaw them? We see these people as simply exercising their civil rights. After all, as with the students who occupied Tiananmen, it is not the activities that produced social instability, but rather the government's reaction to them.

The Authorities' Dilemma

It must be very difficult for the Chinese authorities to "get a handle" on this movement. During the student protests in 1989, they knew with whom they were dealing. The same is true when workers and peasants become restive. But Falun Gong blends pretty seamlessly into a broad spectrum of Chinese society, and until recently one could easily overlook it. Even government, police, and military people have become involved. This summer the government sent more than a thousand cadres to a camp outside Shijiazhuang for anti–Falun Gong deprogramming. In the People's Liberation Army (PLA), Falun Gong gained adherents at the highest levels; most have now been pressured into recanting. By July 23, the top brass could declare: "The PLA has given its firm support to the CCP Central Committee's decision to outlaw Falun Gong." Lieutenant General Li Qihua, a participant in the Long March who held very sensitive positions in the PLA before reportedly becoming Falun Gong's top officer in Beijing, quickly fell into line: "The party's decision is very wise, very correct, and very timely."

The whole movement was little noticed until April 25 of this year, when, surprising everyone, more than 10,000 members turned out for a day-long vigil around Zhongnanhai, the compound where many of China's top leaders live and work. The demonstration was apparently prompted by an anti–Falun Gong article. This had been written by the notorious leftist (in other words, conservative) scientist He Zuoxiu, who, in the 1980s, had campaigned against people like dissident astrophysicist Fang Lizhi. The article was published in Tianjin, and apparently the outraged Falun Gong people hoped for some support from the central authorities. Although the vigil they staged in Beijing was silent, the authorities found it eerie and alarming. Of course, they must have thought, we Communists sometimes condone and encourage demonstrations, even utterly lawless ones involving damage to foreign embassies, but whatever gave these people, who are not following the Party line, the right of assembly? If we Communists cannot control this religious group, how safe will our grip on the other religions be? And if the Party cannot control the religions, which are relatively docile, what can it control? (China has five legal religions: Buddhism, Taoism, Islam, Catholicism, and Protestantism. Spokespersons for all of the officially recognized groups which "represent" these five have been trotted out to attack Falun Gong.)

Paper Tiger?

In all of this, the Communist leadership ends up looking like a bunch of "control freaks." It is hard for us to see what "massive threat to society" Falun Gong could possibly have posed, unless of course one equates "society" with Communist control of all aspects of culture. The seven-year-old movement just does not seem all that awesome. Its presumed founder, Li Hongzhi, is a former provincial grain bureau clerk who now does not even live in China. He told the *New York Times* on August 8 that his own role has been exaggerated. "Were the [real] cultivators of Falun Gong to know that I was ranked among the influential people in the world, they would most likely laugh . . . My masters are all practicing in the mountains. If they don't want to be seen, even I couldn't find them. I 'came out' only because they said that I should."

Since Li's "coming out," Falun Gong has become an international movement, but a rather amorphous one. It has had serious growing pains. Some of Li's earliest disciples have now turned against the organization. There have been charges of financial improprieties. On the other hand, Falun Gong is big; it is not known just how big. On the low end of estimates, we have the Chinese authorities' assertion that there are only two million members. On the high end, Li has implied that he has more than 100 million followers worldwide. Even if there are only half that many in China, that would make the movement roughly the size of the CCP, but it probably is not that large.

In July, when demonstrations by sect members occurred in more than thirty Chinese cities, the CCP's leaders seemed to have become paranoid. They felt that they were under "siege." (By their count, 307 "sieges" took place between April 25 and early August.) They were particularly keen to put a stop to the movement in the capital. The police have demanded that the out-of-town demonstrators leave immediately; otherwise "the nature of the incident will even change." (One cannot help but recall how, on June 4, 1989, the CCP "changed the nature" of another incident.)

According to US-based Falun Gong disciples, police throughout China have ransacked homes of practitioners, confiscating books, videotapes, and posters. It is said that 1.5 million of the movement's publications have been destroyed by crushing or shredding, certainly an act worthy of Mao Zedong and the first emperor Qin Shi Huangdi at their worst. Every effort has been made to block members' access to the Falun Gong site on the Internet, which had been a crucial means of communication within the movement, providing Falun Gong with an amazing ability to turn out its "troops" in highly disciplined demonstrations everywhere from Harbin to Shenzhen. Only the CCP can duplicate that feat and turn out "the masses" from one end of the country to the other.

But the authorities' overreaction in April was counterproductive, and the protests only intensified. Seventy Falun Gong members were reportedly detained on July 20, including movement leaders around the country. Those arrested included Li Chang, who had represented the group in nego- tiations with the government in April. Altogether, according to one police estimate, about 50,000 members of the group were detained in the Beijing area alone; most were released before the end of the fifteen days, when according to the law they would have to be formally charged. But the lead- ers remain in prison and are likely to be put on trial soon. Large rewards have been promised for information leading to the arrest of others (pre- sumably financed by the heavy fines being extracted from the underlings).

Role of the Media

The crackdown on Falun Gong demonstrates how important is the right of freedom of information. This summer the media throughout the coun- try was mobilized to attack the movement. The government has published and heavily promoted a new book, *Exposing the True Face of Falun Gong*. In Shandong, the scientific magazine *Kepu Forum* declared that the sect was superstitious and based on "sham science." The Beijing media on July 22 accused the sect of spreading "superstitious, evil thinking" and under- mining social stability. "The Falun Gong Research Society conducted ille- gal activities, spread superstitious, evil thinking to blind people, all to stir up trouble and sabotage social stability."

Whether or not such charges have any merit, Falun Gong deserves more evenhanded treatment in the media. And, more importantly, the general public have a right to objective and balanced reporting on this and all other subjects, a right that they rarely enjoy in China. Indeed, it was precisely the authorities' abuse of their monopoly control of the media that outraged the Falun Gong followers. In its campaign against the movement, *People's Daily* has emphasized the need for "promoting education in Marxist materialism and atheism, and the basic principles and guidelines of the Chinese Communist Party." Small wonder that the Falun people might want to retaliate. As the paper described their actions, "practitioners . . . besieged the newspaper office . . . Some of them played 'Falun Gong' music all day long outside the media establishments . . . Some wormed their way into the offices en masse to entangle the editors and journalists on duty; some continually made nuisance calls on editors' and journalists' phones and pagers, and even forced editors to change their phone numbers." But had Falun Gong not been subjected to prejudiced reporting, they would not have undertaken their demonstrations in the first place.

The Group's Appeal

It is worth noting that Falun Gong seems to be attracting precisely those who have been the main victims of past human rights abuses: the middle-aged and elderly (both age groups having suffered through the Cultural Revolution), and women (toward whom the Communists fell far short of delivering on revolutionary promises). Now, Chinese "law" again fails such people. Chinese media have attributed the involvement of the elderly to a lack of "healthy" activities being provided for retired people, at the same time berating elderly Falun Gong adherents for engaging in such irresponsible and antisocial behavior. But interviews with some older members of the group by international media have highlighted the fact that many began their practice precisely because they were ill and could not afford escalating medical fees, so were attempting to help themselves.

The authorities were clearly worried that so many women had joined the movement. "With the deepening struggle against Falun Gong," stated an ostensibly reassuring Xinhua News Agency dispatch, "more women now have a clear understanding of the true purpose of this illegal organization, and have broken away from it . . . The Falun Gong incidents make us realize that it is an important duty of women's organizations to help women improve their overall quality and establish a right viewpoint, which is also a long-term task for the women's movement. Women should arm their minds with scientific theories and knowledge, and play key roles in advocating science and fighting against superstition . . . Women's fate is always closely connected with that of their country . . . The two decades since China's opening to the outside world prove that women emancipated themselves only by having confidence in the leadership of the Communist Party, Marxism, and science . . . It is the ultimate role of women to uphold science and break away from superstition, and also their glorious mission." Apparently, recent decades have not taught women that there is much glory in following the CCP, and thus many have now turned to religion.

Indeed, so have many intellectuals. Thus, the government has mobilized its "experts" to attack Falun Gong. The Chinese Academy of Social Science held a much-publicized seminar. One research fellow, Li Chongfu, said that behind Li Hongzhi's desire to convert people was a political goal and ambition to establish a kingdom ruled by himself. "To reach this goal, he dreamed up Falun Dafa . . . to deceive and brainwash Falun Gong practitioners. Li Hongzhi has also set up a tightly run organization with political motives and an agenda that has been involved in numerous illegal activities." Other scholars urged that the country should make every effort to get rid of the social causes of Falun Gong and leave no room for other cults. The professional press has echoed these concerns. *Science and Technology Daily* warned: "We should remain highly vigilant against a few international forces that are trying to push power politics." Note how foreigners are to blame for all of the authorities' problems; they themselves are, of course, blameless.

But in reality, the official media's "scientific" judgments have nothing to do with science. What the Falun Gong movement really shows is that many Chinese are very frustrated about their plight. Sometimes the authorities can channel this frustration into such activities as attacking American diplomatic venues. But sooner or later people will realize that a more appropriate target is a leadership which behaves lawlessly and denies citizens their human rights.

James D. Seymour, senior research scholar at the East Asian Institute of Columbia University, is co-author of New Ghosts, Old Ghosts: Prisons and Labor Reform Camps in China, *and a board member of Human Rights in China.*

* * *

Unprecedented Courage in the Face of Cultural Revolution–Style Persecution
by Liu Binyan

The Chinese Communist Party (CCP) established itself and finally won political power by relying on the support of the masses. "The people" is one of the most commonly used phrases in the CCP's official language. But, unfortunately, this phrase has been turned into an abstract, almost mystical concept designed to control and direct the lives of the real people. Terrorizing and despising the people has been a characteristic of CCP leaders since Mao Zedong. He constantly mobilized mass movements to achieve his political purposes, while at the same time forbidding people from initiating any kind of political activities of their own, so even non-political organizations were strictly banned. In the past, the focus of the repressive apparatus was mainly concentrated on university students and intellectuals, and only in the 1990s did it shift toward farmers and workers. The CCP had never viewed urban people who had become disengaged from the collective structures of society and did not appear to pose any kind of organizational threat as potentially antagonistic to its interests.

People have been practicing qigong (exercises that move the practitioner's non-physical energy, or qi) to improve their health for the past thirty-plus years of the PRC's history. Some of the qigong practice groups have even been allowed to become legitimate organizations, demonstrating that the CCP has not seen them as a threat. However, some particular groups have been disbanded when they have become very large and their leaders were very charismatic. But groups like Falun Gong, which have been able to win tens of millions of followers in the space of a few years, have been a rare occurrence.

It is said that one reason for Falun Gong's astonishing popularity is its highly effective curative powers, which accord with the pragmatic mentality of the Chinese people, especially in the light of the fact that free medical services for employees of state-owned enterprises are being cut, a reality which has greatly increased people's need for alternative forms of health care. Another reason people speak of is the growing moral vacuum in society and the lack of collective values, a trend which started to be seen in the 1970s. In the 1990s the decline in basic human decency has been even more pronounced, while crime has been rising unchecked, leading to a sense of uncertainty in the community. This made the religious character of Falun Gong, with its promotion of the principles of truthfulness, benevolence, and forbearance, even more attractive.

Of course the participation and support of powerful cadres at the top and middle levels of the CCP hierarchy, people with high social status and strong political influence, also increased the legitimacy and appeal of Falun Gong. There is no basis for the claim that these people have any political ambitions. However, it is true that many old and retired officials feel dissatisfied with current CCP policy, official corruption, and the state of society, but think they have no power to intervene. For them, strengthening a movement like Falun Gong could be seen as a way of cleansing the spirit of society, and thus appeared to be a way of addressing some of their concerns.

From April to June this year [1999], Jiang Zemin suddenly seemed determined to treat Falun Gong as a major political enemy, employing all means to destroy the organization. One reason for this was his fear of any people's movement not controlled by the CCP. (It had developed such a large membership and the example of the way followers surrounded the leadership compound, Zhongnanhai, on April 25, 1999, demonstrated a phenomenal level of organization.) Second was his fear of the potential for splits within the Party if those CCP cadres who belonged to Falun Gong decided to transform the movement into an opposition force.

Religion has always been a separate issue from science. The way the Chinese government is attacking Falun Gong teachings as unscientific is unreasonable. Of course, this does not mean one cannot pose challenges both to the teachings and to Li Hongzhi himself, but this is not an acceptable reason to negate Falun Gong. The group's followers have not demonstrated any destructive fanaticism, indeed their behavior has been peaceful, rational, and constructive. The CCP's smear tactics of calling Falun Gong a cult are just absurd.

The membership of Falun Gong is not limited to those people who have too much leisure time on their hands. One of the most important hotbeds of Falun Gong is the Jiang'an Locomotive Factory in Wuhan; it was labeled by the anti–Falun Gong campaign as among "the worst-hit disaster areas." Famous as the center of the "February Seventh" strike campaign launched by the CCP in 1920s, this plant has particular significance for the regime. The crackdown initiated in July 1999 had little effect there. As soon as workers who had been detained were released, they continued all of their activities. The authorities ordered the managers of the factory to help re-educate those workers who are Falun Gong members, but that also did not change anything. Most of the Falun Gong members in the factory are known to be honest, hardworking people who are dissatisfied with the current social environment.

Not long after the Chinese government launched its campaign for the complete suppression of Falun Gong, using all possible means to achieve its aims, the US-based Chinese language newspaper *World Journal* said in a commentary: "With the force of the entire state machine against them, even if Falun Gong members number in the tens of millions, they will find it virtually impossible to resist. The biggest popular movement since June Fourth, 'practicing qigong as a means of protest,' will gradually subside." Many people, including myself, agreed with this sentiment at that time. I did not believe that Falun Gong would be totally exterminated, but that it would become an underground movement. But the reality proved us all wrong.

Falun Gong members inside China have not ceased their protests opposing the regime's treatment of their movement during the past four months, and since October, their campaign of disobedience has actually intensified. It is hard to believe that at least two groups of members managed to break through the strict police blockade to enter Tiananmen Square and practice qigong and meditation while the celebrations for the PRC's fiftieth anniversary were in progress. And since October 25, the number of people staging similar protests has increased; these people insisted on exercising their rights even though they knew perfectly well that they would be arrested and some could even face the death penalty. This kind of attitude is unprecedented in the fifty-year history of the PRC. Another historic first was seen when, on November 30, Falun Gong members successfully held a press conference for the international media in Beijing.

From 1949 onward, with the exception of a few exceptional individuals, those singled out as the targets of the many political campaigns launched by the CCP have been forced to bend their heads and admit their "crimes," following the will of the Party and accepting their punishment, even if they had been the head of state, or the number one in the Party, or if they were just one among the millions of intellectuals and cadres being persecuted. The scale on which the CCP mobilized the propaganda apparatus across the country to attack and slander Falun Gong was comparable to the "great struggle sessions" of the Cultural Revolution. And the threats, detentions, and criminal prosecutions directed toward Falun Gong members were also not much different to the persecution in the Cultural Revolution. It is fair to say that the full panoply of psychological and physical weapons is being used against them. But Falun Gong has not surrendered, becoming the first social organization that the Party dictatorship has been unable to crush in fifty years. This has far-reaching significance, and will have a variety of social and political consequences. One of the most important of these is the widespread resentment the CCP's handling of this issue has caused among the people.

Recently Jiang Zemin said: "I don't believe we can't deal with Falun Gong!" But when Chinese people use this construction, "I don't believe I can't . . . ", on the one hand they are indicating their determination to deal with the matter, and on the other they are acknowledging that they face serious obstacles to achieving their aims. Evidently Jiang Zemin has discovered that Falun Gong is not as easy to deal with as he thought when he ordered the crackdown in July.

One fundamental reason why, in the space of seven years, Falun Gong has became the largest social organization in the PRC's history and why its members are so persistent despite the odds, is that China is beset by a spate of crises created by the CCP, and which the Party has no means of solving. If Falun Gong does not commit any major errors, the existence and development of these crises will mean that it will continue to expand and gain more people's sympathy. For this reason, I and a number of friends have independently come to the conclusion that in his attack on Falun Gong, Jiang Zemin has picked up the stone which will crush his own foot; this campaign may be one of the factors which brings his rule to an end.

Liu Binyan established a tradition of investigative reporting when he worked for People's Daily *in the 1980s. Twice expelled from the CCP, he now lives in the United States, and continues his journalistic work. He is currently working on a book presenting his perspective on Chinese history. This article was translated by Chine Chan.*

* * *

Falun Gong and the Internet
by Stephen D. O'Leary

In 1999, the Chinese government launched a campaign against superstitions and unauthorized spiritual groups. One group targeted was Falun Gong, also known as Falun Dafa, which practices a form of qigong, a slow-motion meditative exercise related to martial arts such as Tai Chi. Members of the group reacted to the government offensive with a daring demonstration, staged in Beijing's Tiananmen Square— the site of the 1989 crackdown on the pro-democracy movement. The demonstration was peaceful, but involved 10,000 of the group's followers, making it the largest demonstration in recent Chinese history. In return, the Chinese government launched an all-out offensive specifically targeted against the group, branding it an "evil cult" and arresting and imprisoning its leaders and members.

Is this just another example of religious repression? Why should we care about the Chinese government's beef with a bunch of people who appear to be devoted to the practice of an ancient meditative exercise regime?

Before we dismiss what appears to be a marginal religious cult, we should remember that estimates of this group's size range from two million to 100 million. We might also recall the last time an unorthodox religious movement swept across China (as Jonathan Spence tells the story in *God's Chinese Son*), the result was a war, the Taiping Rebellion, that killed twenty million people. Imagine if Hong Xiuquan, the messianic leader of that nineteenth-century cultic crusade, had had access to twenty-first century technology—and you'll have a clue as to why the Chinese regime is so scared of this group.

A little web-surfing reveals that there's more to this story than meets the eye. [See Chapter 19: Internet Resource Guide, for a comprehensive listing of Falun Gong–related Internet links.] Falun Gong's Internet savvy was a crucial factor in its ability to organize the unauthorized demonstration under the noses of Chinese intelligence. The group's secretive leader, Li Hongzhi, lives in New York and directs his movement from abroad with Internet, fax, and telephone. The group is thoroughly wired, with Falun Gong websites all over the world, including Asia, the US, UK, Canada, Israel, and Australia.

In response, the Chinese government has set up an anti–Falun Gong website to discredit the group, and, according to an ABC News report, has also hacked into Falun Gong websites worldwide, spamming and causing their servers to crash.

Others have also joined in the fray of the Internet propaganda war between the Chinese government and the Falun Gong, with websites such as CESNUR and AsiaSource following the developments of Chinese persecution of the group closely, and offering overviews, commentaries, and site links.

The Falun Gong story appears to be as much about technology as it is about religion; it offers a fascinating glimpse of an ancient religious tradition that is mutating rapidly as it makes the leap into cyberspace.

The Propaganda War

Let's start with the attacking side in the propaganda war. Why is the Chinese government so upset over this group, and what allegations have they made about it?

A July 23, 1999 article in *China Daily* provides some of the government's justifications of its campaign to arrest and jail Falun Gong followers. Chinese Foreign Ministry spokeswoman Zhang Qiyue is quoted as claiming that "Falun Gong organizations have advocated superstitious beliefs and incited the masses to create disturbances and jeopardize social stability under the banner of practicing Falun Gong."

The official website of the China Internet Information Center, the center of the government's Internet campaign to discredit the group, contains numerous articles detailing the "cult's" alleged crimes.

In one article, "True Face of Li Hongzhi Exposed," Falun Gong is characterized as a "highly organized, fully functional, and unregistered illegal organization," whose leader is alleged to have bilked his followers of massive quantities of money and even their sanity.

Another article with the unambiguous title, "Analysis of Falun Gong Leader's Malicious Fallacies," accuses the group of being a doomsday cult that has supposedly "deceived" and "harmed" many: "Falun Gong has a set of ridiculous ideas, a basic one of which claims that doomsday is coming, that human beings will be extinct soon, that modern science can do nothing to prevent the catastrophe, that only Falun Gong can save mankind, and that Li Hongzhi is the sole 'savior.'" Li Hongzhi is alleged to have warned "that the Earth would explode, that only he could postpone the explosion, and that only 'Falun Dafa' was the 'transcendental law' which could save the entire human race."

This is all very interesting to apocalyptic prophecy buffs. And it's not very often that claims about the impending apocalypse attract the attention of the government of the world's most populous nation. That same government was so afraid of Falun Gong that it continued its crackdown at a sensitive moment, when China's entry into the WTO and the debate over Most Favored Nation status in the US placed it under intense critical scrutiny from anti-China activists eager to publicize evidence of religious repression.

What is perhaps most interesting about the Falun Gong web pages—on both sides of this battle—is that they are quite extensively available in both English and Chinese. This suggests two things: first, that persuading external, Western audiences to either condemn or tolerate this group is an important objective for both sides; second, that some substantial portion of the followers themselves are English-speaking, non-Asian Westerners.

At least one believer's web testimony indicates that it has an appeal for non-Asians; and the many other personal stories posted at Minghui Net, the main site for "Falun Dafa in North America," bear this out. Falun Gong appears to be aggressively attempting to expand its membership beyond China by targeting mystically inclined Westerners.

Most interesting of all to those who follow news about fringe religions around the world is the fact that the Chinese government's campaign against this organization has drawn its justifications directly from the findings of anti-cult authors in the West. The extensive article "Why We Judge 'Falun Gong' to Be a Cultist Organization" is hauntingly familiar to those who remember the press accounts of cult violence from Jonestown to Waco to Heaven's Gate and Aum Shinrikyo.

The article pulls out all the stops in its comparison of Li Hongzhi to Jim Jones and other planners of religious violence, and in its demonization of alternative religious groups as "cultist organizations corroding human society like malignant tumors." It lists a number of symptoms of destructive cultism, as distinguished from legitimate religion: "cult founder worship" and claims of supernatural powers, "hawking the theory of doomsday," "amassing illegal funds by manipulating followers," and "brainwashing."

As the article puts it, "The followers of a cult are re-educated, have their brains washed and start with a clean slate—'Brain washing' means that the founder of a cult, or his organization, instills his ideas into the followers' minds and demands that they accept them."

The Brainwash Debate

The scholarly debate over the brainwashing thesis is conflicted. Academics are divided over whether many standard religious practices of indoctrination are distinguishable from this kind of acute psychological coercion. The fact that the charge of brainwashing is being raised by the Chinese government is particularly ironic, for the term was introduced to our lexicon as a way to describe the coercive pressure applied to American prisoners of war by the Chinese during the Korean War. (The image of evil Chinese Communists brainwashing American soldiers was memorably fixed in public consciousness by the film "Manchurian Candidate.")

Any scholarly validity that attaches to the brainwashing theory today is largely due to Robert Jay Lifton's pioneering study, *Thought Reform and the Psychology of Totalism: A Study of Brainwashing in China*, which certainly does not reflect well on the Chinese government's own persuasive practices. But the irony seems invisible to Falun Gong's official enemies, who are content to paint a picture of Li Hongzhi and his group that depicts them with the standard charges in the anti-cult arsenal.

If Li is the archetypal doomsday cult leader, and his followers are deluded, superstitious victims of sophisticated psychological coercion, then any measures taken by the government would seem to be justifiable. Like many cult leaders, he is supposed to have said that "those who oppose Falun Gong are 'demons.'" He is also accused of encouraging his followers to commit suicide (on closer examination, this charge dwindles to indirectly causing deaths by discouraging members from seeking medical treatment). Finally, Li is portrayed as a corrupt swindler, taking money from his followers and amassing "a large fortune on which he has not paid taxes."

These allusions to the Western ideas of a doomsday cult figure are clearly an attempt by the Chinese government to seek sympathy and empathy from Western countries, particularly from America, where Li now resides. As Western countries may not be familiar with the traditional Chinese religions in which Falun Gong is rooted, the web page also relies on using the voice of state-approved Chinese religious leaders to further discredit Falun Gong and strengthen the "cult" image. For example, the head of the Buddhist Association of China is quoted as saying that "Falun

Gong deceives its followers by misusing Buddhist terminology" and "runs counter to Buddhism and the Communist Party of China's policy of freedom of religious belief."

To American Christians who may be concerned about the implications of the government's campaign for followers of their own religion, the Chinese can also point to statements of support from Christian leaders who support the ban on Falun Gong.

The propagandistic tone of the attacks on Li Hongzhi and Falun Gong seems over the top, recalling the worst excesses of the ideological campaigns of the Cultural Revolution. Li's political ambitions are described as "wicked" and "viperous" while his ideas are "malicious fallacies"; his followers are said to be "an evil group that is fighting against science, the human kind, [and] society."

The official Chinese anti–Falun Gong site on which these attacks appear is entirely self-referential, with not a single link to outside resources that might provide other viewpoints or correct distortions. So, perhaps it's time to turn to the group's own websites, to see if there is any evidence to support the official condemnations that are so strangely aligned with the rhetoric of the American anti-cult movement.

Falun Gong, USA

Visitors to the official USA Falun Gong website, Falun Dafa, will find a distinctly different portrayal of their version of qigong practice and the group's purposes. The "Introduction of Falun Dafa" claims an authoritative ancient lineage, stating that "Much of the teachings are highly classified knowledge that are hitherto imparted exclusively from master to trusted disciples since antiquity in China." A membership of "100 million practitioners in nearly thirty countries around the world" is claimed, and the site's authors proudly note that "Li Hongzhi has worked tirelessly to convey Falun Dafa from China to the rest of the world. Along the way, he has touched the lives of countless people in many countries, earning an acclaimed international reputation."

The website also includes a section "Clarifying Some Misconceptions," which explicitly states that Falun Gong is not a cult, and proceeds to give several examples to refute the Chinese Government's attempts to depict it as a cult. The group rejects the authoritarian characterization of outsiders, claiming the title of "cultivators, not followers or adherents"; they are said to have "complete individual freedom," make their own decisions, and lead "normal lives with families." The site explicitly renounces violence, teaching that killing or suicide violates the supreme principle of "Truthfulness-Benevolence-Forbearance" and teaching that Falun Gong does not "approve any form of punishment or persecution."

Instead of being isolated, "secretive and exclusive," the group is "open to anyone who wants to learn, free of charge." A banner on the home page reinforces the point: "All Falun Dafa Activities Are Free of Charge." The Internet is also the major source of free teaching materials, for instructions in the form of books, audio and videotapes can be downloaded without charge. Indeed, the website itself provides links to full texts of books, lectures and multimedia on Falun Gong. This contradicts the conventional image of cults taking money and possessions from its followers, which is further emphasized with the assertion that Falun Dafa is not a religion and there is "no religious ritual or worship." In addition, "Master Li does not allow donations, fundraising activities, or money to be accumulated in the name of Falun Dafa."

Yet, although the attempt to depict Falun Gong as a non-political, non-religious group appears rather convincing, the fact remains that it is a massive group that is organized, though perhaps not in a clear, structured fashion. The list of Falun Dafa websites that is provided in one of the links is staggering. Lists of volunteers all over the world provide the email addresses and contact numbers of individual members representing groups who practice together. The number of groups in China is claimed to be so large that a disclaimer, almost a boast, is given: "Too many to be listed. Falun Dafa practitioners can be found in public parks in all the cities every morning."

The Internet is clearly being used as a means to keep contact and mobilize members. One comes away from the various Falun Gong websites with a distinct impression of an effective global network that is indeed organized and connected by virtue of the Internet. Is this organization as altruistic and benevolent as it claims to be? Or can any of the charges against Falun Gong and Master Li be substantiated?

It may be that, like some religious groups in the past that have appeared harmless but ultimately turned toward violence, Master Li's deeper designs will be unveiled and found to be malevolent. On one count, however, it seems that the Chinese government has misrepresented his teachings. Oddly, neither the official Falun Dafa websites nor any of the other Falun Gong websites show any reference to doomsday predictions or the end of the world.

The online text of the book *China Falun Gong* states that Falun Dafa is for "cultivation" and "enlightenment." It "offers self-salvation: it makes the person stronger and healthier, more intelligent and wise." There is no mention made in the works available via the Net of impending disasters, the destruction of the world, or the exclusive salvation that Master Li is supposed to offer. These charges seems to come solely from the Chinese government (which, however, may be in possession of lecture tapes or untranslated works that it has yet to share with the world).

If we speculate as to why their attacks focused on doomsday beliefs, it may help to recall that at the time the story broke in the United States, law enforcement agencies and media pundits were embroiled in fearful premillennial speculations about the potential for religious terrorism associated with the apocalyptic year 2000. The Chinese government thus seems to have tried to justify its own repression with the same type of analysis that the FBI was promoting in its now-forgotten "Project Megiddo" report.

A recent survey of the opinions of overseas Chinese regarding Falun Gong and the government's repression yields some rather interesting and equivocal data: while many respondents have unfavorable opinions of Li Hongzhi, many more agreed that both Western and Chinese media have handled the whole case poorly. Those seeking to rectify media bias may find a non-partisan perspective at the online archives of CESNUR, the Italian-based Center for Studies on New Religions, where news items on Falun Gong are regularly collected and updated and some balanced articles may be found. Similarly, the AsiaSource Web page attempts to give a balanced and objective viewpoint of Falun Gong and its practitioners, providing links to interviews with Li, along with other opinions and commentary.

In conclusion, the Falun Gong has used modern technology to its advantage, exploiting the Internet as a tool for teaching, organizing, and mobilizing its global membership, as well as for counteracting the propaganda with which the Chinese government has inundated the world. The examination of websites on the Internet indicates that the Chinese government is clearly on the losing side of this war. Although some articles on the web depict the Falun Gong as a crackpot group with strange spiritual beliefs, most do not swallow their depiction as a nefarious doomsday cult.

Criticism from human rights activists and the US government over the religious persecution of Falun Gong members has clearly forced the Chinese government to proceed with caution. Thus, the power of the Internet can be used to challenge Communist leadership and give religious and spiritual groups a significant voice.

We can be sure that this power will be met with resistance: the November arrest of the Chinese student who was charged with spreading Falun Gong emails is an indication that the war is being fought offline as well as on the Net. One lesson that the Chinese might do well to learn is that persecuting a religion is the surest way to stimulate its growth. Watch for more news as Master Li's students around the world continue their resistance to the Chinese government's oppression.

Stephen D. O'Leary is an associate professor at the USC Annenberg School for Communication.

CHAPTER 16
REACTIONS OF THE US AND OTHER GOVERNMENTS

Congressional Research Service Report for the US Congress
China and "Falun Gong": Implications and Options for US Policy
by Thomas Lum, Analyst in Asian Affairs; Foreign Affairs, Defense, and Trade Division

September 10, 1999

Summary

The "Falun Gong" movement led to the largest public demonstrations in China since the Tiananmen Square demonstrations for democracy in 1989. On April 25, 1999, an estimated 10,000 to 30,000 adherents assembled in front of Zhongnanhai, the Chinese Communist Party leadership compound, and participated in a silent protest against state repression of their activities. Followers assert that Falun Gong provides an exercise regimen and spiritual guide for good health and emotional stability and has no political agenda. Chinese leaders, however, perceived the group as a potential "rival power center" and were concerned about the popularity of Falun Gong among Communist Party members. In the crackdown that began on July 21, 1999, the government has outlawed the practice, imprisoned followers who do not repudiate Falun Gong, and begun to prosecute group leaders. Although the State Department immediately criticized the ban, some members of Congress have pointed to the suppression of Falun Gong as evidence that the Clinton Administration's policy toward China has not gone far enough in promoting human rights. This report will be updated as events warrant.

Background and Recent Events

"Falun Gong" also known as "Falun Dafa" combines an exercise regimen with meditation and a set of moral principles. The practice and beliefs are derived from qigong, a set of movements through which one channels vital energies, and Buddhist and Taoist ideas. Falun Gong promises physical well-being, emotional tranquility, and an understanding of life and one's place in the world. Practitioners claim that by controlling the wheel of dharma, which revolves in the body, one can cure such ailments as high blood pressure, back aches, and even cancer. Falun Gong also teaches people how to be good individuals and citizens. It upholds three main virtues—compassion, forbearance, and truthfulness—and warns against forms of "moral degeneration" such as rock music, drugs, and homosexuality. Adherents believe that through Falun Gong, the problems of society can be resolved and the end of the world can be averted. Some observers attach cult-like qualities to Falun Gong, including an unquestioning obedience to its founder, Li Hongzhi, an obsession with end-of-the-world prophesies, and a rejection of mainstream science. However, followers refute this view, arguing that the practice is voluntary and helps develop healthy, moral, and productive citizens.

Li Hongzhi ("Master Li") developed the motions and philosophy of Falun Gong in the late 1980s, when qigong began to gain popularity in China. In 1992, Li, a former Grain Bureau clerk, explained his "discoveries" in a book, *Zhuan Falun*. During the mid-1990s, Falun Gong acquired a large and diverse following, with membership estimates ranging from 3 million to 100 million, including not only retired persons, but also youth, students, intellectuals, workers, and peasants. In addition, the practice attracted many Party cadres, retired Party members, and military officials and personnel. In 1997, Li traveled throughout China, giving about fifty weeklong lectures. Following the tour, the Chinese government pressured him to leave China and banned the sale of his book. Since 1998, Li, who speaks only Chinese, has lived in New York on permanent visa status. Following the crackdown, Li spoke out against the Chinese government's excessive measures but also expressed hope of opening a dialogue with government leaders to resolve the conflict.

The Chinese government expressed relatively little concern toward practitioners of Falun Gong until the demonstrations of April 1999, which caught the Communist leadership and security forces by surprise. On April 25, 1999, 10,000 to 30,000 Falun Gong practitioners gathered in Beijing. Representatives of Falun Gong associations, notified by telephone and via the movement's websites, came from as far as Zhejiang Province in the south. They arrived in Beijing before dawn and joined local followers in front of Zhongnanhai, the Chinese leadership compound. Clutching Master Li's writings, the demonstrators, many of them elderly, sat silently or meditated. Fearing imminent suppression of their activities, adherents presented an open letter to the government demanding official recognition and legal protections of their rights to free speech, press, and assembly.

Between May and June 1999, Party leaders were reportedly split on whether to ban Falun Gong and conveyed contradictory messages. According to sources close to the movement, Premier Zhu Rongji was sympathetic toward the concerns of Falun Gong practitioners and held discussions with representatives of the group, while Communist Party chief Jiang

Zemin was alarmed by the apparent loss of Party unity and authority and initiated the crackdown. Thus, on the one hand, the government assured Falun Gong leaders and followers that their activities would not be outlawed. On the other hand, the Party produced circulars forbidding its members from participating in Falun Gong activities. State television and newspapers portrayed the Falun Gong following as a religious cult that ruined people's lives and disrupted familial and social stability. Security forces collected the names of instructors, monitored and infiltrated the group, and closed book stalls selling Falun Gong literature. Tensions escalated in July as followers in various cities renewed demonstrations, including occupying a government building in Nanchang, Jiangxi Province and demonstrating in front of China Central Television Station in Beijing. Altogether, between April and July 1999, followers engaged in eighteen major demonstrations.

The crackdown began on July 21, 1999, when Chinese security forces arrested 70-140 Falun Gong leaders, many of whom had met with Zhu Rongji in late April. The Communist Party Central Committee and the State Council issued a joint order that "senior members" of the movement be "punished severely." The state rounded up, detained, and questioned nearly 30,000 participants nationwide, releasing those who promised to quit the group or identified movement organizers. Followers who have not renounced Falun Gong remain in prison. Police raided the homes of adherents and confiscated books, while State Security agencies blocked Falun Gong Internet sites in China and abroad. In Beijing alone, public security officers closed sixty-seven instruction centers and 1,627 exercise areas. The state also ordered work units to obtain signed confessions of Falun Gong practitioners admitting their "mistakes," though enforcement has reportedly been lax. Some 1,200 government officials who had practiced Falun Gong were compelled to sever their ties to the movement and undergo re-education. The state accused the group of advocating superstition, spreading fallacies, and jeopardizing social stability, and issued an arrest warrant for Li Hongzhi. The Ministry of Civil Affairs declared the Falun Gong group an "illegal organization" and outlawed its activities.

The Communist leadership has reduced the group's ability to organize protests but, in the process, further damaged the government's credibility among many Chinese citizens. Many followers have disassociated themselves from the practice out of fear of punishment, some have even begun to accept the government line about Falun Gong's evils. Furthermore, according to some reports, although many non-adherents are bothered by the Party's actions, they are either indifferent toward Falun Gong practitioners or criticize them for carrying their demonstrations too far. However, while the movement may be in disarray and isolated in China, the actions of Chinese leaders have deepened anti-government sentiment among many followers and non-followers.

Adherents of Falun Gong reveal little about their organizational structure. Followers characterize their objectives as individual and limited in scope. Practitioners engage in the exercises for personal purposes and have no political agenda beyond protecting constitutional rights. Followers assert that the group lacks a hierarchical chain of command and has no routine procedures for coordinating activities. According to members, Li Hongzhi has little contact with group leaders in both China and the United States, communicates mostly through written statements, and provides very limited organizational guidance. Li denies that he instigated the April 1999 protests. He was reportedly en route from Hong Kong to Australia when the demonstrations occurred. According to a Falun Gong spokesperson, group efforts in China and abroad have been carried out spontaneously or with little planning. In the United States, practitioners are linked via "contact persons" in several states who have little authority to direct followers as a whole. New York followers have set up a non-profit organization dedicated to Falun Gong, which has been involved mostly in publicizing the plight of adherents in China.

Nonetheless, the size of the demonstrations and the speed with which followers were mobilized in April 1999 indicate that an informal but well-knit and effective network of dedicated leaders and followers had developed. The Research Society of Falun Dafa and exercise instructors may have provided leadership while Falun Gong publications and the Internet enabled group members to communicate. Chinese government, military, and public security officials who practiced Falun Gong may have provided crucial support in initially preventing or delaying government actions against the following. The sale of books and audio-visual products may have generated funds for movement activities.

Implications for Chinese Politics

Although Falun Gong does not represent a political opposition movement, the Chinese government fears the group's harmful effects upon Party unity and social control. First, Chinese leaders fear that the presence of Falun Gong adherents within the Communist Party and other political institutions undermines cohesion within the regime at a time when the government's basis of legitimacy—economic growth—is faltering. For many Party members, Falun Gong not only offers physical benefits but also a belief system that is more appealing than Jiang Zemin's "socialist spiritual civilization." Before the April 1999, many members of the Party, People's Liberation Army, and Public Security apparatus became involved in the movements. Vice President Hu Jintao stated that of 2.1 million known members of Falun Gong group, one-third belonged to the Communist Party. According to reports, the practice enjoyed strong support among soldiers and officers in such major northeastern cities as Dalian and

Shijiazhuang, while the Chinese Navy published the Falun Gong bible, *Zhuan Falun*. High-ranking Party, state, and military officials were among those who met with Zhu Rongji in April 1999. The government has referred to a few Party members as the "backbone" of the group and may use them as scapegoats if they are put on trial.

Second, the size, diversity, and fervor of Falun Gong adherents make them difficult to suppress. The large number of persons involved and the simplicity of their aims enable them to mount collective actions on a national scale. Moreover, several thousand followers practice and teach Falun Gong in the United States and other countries and are lobbying these governments to apply diplomatic pressure upon China. Since practitioners cross social, occupational, regional, and national boundaries, the government cannot control the movement by focusing upon only a few social groups, work units, or geographical areas. Because their reasons for pursuing Falun Gong are largely non-materialistic, pecuniary incentives and sanctions, such as offering or denying promotions at work or licenses and loans to operate businesses, are often ineffectual.

Third, any social movement, no matter how non-political on its face, can attract or encourage the rise of other movements. Li Hongzhi and his followers claim to have rejected ties to political and religious organizations in China and abroad. However, the group's talk of constitutional rights may strike familiar chords among other Chinese suffering from economic stagnation or from political, ethnic, or religious persecution. Falun Gong's core, traditional values of compassion, forbearance, and truthfulness could be adopted by other groups to criticize government coercion and corruption. Finally, some analysts note that in Chinese history, quasi-religious upheavals, such as the Taiping and Boxer rebellions of the last century, tapped into popular discontent and gave rise to mass political movements.

Policy Options for the United States

On July 22, 1999, State Department spokesman James Rubin announced that the United States was "disturbed" by the ban and by reports of "heavy-handed tactics" used against demonstrators, and he urged the Chinese government to guarantee fundamental rights and freedoms. On August 16, 1999, at a meeting of the Association of Southeast Asian Nations in Singapore, Secretary of State Madeleine Albright conveyed US disapproval of China's denial of the rights of peaceful expression and assembly to Chinese Foreign Minister Tang Jiaxuan. In an August 26, 1999, press briefing, State Department spokesman James Foley urged the Chinese government to "live up to obligations under international human rights instruments and protect freedom of thought, conscience, and religion." The State Department also stated that the US government was neither legally nor morally bound to extradite Li Hongzhi. Senator Richard

Durbin submitted a letter to President Jiang Zemin, dated August 6, 1999, and co-signed by Senators Moynihan, Schumer, Kerry, Edwards, Boxer, Levin, and Kennedy, expressing concern and dismay over the arrests of practitioners and demanding their release. In addition, other Senators and several House members have met with Falun Gong followers in the United States or expressed their interest or support. The Chinese government has accused the United States of interference in its domestic affairs.

Chinese progress on human rights is a condition of United States cooperation with the PRC on many issues, including trade, resolution of disputes between China and Taiwan, and bilateral agreements. Critics of the Clinton Administration's policy of "constructive engagement" with the PRC have pointed to the arrests of Falun Gong practitioners as evidence of the lack of progress in human rights in China and argue for a stronger or more formal verbal response or even economic sanctions. Some have suggested applying Public Law 105-292 (H.R. 2431), the *Freedom from Religious Persecution Act of 1998*, or using the Act as model for preventing other forms of human rights abuse. P.L. 105-292 promotes the rights to free speech and assembly for the purpose of cultivating spiritual beliefs. However, the law does not directly apply to groups such as Falun Gong. The Act was designed to protect adherents of established denominations under persecution, such as Christians in Indonesia, Muslims in India, Buddhists in Tibet, and Bahais in Iran. Furthermore, most followers of Falun Gong regard their practice primarily as a form of exercise rather than religion. They note, for example, that there is no worship of a deity, all-inclusive system of beliefs, church, or formal organizational structure.

Some supporters of constructive engagement argue that the US response to the suppression of Falun Gong should not undermine US-China relations as a whole. The movement's reference to constitutional rights and freedoms, use of the Internet, and foreign connections are products of American influence and strong US-China ties; i.e. they show that engagement is working. Furthermore, economic sanctions, such as restricting trade or credit to China, would not only harm China's economy but may also weaken the political standing of Zhu Rongji and other political and economic reformers. Finally, others contend that the crackdown might reflect short-term political considerations of Chinese leaders rather than long-term Party policy; that the arrests were timed to rid the country of dissent and strengthen Jiang Zemin's hold on power prior to the fiftieth anniversary of the founding of the PRC, which takes place in October 1999. Moreover, the state has released most detainees from custody and appears to be focusing only upon the movement's organizers. According to this view, since the Chinese government's actions against Falun Gong may be short-lived or limited in scope, the most appropriate response is to monitor developments until the outcome becomes clear.

* * *

US State Department
1999 Country Reports on Human Rights Practices: China
Released by the Bureau of Democracy, Human Rights, and Labor

February 25, 2000

What follows are excerpts from this report, which may be accessed via the Internet at www.state.gov. The State Department's 2000 report on China, released in February 2001, can also be found on this website.

The People's Republic of China (PRC) is an authoritarian state in which the Chinese Communist Party (CCP) is the paramount source of power. At the national and regional levels, Party members hold almost all top government, police, and military positions. Ultimate authority rests with members of the Politburo. Leaders stress the need to maintain stability and social order and are committed to perpetuating the rule of the CCP and its hierarchy. Citizens lack both the freedom peacefully to express opposition to the Party-led political system and the right to change their national leaders or form of government. Socialism continues to provide the theoretical underpinning of Chinese politics, but Marxist ideology has given way to economic pragmatism in recent years, and economic decentralization has increased the authority of regional officials. The Party's authority rests primarily on the government's ability to maintain social stability, appeals to nationalism and patriotism, Party control of personnel and the security apparatus, and the continued improvement in the living standards of most of the country's 1.27 billion citizens. The Constitution provides for an independent judiciary; however, in practice, the government and the CCP, at both the central and local levels, frequently interfere in the judicial process, and decisions in a number of high-profile political cases are directed by the government and the CCP.

The security apparatus is made up of the Ministries of State Security and Public Security, the People's Armed Police, the People's Liberation Army, and the state judicial, procuratorial, and penal systems. Security policy and personnel were responsible for numerous human rights abuses.

China is making a difficult transition from a centrally planned to a market-based economy. The economy continues to expand. The country is a leading world producer of coal, steel, textiles, and grains. Trade and foreign investment are helping to modernize the economy. Major exports include electronic goods, toys, apparel, and plastics. According to official government statistics, the official gross domestic product (GDP) growth rate during the year was just over seven percent, but the actual rate was widely considered to be lower by experts. The economy faces growing problems, including state enterprise reform, unemployment, underemployment, and regional economic disparities. Rural unemployment and underemployment combined are estimated to be over thirty percent. Tens of millions of peasants have left their homes in search of better jobs and living conditions. Demographers estimate that between 80 and 130 million persons make up this "floating population," with many major cities counting 1 million or more such persons. Urban areas also are coping with millions of state workers idled on partial wages or unemployed as a result of industrial reforms. In the industrial sector, downsizing in state-owned enterprises prompted 6 million layoffs in the first half of 1999, bringing the total number of urban unemployed to well over 15 million. Industrial workers throughout the country sporadically protested layoffs and demanded the payment of overdue wages and benefits. Overall, however, economic reforms have raised living standards for many, provided greater independence for entrepreneurs, and diminished state control over the economy and over citizens' daily lives. Despite serious economic difficulties in the state sector, individual economic opportunities expanded in the non-state sectors, resulting in increased freedom of employment and mobility. A constitutional amendment passed in March recognized the private sector as equal in status to the state sector. The total number of citizens living in absolute poverty continues to decline; estimates range from official figures of 42 million to World Bank figures of 150 million. However, the income gap between coastal and interior regions, and between urban and rural areas, is wide and growing. Chinese economists put the ratio of urban to rural income at 12 to 1. Urban per capita disposable income for 1998 was $656, while rural per capita net income was $261.

The government's poor human rights record deteriorated markedly throughout the year, as the government intensified efforts to supress dissent, particularly organized dissent. A crackdown against a fledgling opposition party, which began in the fall of 1998, broadened and intensified during the year. By year's end, almost all of the key leaders of the China Democracy Party (CDP) were serving long prison terms or were in custody without formal charges, and only a handful of dissidents nationwide dared to remain active publicly. Tens of thousands of members of the Falun Gong spiritual movement were detained after the movement was banned in July; several leaders of the movement were sentenced to long prison terms in late December and hundreds of others were sentenced administratively to re-education–through–labor in the fall. Late in the year, according to some reports, the government started confining some Falun Gong adherents to psychiatric hospitals. The government continued to commit widespread and well-documented human rights abuses, in violation of internationally accepted norms. These abuses stemmed from the authorities' extremely limited tolerance of public dissent aimed at the government, fear of unrest, and the limited scope or inadequate implementation of laws protecting basic freedoms. The Constitution and laws provide for fundamental human rights; however, these protections often are ignored in practice.

Abuses included instances of extrajudicial killings, torture and mistreatment of prisoners, forced confessions, arbitrary arrest and detention, lengthy incommunicado detention, and denial of due process. Prison conditions at most facilities remained harsh. In many cases, particularly in sensitive political cases, the judicial system denies criminal defendants basic legal safeguards and due process because authorities attach higher priority to maintaining public order and suppressing political opposition than to enforcing legal norms. The government infringed on citizens' privacy rights. The government tightened restrictions on freedom of speech and of the press, and increased controls on the Internet; self-censorship by journalists also increased. The government severely restricted freedom of assembly, and continued to restrict freedom of association. The government continued to restrict freedom of religion, and intensified controls on some unregistered churches. The government continued to restrict freedom of movement. The government does not permit independent domestic nongovernmental organizations (NGOs) to monitor publicly human rights conditions. Violence against women, including coercive family planning practices—which sometimes include forced abortion and forced sterilization; prostitution; discrimination against women; trafficking in women and children; abuse of children; and discrimination against the disabled and minorities are all problems. The government continued to restrict tightly worker rights, and forced labor in prison facilities remains a serious problem. Child labor persists. Particularly serious human rights abuses persisted in some minority areas, especially in Tibet and Xinjiang, where restrictions on religion and other fundamental freedoms intensified.

Beginning in the spring, Communist Party leaders moved quickly to suppress what they believed to be organized challenges that threatened national stability and Communist Party authority. In the weeks before the tenth anniversary of the June 4 Tiananmen massacre, the government also moved systematically against political dissidents across the country, detaining and formally arresting scores of activists in cities and provinces nationwide and thwarting any attempts to commemorate the sensitive anniversary . . .

Control and manipulation of the press by the government for political purposes increased during the year. After authorities moved at the end of 1998 to close a number of newspapers and fire several editors, a more cautious atmosphere in general pervaded the press and publishing industries during the year. As part of its crackdown against the popular Falun Gong spiritual movement, the government employed every element of the state-controlled media to conduct a nationwide anti–Falun Gong propaganda campaign reminiscent of the campaigns against the democracy movement that followed the Tiananmen massacre of 1989. The press continued to report on cases of corruption and abuse of power by some local officials.

Unapproved religious groups, including Protestant and Catholic groups, continued to experience varying degrees of official interference, repression, and persecution. The government continued to enforce 1994 State Council regulations requiring all places of religious activity to register with the government and come under the supervision of official, "patriotic" religious organizations. There were significant differences from region to region, and even locality to locality, in the attitudes of government officials toward religion. In some areas, authorities guided by national policy made strong efforts to control the activities of unapproved Catholic and Protestant churches; religious services were broken up and church leaders or adherents were harassed, and, at times, fined, detained, beaten, and tortured . . . The government launched a crackdown against the Falun Gong spiritual movement in July. Tens of thousands of Falun Gong members were reported detained in outdoor stadiums and forced to sign statements disavowing Falun Gong before being released; according to official sources, practitioners of Falun Gong had 35,000 confrontations with police between late July and the end of October. A number of practitioners were detained multiple times. An unknown number of members who refuse to recant their beliefs remain detained; others are serving prison or re-education–through–labor sentences. An intensive pro–Atheism, "anti-superstition" media campaign also accompanied the suppression of Falun Gong. In October, new legislation banning cults was passed. Adherents of some unregistered religious groups reported that these new laws are used against them.

Although the government denies that it holds political or religious prisoners, and argues that all those in prison are legitimately serving sentences for crimes under the law, an unknown number of persons, estimated at several thousand, are detained in violation of international human rights instruments for peacefully expressing their political, religious, or social views . . .

Despite intensified suppression of organized dissent, some positive trends continued. Non-governmental-level village committee elections proceeded, giving citizens choices about grassroots representatives, as well as introducing the principle of democratic elections. Additional experiments with higher level township elections were conducted without fanfare (or official approval by the central government). Social groups with economic resources at their disposal continued to play an increasing role in community life. As many as 8.9 million citizens had access to the Internet, although the government increased its efforts to try to control the content of material available on the Internet. Most average citizens went about their daily lives without significant interference from the government, enjoying looser economic controls, increased access to outside sources of information, greater room for individual choice, and more diversity in cultural life. However, authorities significantly stepped up efforts to suppress those perceived to be a threat to government power or to national stability, and citizens who sought to express openly dissenting political and religious views continued to live in an environment filled with repression . . .

Falun Gong (or Wheel of the Law, also known as Falun Dafa) blends aspects of Taoism, Buddhism, and the meditation techniques of qigong (a traditional martial art) with the teachings of Li Hongzhi, who left the country in 1998. The government estimates that there may be as many as 2.1 million adherents of Falun Gong; Falun Gong followers estimate that there are over 100 million adherents. Some experts estimate that the true number of Falun Gong adherents lies in the tens of millions. Falun Gong does not consider itself a religion and has no clergy or formal places of worship.

On April 25, more than 10,000 adherents of Falun Gong gathered in front of the Zhongnanhai leadership compound, where most of the country's top officials live and work, to protest the detention of some Falun Gong practitioners and to seek government acknowledgment of the legitimacy of their practice. The sudden appearance of such a large crowd of organized demonstrators caught the government by surprise; however, it allowed the peaceful protest to continue for more than twelve hours and publicly stated that the organization was not illegal. Following the April demonstration, the government decided that Falun Gong was a threat to stability. In June, despite a government warning against disturbing social stability or holding large gatherings, Falun Gong practitioners continued to hold demonstrations in cities throughout the country. On July 22 the government officially declared Falun Gong illegal and began a nationwide crackdown against the movement. Around the country, tens of thousands of practitioners were rounded up and detained for several days, often in open stadiums with poor, overcrowded conditions with inadequate food, water, and sanitary facilities. Practitioners who refused to renounce their beliefs were expelled from their schools or fired from their jobs. Some of those detained were government officials and Communist Party members. Some high-ranking practitioners were forced to disavow their ties to Falun Gong on national television. There also were reports that the Public Security Bureau forbade the renting of apartments to members of the Falun Gong, and that local government leaders and heads of institutions in the northeast were summoned to Beijing or fired if too many persons under their jurisdictions participated in Falun Gong demonstrations.

In addition to detaining Falun Gong practitioners, in July the government also launched a massive propaganda campaign against the group and its leader. As part of its crackdown on Falun Gong, the government seized and destroyed Falun Gong literature, including over one million books, in well-publicized sweeps of homes and bookstores. A Falun Gong website designed and operated by computer engineer Zhang Haitao of Jilin Province was shut down by the government on July 24; Zhang himself reportedly was arrested on July 29. Police in Dandong City, Liaoning Province, reported that they had arrested six workers and a factory boss for printing outlawed Falun Gong material. On October 28, several Falun Gong practitioners held a clandestine press conference for foreign reporters in which they described an increase in harassment and in physical abuse by the police. Many of the practitioners involved later reportedly were arrested; the authorities questioned some of the foreign journalists who attended the press conference and temporarily confiscated their press credentials and residence permits.

In spite of the harshness of the crackdown, Falun Gong demonstrations continued around the country throughout the summer and into the fall. Authorities responded quickly by breaking up demonstrations—at times forcibly—and detaining demonstrators. In September, the state-run press reported a raid on a gathering of nineteen Falun Gong followers during which five were arrested formally. In mid-September, one NGO reported that at least 300 Falun Gong adherents were arrested in nine cities over the course of one week. In late October, the pace of protests and detentions picked up as Falun Gong practitioners from around the country converged on Beijing and began a series of peaceful, low-key demonstrations in Tiananmen Square to protest a new anti-cult law being considered by the Standing Committee of the National People's Congress. Most of the protests were small and short-lived, as the police, who roamed the square in increased numbers, questioned persons and quickly arrested anyone who admitted to being or appeared to be a practitioner. On some days, scores of practitioners were arrested as they entered the square in small groups to protest. During the last week of October, a Communist Party official told the foreign press that 3,000 persons from other parts of the country were detained in police sweeps of Beijing for non-residents. On November 16, during a visit to Beijing by UN Secretary General Kofi Annan, more than a dozen Falun Gong practitioners who unfurled a Falun Gong banner were detained forcibly in Tiananmen Square. On November 30, Vice Premier Li Lanqing reportedly stated in a speech to Communist Party members that over 35,000 detentions of Falun Gong practitioners were made by the authorities between July 22 and October 30 (the government later clarified Li's remarks by stating that this figure represented the total number of confrontations that police had with adherents of Falun Gong, pointing out that many persons had multiple encounters with police.)

Authorities also detained foreign practitioners. For example, on November 24, four foreign practitioners of Falun Gong were detained along with other practitioners in Guangzhou. The foreigners were released a few days later and expelled from the country; the Chinese citizens arrested with them remained in custody. On December 15, three Chinese nationals with foreign residency were detained in Shenzhen for visiting other Falun Gong practitioners; they were sentenced to fifteen days of administrative detention.

There were credible reports of beatings and deaths of practitioners in detention who refused to recant their beliefs; according to Amnesty International, some adherents also were tortured by electric shocks and by having their hands and feet shackled and linked with crossed steel chains. In October a Falun Gong website reported that a Falun Gong practitioner from Shandong Province, Zhao Jinhua, died as a result of beatings received while in police custody. The official media reported that Zhao died of a heart attack while in custody. On October 27, police in Heilongjiang Province stated that Chen Ying, an eighteen-year-old practitioner of Falun Gong who died while in police custody in August, had jumped to her death from a moving train. Zhao Dong also allegedly jumped from a train while in police custody; he reportedly died in late September.

Although the vast majority of ordinary Falun Gong practitioners who were detained later were released, authorities acted more forcefully against practitioners it identified as leaders. On October 25, the official media reported that at least thirteen Falun Gong leaders had been charged with stealing and leaking state secrets. On October 31, a new anti-cult law was passed, which specifies prison terms of three to seven years for cult members who "disrupt public order" or distribute publications. Under the new law, cult leaders and recruiters can be sentenced to seven years or more in prison. On November 3, the authorities used the new law to charge six Falun Gong leaders, some of whom, it is believed, were arrested in July. Also, on November 8, the government confirmed that 111 Falun Gong practitioners had been charged with serious crimes including, among others, disturbing social order and stealing state secrets. The government issued a warrant for the arrest of Falun Gong leader Li Hongzhi, and requested Interpol's assistance in apprehending him. Interpol declined to do so, on the grounds that the request was political in nature.

Many others not formally arrested reportedly were sentenced administratively, without trial, to up to three years in re-education–through–labor camps. For example, on October 12, authorities reportedly sentenced five Falun Gong practitioners to a one-year sentence in a re-education–through–labor camp for "disturbing the social order." The exact number of persons sentenced in this manner is unknown, although the Hong Kong-based Information Center for Human Rights and Democratic Movements in China reported that at least 500 persons were sentenced to terms of re-education- through-labor. Late in the year, according to some reports, the government started confining some Falun Gong adherents to psychiatric hospitals.

Some of the leaders of Falun Gong were brought to trial by year's end. On December 26, four practitioners of Falun Gong were sentenced by a Beijing court for using a cult "to obstruct justice, causing human deaths in the process of organizing a cult, and illegally obtaining state secrets." Li Chang, a former official at the Public Security Ministry, was sentenced to eighteen years in prison; former Railways Ministry official Wang Zhiwen was sentenced to sixteen years in prison. Two other high-ranking Falun Gong members, Ji Liewu and Yao Jie, were sentenced to twelve years and seven years in prison. According to one international human rights organization, the Ministry of Justice required attorneys who wished to represent Falun Gong practitioners to obtain government permission.

There were reports that qigong groups not associated with the Falun Gong have experienced an increase in harassment as well, particularly since the ban on Falun Gong was announced in July. Two leaders of such groups reportedly were arrested, and the government banned the practice of qigong exercises on public or government property. This has created an atmosphere of uncertainty for many, if not most, qigong practitioners.

* * *

Statements by US Presidents

"[China's] progress is still being held back by the government's response to those who test the limits of freedom. A troubling example, of course, is the detention by Chinese authorities of adherents of the Falun Gong movement. Its targets are not political dissidents . . . But the principle still, surely, must be the same: freedom of conscience and freedom of association."
—President Bill Clinton, December 6, 1999

"We hear alarming reports of the detention of worshippers and religious leaders [in China]. These acts of persecution are acts of fear—and therefore of weakness . . . Churches and mosques have been vandalized or demolished. Traditional religious practices in Tibet have long been the target of especially harsh and unjust persecution. And most recently, adherents of the Falun Gong spiritual movement have been singled out for arrest and abuse . . . This persecution is unworthy of all that China has been—a civilization with a history of tolerance. And this persecution is unworthy of all that China should become—an open society that respects the spiritual dignity of its people."
—President George W. Bush, May 3, 2001 (in a speech to the American Jewish Committee)

* * *

Letter from US Congress to Secretary of State Madeleine Albright

September 10, 1999

The Honorable Madeleine K. Albright
Secretary of State

Department of State
2201 C Street, N.W.
Washington, DC 20520

Dear Madam Secretary:

We write out of concern over the current crackdown against Falun Gong practitioners in China. As you know, the recent arrest of hundreds of Falun Gong practitioners provides fresh and disturbing evidence of the lack freedom of expression and assembly in China and of the Chinese government's blatant disregard for human rights.

When over 10,000 Falun Gong practitioners assembled peacefully in April to ask for official recognition, the Chinese government reacted by viewing the request as a threat to its power. As a result, on July 22, the Chinese Ministry of Civil Affairs denounced Falun Gong as an illegal organization and banned its practice in public or private throughout China. On the same day the Ministry of Public Security issued a decree declaring a wide range of activities illegal and subject to prosecution, including distribution of Falun Gong materials, gatherings, silent sit-ins, marches, demonstrations, and other activities which promote Falun Gong.

We are extremely concerned about these actions by the Ministry of Civil Affairs and the Ministry of Public Security. The scope of the arbitrary detentions of the members of this non-political organization is astounding, and the decree issued by the Public Security Bureau violates the rights to freedom of belief, association, and assembly, which are guaranteed by the Chinese Constitution and international law.

We ask you to speak out against this recent crackdown and to work with the international community to secure the release of the hundreds of the organization's members arbitrarily detained during recent weeks.

Thank you for your attention to this matter. We look forward to your reply.

Sincerely,

(Letter signed by forty members of Congress:)
John Edward Porter (IL), Tom Lantos (CA), James A. Traficant (OH), Eleanor Holmes Norton (DC), Stephen Horn (CA), Edolphus Towns (NY), Barney Frank (MA), Edward J. Markey (MA), Chrispher Shays (CT), Eliot L. Engel (NY), Nita M. Lowey (NY), Howard L. Berman (CA), Ron Lewis (KY), David Price (NC), Henry Waxman (CA), Barbara Lee (CA), Rod R. Blagojevich (IL), James H. Maloney (CT), Louise M. Slaughter (NY), Robert L. Ehrlich (MD), Contance A. Morella (MD), Christopher H. Smith (NJ), Julian C. Dixon (CA), Bruce F. Vento (MN), Bob Clement (TN), James Moran (VA), John W. Olver (MA), Joseph R. Pitts (PA), John

Joseph Moakley (MA), David Dreier (CA), James P. McGovern (MA), Robert Wexler (FL), Spencer Bachus (AL), Frank Wolf (VA), James M. Talent (MO), Kenny C. Hulshof (MO), Neil Abercrombie (HI), Janice Schakowsky (IL), John F. Tierney (MA), Dennis J. Kucinich (OH).

* * *

Secretary of State Madeleine K. Albright's Address to the UN Human Rights Commission
Palais des Nations, Geneva, Switzerland

March 23, 2000

What follows are excerpted passages from this statement, which may be viewed in its entirety via the Internet at www.state.gov.

Thank you, Mr. Chairman. Madam High Commissioner, excellencies and colleagues, it is not often that someone on the way from India to Pakistan stops off in Geneva. But I wanted very much to be here today personally to affirm America's commitment to international standards of human rights and to the work of this Commission.

This body was forged in the aftermath of global war and Holocaust. Its founders were determined to build a better future in which the world would not simply stand by and watch while countries were invaded and entire peoples annihilated.

They sought to make real the principles enshrined in the UN Charter. They began by drafting the Universal Declaration of Human Rights.

And they created this Commission as a practical instrument for investigating and calling attention to violations of human rights, and as a forum for international discussion, consensus-building, and action.

It is our responsibility to carry forward their vision and do all we can to fulfill the high purpose of the Commission's founders. In that spirit, the United States looks forward to working with each delegation, for when it comes to the protection of human rights, every nation counts and there is always more to do.

Two main themes are at the heart of my presentation today. First, for all its imperfections, democracy is the single surest path to the preservation and promotion of human rights.

Second, no nation should feel threatened by this Commission's work, for our task is to support the right of people everywhere to control their own destinies. Moreover, the standards we apply are not narrow, but rather universal. They embody norms voluntarily affirmed by governments almost everywhere. This Commission asks only that its members play by global rules.

Mr. Chairman, the world today is freer now than ever. For the first time in history, a majority of people live under elected governments. This provides no guarantee of prosperity or progress. But it makes both more likely.

People who are free to exchange ideas, publish their thoughts, organize their labor and invest their capital will contribute far more to their societies than people stunted and held back by repression. As Aung San Suu Kyi has written, "it is difficult to dispel ignorance unless there is freedom to pursue the truth."

Last year, this Commission took a major step forward when it approved a landmark resolution affirming, without dissent, the universal right to democracy. This reflects the power of the democratic tide that has been sweeping the world for the past quarter century.

During that time, the number of democratically elected governments has increased from 30 to 120. More than two billion people, on five continents, have moved towards more open economic and political systems.

Still, our mission is far from complete. While the forms of democracy are more widely accepted than ever, the true substance of democracy remains too often absent.

For this reason, it is important that the Commission build on last year's achievement and approve the resolution on the Promotion and Consolidation of Democracy that Romania has drafted. As this Resolution makes clear, democracy requires far more than elections; and when we speak about the right to democracy, we include all the privileges and responsibilities that democracy entails . . .

This body will also vote on whether to consider a Resolution expressing concern about widespread denials of political, cultural, labor, and religious freedom in China. The United States strongly believes that favorable action on this Resolution is needed.

In recent years, China has made great progress in expanding social choices, building a new economy and lifting millions of people out of poverty. But its human rights record does not match the obligations it has accepted.

China is one of five permanent members of the UN Security Council. It is bound by the UN Charter and recently reaffirmed its commitment to the Universal Declaration of Human Rights. It has signed the International Covenant on Civil and Political Rights. Unfortunately, its official policies have always fallen well short of these standards, and deteriorated markedly this past year.

During that period, there were widespread arrests of those seeking to exercise their right to peaceful political expression. Thousands of members of the Falun Gong movement were detained. Authorities continued to limit the ability of Christians, Muslims, and Buddhists to worship in accordance with custom and conscience. Minority groups such as the Tibetans and Uighurs were barred from fully exercising their cultural and linguistic heritage.

In light of such a record, Mr. Chairman, it is both necessary and appropriate that this Commission express its concern and call for improvements.

We owe it to the Chinese people and to the credibility of this Commission and its members not to shy away from the whole truth, or to hide behind procedural motions. I hope very much that all of you will be willing to work with us and give us your support for the resolution on China that we will offer . . .

Mr. Chairman, the work of this Commission, like the Universal Declaration of Human Rights, draws upon the moral and legal traditions of every great culture on earth. It speaks to the best within us all. And it matters to people everywhere.

Accordingly, my government appeals to all governments to support the work and promote the purposes of this Commission.

Let us work together, as the UN Charter suggests, with "faith in fundamental human rights, in the worth of every human person, in the equal rights of men and women, and of nations large and small."

Let us respect the dignity of our citizens and all others who come within our power. And let us not rest until we have established a foundation of humanity, democracy, and law that will secure for our children in the new century the peace and justice so often lacking in the old.

Thank you all very much.

* * *

Statement Before the Human Rights Caucus
by Robert A. Seiple, Ambassador-at-Large for International Religious Freedom

April 6, 2000, Washington, DC

What follows are excerpted passages from this statement, which may be viewed in its entirety via the Internet at www.state.gov.

Religious Freedom in China

Mr. Chairman and Members of the Human Rights Caucus, it is indeed a pleasure to appear before you today to report on the status of religious freedom in China. China is a nation of ancient and modern religions whose governments historically have attempted to control the worship of its citizens and, at their worst, acted as if religion threatened their survival. What I would like to do this afternoon is give you a detailed assessment of where things stand in China with respect to religious freedom, and then describe to you how we are attempting to address the substantial problems that exist.

The Current Status

Religious freedom—meaning the internationally acknowledged right of every human being to believe and practice as he sees fit—does not exist in China. It is true that millions of Chinese citizens worship without substantial interference by the state, but they do so under carefully defined limits—limits sufficiently burdensome that their very presence precludes the emergence of what we and the international community recognize as religious freedom.

Before I address these problems, however, let me sketch for you a bit of context and acknowledge the existence of certain positive elements in the Chinese political-religious structure. Fairness demands as much, but it is also important to recognize structures and practices that could encourage better policy should the Chinese government decide to embrace and fully implement religious freedom.

Seeds of Hope

The Chinese constitution provides for freedom of religious belief, as well as the protection of what the constitution refers to as "normal religious activities." It thus appears to acknowledge the sanctity of conscience and belief on the one hand, but not of religious practice on the other. In fact, freedom of religious practice and expression are not protected in China. But the concept of religious freedom is there—however imperfectly rooted—to be exploited by the voices of democracy and civil society. Such voices are heard only faintly now, but they will not be silenced. Indeed, they are likely to continue growing as the great economic forces now at work in China loosen political restraints.

Nor should we ignore the voices of religious piety that are undeniably at work in this great and ancient land. Scarcely two decades ago, those voices were still, the victims of the general political terror and the ruthless religious persecution of the Cultural Revolution. Over the past twenty years, there has been a loosening of government controls. There has been a dramatic resurgence of religious activity. Today, most estimates suggest some 200 million Chinese people are members of some religion. They are Buddhists, Muslims, Taoists, and Christians, as well as adherents to other religious groups such as traditional folk religions often having connections to Buddhism or Taoism. And their numbers are growing. Despite the continuance of serious religious discrimination and persecution, more and more Chinese are thirsting for ultimate meaning and purpose beyond the decaying ideology of Chinese Communism. Many are turning to religion to address that universal, and very human, yearning.

Therein, of course, lies a fundamental dilemma for the Communist authorities. On the one hand, the Chinese government has, since the end of the Cultural Revolution, rebuilt or restored thousands of damaged or confiscated temples, churches, mosques, and monasteries. Chinese Muslims are permitted to make the hajj pilgrimage to Mecca, and in some cases the government even subsidizes the trips. Seminaries have been reopened, and occasionally seminarians are permitted to study abroad. Typically, however, Chinese seminarians must demonstrate political reliability in order to graduate and are viewed by the government as agents of religious management, rather than free agents of religion. The problem, Mr. Chairman, is that the Chinese Communists do not value religion. They fear it and tolerate it only insofar as it serves—or at least does not in their judgment undermine—the purposes of the state . . .

It should also be noted that there are substantial regional variations in the actions of Chinese officials with respect to religion. As we note in the 1999 International Religious Freedom Report, some areas of China are reasonably free of religious persecution. These tend to be areas where there are fewer religious adherents or where Chinese believers do not directly challenge the controls imposed by the state.

The Structure of Religious Persecution in China

Despite these and other hopeful signs in China, it must be said that the overall picture for human rights, and for religious freedom, remains poor. Beneath the constitutional veneer of religious freedom lies a substratum of laws and regulations which provide a juridical basis for state control and, in some cases, persecution of religious believers. The driving force behind these laws and regulations is, of course, the Communist Party. It controls the top positions in government at all levels, as well as in the Ministries of State Security and Public Security, the People's Armed Police; the People's Liberation Army; and the state judicial, prosecutorial, and penal systems. Officially, no member of the Communist party may be a religious believer, much less practice religion. If their membership in a religious organization is discovered, they are expelled from the party, and from any official position they hold. While there appear to be some believers among local authorities, and at least one in the National People's Congress, these seem to be the exceptions that prove the rule. And the "rule" remains one of official hostility to religion—the conviction that religion cannot be permitted to grow unchecked, that it must be adapted to socialism, and that it must be free of foreign influence which might destabilize the Communist regime . . .

The Face of Persecution

. . . Falun Gong has a spiritual ethic which has captured the minds and hearts of millions of Chinese. Clearly, this aspect of Falun Gong threatens the Chinese government. Whenever thousands of people are attracted by a particular way of thinking about life and purpose, and are willing to manifest it publicly, the Communist Party of China is alarmed. As you know, Chinese authorities have detained for short periods of time thousands of Falun Gong adherents over the past eight months, and Falun Gong leaders have been sentenced to prison terms as long as eighteen years, or sentenced to "re-education." What a lousy synonym that is for the abuse of human dignity. We recently received a report of a sixty-year-old woman who died as a result of beatings administered to her for being a practitioner of Falun Gong.

US Policy

Mr. Chairman, I know that people of good will can, and do, disagree over where this analysis of Chinese human rights abuses ought to take US policy. Some believe that it should prevent the establishment of "Permanent Normal Trade Relations" (PNTR), or cause us to oppose Chinese entry into the World Trade Organization. I understand and respect this point of view. It is premised on the belief that we can change Chinese human rights behavior by withholding US trade.

Diplomacy, of course, is not a science. I cannot prove that people who hold such views—many of whom are my friends—are wrong. I can only say, with great respect, that I believe we must increase our engagement with the Chinese, not decrease it. In order to influence Chinese behavior, we must have Chinese attention—in both a positive and, if necessary, a negative sense. We must have a sustained relationship on many levels in order to help convince Chinese leaders that eighty-year-old bishops are a boon, not a threat, to the Chinese nation.

My job, and that of the Bureau of Democracy, Human Rights and Labor at the State Department, is to ensure that our trade relationship is not the only level at which we communicate, and that our diplomatic intercourse always includes the issue of human rights. I view it as my responsibility—as does Assistant Secretary Koh—to let the Chinese leaders know that China will never be considered a member in good standing of the world community until the day comes when they move beyond words and implement policies that protect human dignity.

One bellweather of such a day would, of course, be the full acceptance of freedom of religion and conscience by the Chinese government. Such a policy would signal, as it does in other countries, that the government of China recognizes a fundamental distinction between the individual and the state that is essential in any just society. It is the recognition—as political scientists might put it—that society precedes the state, not vice versa. Because religious freedom entails the inviolable right of every human being to seek the truth, no government should consider the control or management of that process within its province.

Quite frankly, Mr. Chairman, I believe that the Chinese government will not come readily to the acceptance of these policies. Indeed, to the extent that the leadership is still under the influence of a Communist worldview, true religious freedom will be that much more difficult to attain. Communists consistently have treated religion as a powerful and deadly enemy. Under Mao, they created a daunting propaganda machine to combat it and ruthlessly suppressed those clergy who were most committed to the proletariat and the peasantry. In the economic and social spheres, the Chinese have moved a long way from the deadening effects of Maoism. In the religious sphere, their continuing attempts to control religious belief and practice constitute an unstable half-way house between Communism and religious freedom.

The real question for us is how to keep the train moving in the right direction. A policy aimed at isolating China through economic sanctions or the withholding of trade cannot work, if for no other reason than the international economy would quickly fill the void should the United States leave the field. But there is another reason—one grounded in human rights—for us to encourage trade. It is the need to encourage the spread of those economic forces which are broadening the entrepreneurial class in China and bringing pressures against the creaking post-Maoist structure of control and persecution.

However, a policy of engagement in trade must be complemented by a strong and consistent human rights policy. As our economic relationships with China broaden and deepen, we must press Chinese leaders ever harder to accept and implement human rights based on the universal dignity of the human person. We must hold them accountable on all fronts—religious freedom, labor rights, freedom of association, free speech, rule of law, and the other core human rights. When China abuses these rights, we must hold its government up to the world in which it is increasingly engaged. We must do so swiftly and relentlessly.

This is our policy. As you know, Mr. Chairman, we have used the International Religious Freedom Act of 1998 as one vehicle against Chinese human rights abuses. In October of last year, the Secretary of State designated China a "country of particular concern" for having engaged in particularly severe violations of religious freedom. This designation put China in very bad company. Secretary Albright also named Burma, Iran, Iraq, Sudan, Serbi, and the Taliban regime in Afghanistan. The Chinese were very unhappy with this designation; it stigmatized them, in effect, as among the worst religious persecutors of today. The Human Rights Caucus is also aware that the Administration has introduced a resolution on China at the current UN Human Rights Commission session in Geneva. We have not been able to pass this resolution in the past, but I was in Geneva last week and I can tell you that we have implemented a "full court press" to convince other members of the Commission to vote with us. The Secretary also flew to Geneva from India to press this issue.

But whether we win this resolution or not, Mr. Chairman, we will not back down from telling the truth about Chinese human rights abuses. China seeks to become a member in good standing of the international community of nations. It places a great deal of store on "face," by which it means respect. Our message to China is that it will not have the respect of the world until it changes its policies on human rights in general, and freedom of religion, and conscience in particular.

I want again to thank the Caucus for holding this hearing and giving me the opportunity to report . . .

* * *

US Response to Decision of UN Commission on Human Rights to Adopt "No-Action" Motion on the US-Sponsored China Resolution
Press Statement by James P. Rubin, Spokesman for US Department of State

April 18, 2000

The following statement was issued by Harold Hongju Koh, Assistant Secretary of State for Democracy, Human Rights, and Labor, and Nancy Rubin, US Ambassador to the UN Commission on Human Rights, at the Commission in Geneva, in response to the Commission's decision to accept a Chinese motion to take no action on a US-sponsored resolution:

"The United States notes that the United Nations Commission on Human Rights today passed a procedural motion made by China not to take action on a resolution on human rights sponsored by the United States. We sponsored the China resolution as part of our principled, purposeful policy of engagement with China. Our goals were to speak up for the Chinese people and to focus international attention on the marked deterioration in the human rights situation in China during the past year. We believe that we have accomplished these goals. We would like to thank those countries that joined us in opposing the no-action motion on the grounds that it would prevent the Commission from addressing an important human rights concern that clearly falls well within its jurisdiction.

"The gap by which the no action motion passed narrowed once again this year. A growing number of countries now recognize that China should not be permitted to escape scrutiny of its human rights record and that China should not prevent the Commission from fulfilling its mandate.

"Over the past year, the government of China has expanded and intensified its crackdown on organized political dissent and initiated a full-scale campaign to suppress the Falun Gong spiritual movement. Chinese authorities have also intensified controls on unregistered churches and ethnic minorities, especially Tibetans and Uighurs. In addition, the government also tightened controls on the media, academia, and the Internet.

"The Chinese government understands its international human rights obligations. It has signed the International Covenant on Civil and Political Rights (ICCPR) and has acceded to the UN Convention against Torture. China has stated its intention to fulfill its international obligations. However, it has not taken significant, concrete steps to bring its human rights practices into compliance with that convention or with other international human rights instruments.

"The Commission is the appropriate venue for members of the United Nations to discuss violations of international human rights standards. No Commission member should have the right to judge all others yet never be judged itself. By sponsoring a resolution on China, we have helped draw the attention of the world and the Chinese authorities themselves to China's poor human rights record, and the plight of the Chinese people. We hope this will help to improve human rights conditions in China."

* * *

Canada
Letter to Falun Gong from Lloyd Axworthy, Canadian Minister of Foreign Affairs

Xun Li
Falun Dafa Ottawa
90 Belleview Drive
Kanata, Ontario
K2L 1W3

September 3, 1999

Dear Xun Li:

The Prime Minister has forwarded to me your letter of July 22, 1999, and enclosed a report concerning the situation of Falun Gong practitioners in China.

The government of Canada regrets the detention of Falun Gong members and the banning of the organization. We are very concerned about this suppression of the basic rights of freedom of expression and spiritual practice and call on the Chinese government to respect these essential human rights.

The Canadian Embassy in Beijing has raised our concerns about the treatment of Falun Gong members with the Chinese Foreign Ministry. Departmental officials have expressed our views on this matter to the Chinese Ambassador in Canada. We have also registered our concerns at the Plurilateral Symposium on Human Rights, which was held in Qingdao, China, on July 26 and 27. This event was co-hosted by Canada, China, and Norway. For your information, I enclose a news release concerning this symposium. In addition, Falun Gong members met with officials of the Department of Foreign Affairs and International Trade on July 26 to voice their concerns about the arrest of their fellow practitioners.

Please be assured that we will continue to monitor the situation. Thank you for writing on behalf of Falun Gong practitioners in Canada.

Sincerely,
Lloyd Axworthy
Canadian Minister of Foreign Affairs

* * *

Australia
Excerpt from statement by Miles Kupa, Australian Department of Foreign Affairs and Trade

"The ban on Falun Gong does raise some serious questions about China's international commitments relating to freedom of assembly, freedom of association, freedom of expression."

CHAPTER 17
CONSTITUTION OF THE PEOPLE'S REPUBLIC OF CHINA
(AND ADDITIONAL ANTI-CULT LEGISLATION)

Four constitutions have been enacted since the establishment of the People's Republic of China (1954, 1975, 1978, and 1982). What follows are the preamble and selected Articles from the most recent version.

Adopted on December 4, 1982

Preamble: China is one of the countries with the longest histories in the world. The people of all nationalities in China have jointly created a splendid culture and have a glorious revolutionary tradition. Feudal China was gradually reduced after 1840 to a semi-colonial and semi-feudal country. The Chinese people waged wave upon wave of heroic struggles for national independence and liberation and for democracy and freedom. Great and earth-shaking historical changes have taken place in China in the twentieth century. The Revolution of 1911, led by Dr. Sun Yat-Sen, abolished the feudal monarchy and gave birth to the Republic of China. But the Chinese people had yet to fulfill their historical task of overthrowing imperialism and feudalism. After waging hard, protracted, and tortuous struggles, armed and otherwise, the Chinese people of all nationalities, led by the Communist Party of China with Chairman Mao Zedong as its leader, ultimately, in 1949, overthrew the rule of imperialism, feudalism, and bureaucrat capitalism, won the great victory of the new-democratic revolution, and founded the People's Republic of China. Thereupon the Chinese people took state power into their own hands and became masters of the country. After the founding of the People's Republic, the transition of Chinese society from a new-democratic to a socialist society was effected step by step. The socialist transformation of the private ownership of the means of production was completed, the system of exploitation of man by man eliminated, and the socialist system established. The people's democratic dictatorship led by the working class and based on the alliance of workers and peasants, which is in essence the dictatorship of the proletariat, has been consolidated and developed. The Chinese people and the Chinese People's Liberation Army have thwarted aggression, sabotage, and armed provocations by imperialists and hegemonists, safeguarded China's national independence and security, and strengthened its national defense. Major successes have been achieved in economic development. An independent and fairly comprehensive socialist system of industry has in the main been established. There has been a marked increase in agricultural production. Significant progress has been made in educational, scientific, cultural, and other undertakings, and socialist ideological education has yielded noteworthy results. The living standards of the people have improved considerably. Both the victory of China's new-democratic revolution and the successes of its socialist cause have been achieved by the Chinese people of all nationalities under the leadership of the Communist Party of China and the guidance of Marxism-Leninism and Mao Zedong Thought, and by upholding truth, correcting errors, and overcoming numerous difficulties and hardships. The basic task of the nation in the years to come is to concentrate its effort on socialist modernization. Under the leadership of the Communist Party of China and the guidance of Marxism-Leninism and Mao Zedong Thought, the Chinese people of all nationalities will continue to adhere to the people's democratic dictatorship and follow the socialist road, steadily improve socialist institutions, develop socialist democracy, improve the socialist legal system, and work hard and self-reliantly to modernize industry, agriculture, national defense, and science and technology step by step to turn China into a socialist country with a high level of culture and democracy. The exploiting classes as such have been eliminated in our country. However, class struggle will continue to exist within certain limits for a long time to come. The Chinese people must fight against those forces and elements, both at home and abroad, that are hostile to China's socialist system and try to undermine it. Taiwan is part of the sacred territory of the People's Republic of China. It is the lofty duty of the entire Chinese people, including our compatriots in Taiwan, to accomplish the great task of reunifying the motherland. In building socialism it is imperative to rely on the workers, peasants, and intellectuals, and unite with all the forces that can be united. In the long years of revolution and construction, there has been formed under the leadership of the Communist Party of China a broad patriotic united front that is composed of democratic parties and people's organizations and embraces all socialist working people, all patriots who support socialism, and all patriots who stand for reunification of the motherland. This united front will continue to be consolidated and developed. The Chinese People's Political Consultative Conference is a broadly representative organization of the united front, which has played a significant historical role and will continue to do so in the political and social life of the country, in promoting friendship with the people of other countries and in the struggle for socialist modernization and for the reunification and unity of the country. The People's Republic of China is a unitary multinational state built up jointly by the people of all its nationalities. Socialist relations of equality, unity, and mutual assistance have been established among them and will continue to be strengthened. In the struggle to safeguard the unity of the nationalities, it is necessary to combat big-nation chauvinism, mainly Han chauvinism, and also necessary to combat local-national chauvinism. The state does its utmost to promote the common prosperity of all nationalities in the country. China's achievements in revolution and construction are inseparable from support by the people of the world. The future of China is closely linked with that of the whole world. China adheres to an independent foreign policy as well as to the five principles of mutual respect for sovereignty and territorial integrity, mutual non-aggression, non-interference in each other's internal affairs, equality and mutual benefit, and peaceful coexistence in developing diplomatic relations and economic and cultural exchanges with other countries; China consistently opposes imperialism, hegemonism, and colonialism, works to strengthen unity with the people of other countries, supports the oppressed nations and the developing countries in their just struggle to win and preserve national independence and develop their national economies, and strives to safeguard world peace and promote the cause of human progress. This Constitution affirms the achievements of the struggles of the Chinese people of all nationalities and defines the basic system and basic tasks of the state in legal form; it is the fundamental law of the state and has supreme legal authority. The people of all nationalities, all state organs, the armed forces, all political parties and public organizations, and all enterprises and undertakings in the country must take the Constitution as the basic norm of conduct, and they have the duty to uphold the dignity of the Constitution and ensure its implementation.

Chapter 1: General Principles

Article 1. The People's Republic of China is a socialist state under the people's democratic dictatorship led by the working class and based on the alliance of workers and peasants. The socialist system is the basic system of the People's Republic of China. Sabotage of the socialist system by any organization or individual is prohibited.

Article 2. All power in the People's Republic of China belongs to the people. The organs through which the people exercise state power are the National People's Congress and the local people's congresses at different levels. The people administer state affairs and manage economic, cultural, and social affairs through various channels and in various ways in accordance with the law.

Article 5. The state upholds the uniformity and dignity of the socialist legal system. No law or administrative or local rules and regulations shall contravene the constitution. All state organs, the armed forces, all political parties and public organizations and all enterprises and undertakings must abide by the Constitution and the law. All acts in violation of the Constitution and the law must be investigated. No organization or individual may enjoy the privilege of being above the Constitution and the law.

Article 21. The state develops medical and health services, promotes modern medicine and traditional Chinese medicine, encourages and supports the setting up of various medical and health facilities by the rural economic collectives, state enterprises and undertakings, and neighborhood organizations, and promotes sanitation activities of a mass character, all to protect the people's health. The state develops physical culture and promotes mass sports activities to build up the people's physique.

Article 22. The state promotes the development of literature and art, the press, broadcasting and television undertakings, publishing and distribution services, libraries, museums, cultural centers, and other cultural undertakings that serve the people and socialism, and sponsors mass cultural activities. The state protects places of scenic and historical interest, valuable cultural monuments and relics, and other important items of China's historical and cultural heritage.

Article 24. The state strengthens the building of socialist spiritual civilization through spreading education in high ideals and morality, general education and education in discipline and the legal system, and through promoting the formulation and observance of rules of conduct and common pledges by different sections of the people in urban and rural areas. The state advocates the civic virtues of love for the motherland, for the people, for labor, for science, and for socialism; it educates the people in patriotism, collectivism, internationalism, and communism, and in dialectical and historical materialism; it combats the decadent ideas of capitalism and feudalism and other decadent ideas.

Article 28. The state maintains public order and suppresses treasonable and other counterrevolutionary activities; it penalizes actions that endanger public security and disrupt the socialist economy and other criminal activities, and punishes and reforms criminals.

Chapter 2: The Fundamental Rights and Duties of Citizens

Article 33. All persons holding the nationality of the People's Republic of China are citizens of the People's Republic of China. All citizens of the People's Republic of China are equal before the law. Every citizen enjoys the rights and at the same time must perform the duties prescribed by the Constitution and the law.

Article 35. Citizens of the People's Republic of China enjoy freedom of speech, of the press, of assembly, of association, of procession, and of demonstration.

Article 36. Citizens of the People's Republic of China enjoy freedom of religious belief. No state organ, public organization, or individual may compel citizens to believe in, or not to believe in, any religion; nor may they discriminate against citizens who believe in, or do not believe in, any religion. The state protects normal religious activities. No one may make use of religion to engage in activities that disrupt public order, impair the health of citizens, or interfere with the educational system of the state. Religious bodies and religious affairs are not subject to any foreign domination.

Article 37. The freedom of person of citizens of the People's Republic of China is inviolable. No citizen may be arrested except with the approval or by decision of a people's procuratorate or by decision of a people's court, and arrests must be made by a public security organ. Unlawful deprivation or restriction of citizens' freedom of person by detention or other means is prohibited; and unlawful search of the person of citizens is prohibited.

Article 38. The personal dignity of citizens of the People's Republic of China is inviolable. Insult, libel, false charge, or frame-up directed against citizens by any means is prohibited.

Article 39. The home of citizens of the People's Republic of China is inviolable. Unlawful search of, or intrusion into, a citizen's home is prohibited.

Article 40. The freedom and privacy of correspondence of citizens of the People's Republic of China are protected by law. No organization or individual may, on any ground, infringe upon the freedom and privacy of citizens' correspondence except in cases where, to meet the needs of state security or of investigation into criminal offenses, public security or procuratorial organs are permitted to censor correspondence in accordance with procedures prescribed by law.

Article 41. Citizens of the People's Republic of China have the right to criticize and make suggestions to any state organ or functionary. Citizens have the right to make to relevant state organs complaints and charges against, or exposures of, violation of the law or dereliction of duty by any state organ or functionary; but fabrication or distortion of facts with the intention of libel or frame-up is prohibited. In case of complaints, charges, or exposures made by citizens, the state organ concerned must deal with them in a responsible manner after ascertaining the facts. No one may suppress such complaints, charges, and exposures, or retaliate against the citizens making them. Citizens who have suffered losses through infringement of their civil rights by any state organ or functionary have the right to compensation in accordance with the law.

Article 45. Citizens of the People's Republic of China have the right to material assistance from the state and society when they are old, ill, or disabled. The state develops the social insurance, social relief, and medical and health services that are required to enable citizens to enjoy this right. The state and society ensure the livelihood of disabled members of the armed forces, provide pensions to the families of martyrs, and give preferential treatment to the families of military personnel. The state and society help make arrangements for the work, livelihood, and education of the blind, deaf-mute, and other handicapped citizens.

Article 46. Citizens of the People's Republic of China have the duty as well as the right to receive education. The state promotes the all-round moral, intellectual, and physical development of children and young people.

Article 47. Citizens of the People's Republic of China have the freedom to engage in scientific research, literary and artistic creation, and other cultural pursuits. The state encourages and assists creative endeavors conducive to the interests of the people made by citizens engaged in education, science, technology, literature, art, and other cultural work.

Article 51. The exercise by citizens of the People's Republic of China of their freedoms and rights may not infringe upon the interests of the state, of society, and of the collective, or upon the lawful freedoms and rights of other citizens.

Article 52. It is the duty of citizens of the People's Republic of China to safeguard the unity of the country and the unity of all its nationalities.

Article 53. Citizens of the People's Republic of China must abide by the Constitution and the law, keep state secrets, protect public property, and observe labor discipline and public order, and respect social ethics.

Article 54. It is the duty of citizens of the People's Republic of China to safeguard the security, honor, and interests of the motherland; they must not commit acts detrimental to the security, honor, and interests of the motherland.

Chapter 6: The People's Court and the People's Procuratorates

Article 125. All cases handled by the people's courts, except for those involving special circumstances as specified by law, shall be heard in public. The accused has the right of defense.

Article 126. The people's courts shall, in accordance with the law, exercise judicial power independently and are not subject to interference by administrative organs, public organizations, or individuals.

* * *

Following is the full text of a Chinese legislative resolution banning cults, announced on October 30, 1999:

To maintain social stability, protect the interests of the people, safeguard reform and opening up, and the construction of a modern socialist country, it is necessary to ban heretic cult organizations and prevent and punish cult activities.

Based on the constitution and other related laws, the following decision is hereby made:

1. Heretic cult organizations shall be resolutely banned according to law and all of their criminal activities shall be dealt with severely. Heretic cults, operating under the guise of religion, qigong, or other illicit forms, which disturb social order and jeopardize people's life and property, must be banned according to law and punished resolutely. People's courts, people's procuratorates, public security, national security, and judicial administrative agencies shall fulfill their duties in carrying out these tasks.

To be severely dealt with according to law are those who manipulate members of cult organizations to violate national laws and administrative regulations, organize mass gatherings to disrupt social order and fool others, cause deaths, rape women, swindle people out of their money and property, or commit other crimes with superstition and heresy.

2. The principle of combining education with punishment should be followed in order to unify and instruct the majority of the deceived public and to mete out severe punishment to the handful of criminals. During the course of handling cult groups according to law, people who joined cult organizations but were unaware of the lies being spread by the group shall be differentiated from criminal elements who organize and take advantage of cult groups for illegal activities and/or to intentionally destroy social stability.

The majority of the deceived members shall not be prosecuted, while those organizers, leaders, and core members who committed crimes shall be investigated for criminal conduct; those who surrender to the authorities or contribute to the investigations shall be given lesser punishments in accordance with the law or be exempt from punishment.

3. Long-term, comprehensive instruction on the Constitution and the law should be carried out among all citizens, knowledge of science and technology should be popularized, and the national literacy level raised.

Banning cult organizations and punishing cult activities according to law goes hand-in-hand with protecting normal religious activities and people's freedom of religious belief. The public should be exposed to the inhumane and anti-social nature of heretic cults, so they can knowingly resist influences of cult organizations, enhance their awareness of the law, and abide by it.

4. All corners of society shall be mobilized in preventing and fighting against cult activities, and a comprehensive management system should be put in place.

People's governments and judicial bodies at all levels should be held responsible for guarding against the creation and spread of cult organizations and combating cult activities.

This is an important, long-term task that will ensure social stability.

CHAPTER 18
TEACHINGS OF LI HONGZHI

Selection from Falun Gong *by Li Hongzhi (The Universe Publishing NY Corp., 2000; originally titled* China Falun Gong*).*

CHAPTER 3: CULTIVATION OF XINXING

All cultivators of Falun Gong must make cultivation of xinxing their top priority and regard xinxing as the key to developing gong. This is the principle for cultivating at high levels. Strictly speaking, the gong potency that determines one's level isn't developed through performing exercises but through xinxing cultivation. Improving xinxing is easier said than done. Cultivators must be able to abandon many things, improve their enlightenment quality, bear hardships upon hardships, endure almost unendurable things, and so on. Why haven't some people's gong grown even though they have practiced for years? The fundamental causes are: first, they disregard xinxing; second, they do not know a high-level righteous cultivation way. This point must be brought to light. Many masters who teach a practice system talk about xinxing—they are teaching genuine things. Those who only teach movements and techniques without ever discussing xinxing are actually teaching evil cultivation. So practitioners must exert great effort in improving their xinxing before they can start cultivation at higher levels.

1. Xinxing's Inner Meaning

The "xinxing" referred to in Falun Gong cannot be fully summarized by "virtue" alone. It encompasses much more than virtue. It encompasses many different facets of things, including those of virtue. Virtue is only one manifestation of one's xinxing, so using only virtue to understand the meaning of xinxing is inadequate. Xinxing encompasses how to deal with the two issues of gain and loss. "Gain" is to gain conformity to the nature of the universe. The nature that comprises the universe is Zhen-Shan-Ren. A cultivator's degree of conformity to the nature of the universe is reflected in the amount of his or her virtue. "Loss" is to abandon negative thoughts and behaviors, such as greed, the pursuit of personal gain, lust, desire, killing, fighting, theft, robbery, deception, jealousy, etc. If one is to cultivate to high levels one also needs to abandon the pursuit of desires, something inherent in human beings. In other words, one should let go of all one's attachments and take lightly all matters of personal gain and reputation.

A complete person is composed of a physical body and character. The same is true with the universe: In addition to the existence of substances, there also simultaneously exists the nature Zhen-Shan-Ren. Every particle of air contains this nature. This nature is made manifest in human society in the fact that good actions are met with rewards and bad ones with punishment. At a high level this nature also manifests as supernormal abilities. People who align themselves with this nature are good people; those who depart from it are bad. People who comply with it and assimilate to it are those who achieve the Dao. In order to conform to this nature, practitioners must have extremely high xinxing. Only this way can one cultivate to high levels. It is easy to be a good person, but it is none too easy to cultivate xinxing—cultivators must prepare mentally. Sincerity is prerequisite if you are to rectify your heart. People live in this world in which society has become very complicated. Though you want to do good deeds, there are some people who don't want you to; you do not want to harm others, but others might harm you for various reasons. Some of these things happen for unnatural reasons. Will you understand the reasons? What should you do? The struggles in this world test your xinxing at every moment. When confronted with indescribable humiliation, when your vested interests are infringed upon, when faced with money and lust, when in a power struggle, when rage and jealousy emerge in conflicts, when various conflicts in society and in the family take place, and when all kinds of suffering occur, can you always handle yourself in accordance with the strict xinxing criteria? Of course, if you can handle everything you are already an Enlightened Being. Most practitioners start as everyday people after all, and cultivation of xinxing is gradual; it moves upward little by little. Determined cultivators will eventually gain the Righteous Attainment if they are prepared to endure great hardships and to face difficulties with a firm mind. I hope that each of you cultivators maintains your xinxing well and improves your gong potency rapidly!

2. Loss and Gain

Both qigong and religious circles talk about loss and gain. Some people take "loss" to mean being charitable, doing some good deeds, or giving a hand to people in need, and "gain" to mean gaining gong. Even monks in temples also say that one should be charitable. This understanding narrows the meaning of loss. The loss we talk about is much broader—it is something of a larger scale. The things we require you to lose are the attachments of everyday people and the mindset that doesn't let go of those attachments. If you can abandon the things you consider important and part with the things you think you can't part with, that is loss in the truest sense. Offering help and displays of charity are only a part of loss.

An everyday person wants to enjoy prestige, personal gain, a better standard of living, more comfort, and more money. These are everyday people's goals. As practitioners, we are different, for what we acquire is gong, not those things. We need to care less about personal gain and take it lightly, but we are not really asked to lose any material things; we cultivate in human society and need to live as everyday people do. The key is for you to let go of your attachments—you aren't really required to lose anything. Whatever belongs to you won't be lost, while the things that don't belong to you cannot be acquired. If they are acquired they will have to be returned to others. To gain, you must lose. Of course, it's impossible to immediately handle everything very well, just as it's impossible to become an Enlightened Being overnight. Yet by cultivating little by little and improving step by step it is attainable. You will gain however much you lose. You should always take matters of personal gain lightly and prefer to gain less in order to have peace of mind. When it comes to material things you might suffer some losses, but you will gain in terms of de and gong. Herein lies the truth. You are not to intentionally gain de and gong by exchanging your prestige, money, and personal gain. This should be understood further using your enlightenment quality.

A cultivator of the great Dao once said: "I don't want the things others want, and I don't possess the things others possess; but I have things others don't, and I want things others don't." An everyday person hardly has a moment when he or she feels satisfied. This kind of person wants everything except the rocks lying on the ground that no one wants to pick up. Yet this Daoist cultivator said, "Then I'll pick up those rocks." A proverb goes like this: "Rarity produces preciousness, scarcity produces uniqueness." Rocks are worthless here but could be most valuable in other dimensions. This is a principle that an everyday person can't understand. Many enlightened, high-level masters with great de have no material possessions. For them, there is nothing that cannot be given up.

The path of cultivation is the most correct one and practitioners are actually the most intelligent people. The things that everyday people struggle for and the minute benefits they gain only last a short while. Even if you obtain through struggling, find something for free, or profit a little, so what? There is a saying among everyday people: "You can't bring anything with you when you are born, and you can't take anything away with you when you die." You enter the world having nothing, and you take nothing away when you leave it—even your bones will be burned to ashes. It doesn't matter if you have tons of money or are a dignitary—nothing can be taken with you when you leave. Yet since gong grows on the body of your Main Consciousness, it can be taken forth. I am telling you that gong is hard to earn. It is so precious and so hard to acquire that it can't be exchanged for any amount of money. Once your gong has reached a very advanced level, should you one day decide not to cultivate anymore, as long as you don't do anything bad, your gong will be converted into any material thing you want—you will be able to have them all. But you will no longer have the things that cultivators possess. You will instead have only the things that one can acquire in this world.

Self-interest leads some people to use improper means to take things that belong to others. These people think that they get a good deal. The truth is that they gain such profit by exchanging their de with others—only they don't know it. For a practitioner, this would have to be deducted from his or her gong. For a nonpractitioner, it would have to be deducted from his or her life expectancy or from something else. In short, the books will be balanced. This is the principle of the universe. There are also some people who always push others around, harm others with abusive words, and so on. With these actions they throw a corresponding portion of their de to the other party, exchanging their de for the act of insulting others.

Some people think it is disadvantageous to be a good person. From an everyday person's viewpoint, such people are at a disadvantage. But what they acquire is something that everyday people cannot: de, a white substance that is extremely precious. Without de one cannot have gong—this is an absolute truth. Why is it that many people cultivate but their gong fails to develop? It's precisely because they don't cultivate de. Many people emphasize de and require cultivation of de, yet they fail to disclose the real principles of how de is transformed into gong. It is left for the individual to comprehend. The close to ten thousand volumes of the Tripitaka and the principles that Shakyamuni taught for over forty some years all talked about one thing: de. The ancient Chinese books of Daoist cultivation all discuss de. The five-thousand-word book by Lao Zi, *Dao De Jing,* also contemplates de. Some people still fail to understand this.

We talk about "loss." When you gain, you must lose. You will encounter some tribulations when you genuinely want to cultivate. When they manifest in your life, you might experience a little suffering of the physical body or feel uncomfortable here or there—but it's not sickness. The hardships can also manifest in society, in the family, or in the workplace—anything is possible. Conflicts will suddenly arise over personal gain or emotional tensions. The goal is to enable you to improve your xinxing. These things usually happen very suddenly and seem extremely intense. If you encounter something that is very tricky, embarrassing for you, that makes you lose face, or puts you in an awkward position, how are you going to handle it at that point? If you stay calm and unruffled—if you're able to do that—your xinxing will be improved through the tribulation and your gong will develop proportionately. If you can achieve a little, you will gain a little.

However much you expend is however much you gain. Typically, when we are in the middle of a tribulation we might not be able to realize this, yet we must try. We shouldn't regard ourselves as everyday people. We should hold ourselves to higher standards when conflicts arise. Our xinxing will be tempered among everyday people since we cultivate amidst them. We are bound to make some mistakes and to learn something from these. It's impossible for your gong to develop while you are comfortable and not encountering any problems.

3. Simultaneous Cultivation of Zhen, Shan, and Ren

Our cultivation way cultivates Zhen, Shan, and Ren simultaneously. "Zhen" is about telling the truth, doing truthful things, returning to one's origin and true self, and ultimately becoming a true person. "Shan" is about developing great compassion, doing good things, and saving people. We particularly emphasize the ability of "Ren." Only with Ren can one cultivate to become a person with great de. Ren is a very powerful thing and transcends Zhen and Shan. Throughout the entire cultivation process you are asked to forbear, to watch your xinxing, and to exercise self-control.

It's not easy to forbear when confronted with problems. Some say, "If you don't hit back when beaten, don't talk back when slandered, or if you forbear even when you lose face in front of your family, relatives, and good friends, haven't you turned into Ah Q?! I say that if you act normal in all regards, if your intelligence is no less than that of others, and if it's only that you have taken lightly the matter of personal gain, no one is going to say you are foolish. Being able to forbear is not weakness, and neither is it being Ah Q. It is a display of strong will and self-restraint. There was a person in Chinese history named Han Xin who once suffered the humiliation of crawling between someone's legs. That was great forbearance.

There is an ancient saying: "When an everyday person is humiliated, he will draw his sword to fight." It means that when a common person is humiliated, he will draw his sword to retaliate, will swear at others, or will throw punches at them. It's not an easy thing for a person to come and live a lifetime. Some people live for their ego—it's not worth it whatsoever, and it is also extremely tiring. There is a saying in China: "With one step back, you will discover a boundless sea and sky." Take a step back when you are confronted with troubles, and you will find a whole different scenario.

A practitioner should not only show forbearance towards the people with whom he has conflicts and those who embarrass him directly, but should also adopt a generous attitude and even thank them. How could you improve your xinxing if it weren't for your difficulties with them? How could the black substance be transformed into the white substance during suffering? How could you develop your gong? It is very difficult when you are in the midst of a tribulation, yet you must exercise self-restraint at that point. The tribulations will get continually stronger as your gong potency increases. Everything depends on whether you can improve your xinxing. That tribulation may be upsetting to you at the beginning and make you unbearably angry—so angry that your veins bulge. Yet you don't erupt and you are able to contain your anger—that's good. You have started to forbear, to intentionally forbear. You will then gradually and continuously improve your xinxing, truly taking these things lightly; that is an even greater improvement.

Everyday people take certain conflicts and minor problems very seriously. They live for their ego and tolerate nothing. They will dare to do anything when they are angered to an unbearable point. Yet as a practitioner you will find the things that people take seriously very, very trivial—even too trivial—because your goal is extremely long-term and far-reaching. You will live as long as this universe. Then think about those things again: it doesn't matter if you have them or not. You can put them all behind you when you think from a broader perspective.

4. Eliminating Jealousy

Jealousy is a very big obstacle in cultivation and one that has a large impact on practitioners. It directly impacts a practitioner's gong potency, harms fellow cultivators, and seriously interferes with our ascension in cultivation. As a practitioner, you must eliminate it one hundred percent. Some people have yet to forgo their jealousy even though they have cultivated to a certain level. Moreover, the harder it is to abandon, the easier it is for jealousy to grow stronger. The negative effects of this attachment make the improved parts of one's xinxing vulnerable. Why is jealousy being singled out for discussion? It's because jealousy is the strongest, most prominent thing that manifests among Chinese; it weighs most heavily in people's thinking. Many people are nonetheless unaware of this. Called "Oriental jealousy" or "Asian jealousy," it is characteristic of the East. The Chinese people are very introverted, very reserved, and don't express themselves openly. All of this easily leads to jealousy. Everything has two sides. Accordingly, an introverted personality has its pros and cons. Westerners are relatively extroverted. For example, a child who scored a one hundred in school might happily call out on his way home, "I got a hundred!" Neighbors would open their doors and windows to congratulate him, "Congratulations, Tom!" All of them would be happy for him. If this happened in China—think about it—people would feel disgusted once they heard it: "He scored a hundred. So what? What's there to show off about?" The reaction is completely different when one has a jealous mentality.

Jealous types look down upon others and don't allow others to surpass them. When they see someone more capable than they, their minds lose all perspective, they find it unbearable, and they deny the fact. They want to get pay raises when others do, get equal bonuses, and share the same burden when something goes wrong. They get green-eyed and jealous when they see others making more money. At any rate, they find it unacceptable if others do better than they. Some people are afraid of accepting a bonus when they have made certain achievements in their scientific research; they are afraid of others becoming jealous. Some people who have been awarded certain honors don't dare reveal them for fear of jealousy and sarcasm. Some qigong masters can't stand to see other qigong masters teach, so they go make trouble for them. This is a xinxing problem. Suppose that in a group that does qigong exercises together, some people develop supernormal abilities first even though they started later. There are people who would then say: "What's he got to brag about? I've practiced for so many years and have a huge pile of certificates. How could he develop supernormal abilities before me?" His jealousy would then emerge. Cultivation focuses inward, and a cultivator should cultivate him or herself and find the source of problems within. You should work hard on yourself and try to improve in the areas you haven't done enough with. If you look hard at others to find the source of conflict, others will complete cultivation and ascend, while you will be the only one left here. Won't you have wasted all of your time? Cultivation is for cultivating oneself!

Jealousy also harms fellow cultivators, such as when one's bad-mouthing makes it hard for others to enter tranquility. When this type of person has supernormal abilities, he or she might use them out of jealousy to harm fellow cultivators. For example, a person sits there meditating, and he has been cultivating fairly well. He sits there like a mountain since he has gong. Then two beings float by, one of whom used to be a monk but who, due to jealousy, didn't achieve Enlightenment; even though he possesses a certain gong potency, he has not reached Completion. When they arrive at where the person is meditating, one says, "So-and-so is meditating here. Let's go around him." But the other says, "In the past, I chopped off a corner of Mount Tai." He then tries to hit the practitioner. Yet when he raises his hand he can't bring it down. That being is unable to hit the practitioner because he is cultivating in a righteous practice and has a protective shield. He wants to harm a cultivator of the righteous way, so it becomes a serious matter and he will be punished. People who are jealous harm themselves as well as others.

5. Abandoning Attachments

"Having attachments" refers to the relentless, zealous pursuit of a particular object or goal by those practitioners who are unable to liberate themselves or too stubborn to heed any advice. Some people pursue supernormal abilities in this world, and this will certainly impact their cultivating to high levels. The stronger the feelings, the more difficult they are to abandon. Their minds will become ever more unbalanced and unstable. Later on these people will feel that they have gained nothing, and they will even start to doubt the things that they have been learning. Attachments stem from human desires. These attachments' attributes are that their targets or goals are obviously limited, fairly clear and particular, and frequently the person might be unaware of the attachments. An everyday person has many attachments. He might use any means necessary in order to pursue something and obtain it. A cultivator's attachments manifest differently, such as in his pursuing a particular supernormal ability, his indulging in a certain vision, his obsessing over a certain phenomenon, and so on. No matter what you, a practitioner, pursue, it is incorrect—pursuit must be abandoned. The Dao School teaches nothingness. The Buddha School teaches emptiness and how to enter the gate of emptiness. We ultimately want to achieve the state of nothingness and emptiness, letting go of every attachment. Anything that you cannot let go of—such as the pursuit of supernormal abilities—must be relinquished. If you pursue them it means you want to use them. In reality, that is going against our universe's nature. It is actually still an issue of xinxing. If you want to have them, then you in fact want to flaunt them and show them off in front of others. Those abilities aren't something to showcase for others' viewing. Even if the purpose of your using them was very innocent and you just wanted to use them to do some good deeds, the good deeds that you did could turn out to be not so good. It's not necessarily a good idea to handle matters of everyday people using supernormal means. After some people hear me remark that seventy percent of the class has had their Third Eye opened, they start to wonder, "Why can't I sense anything?" Their attention focuses on the Third Eye when they return home and do the exercises—even to the point of getting a headache. They still can't see anything in the end. This is called an attachment. Individuals differ in physical state of being and inborn quality. It isn't possible that all of them come to see through their Third Eye at the same time, and neither can their Third Eye be at the same levels. Some people might be able to see and some might not. It is all normal.

Attachments can bring the development of a cultivator's gong potency to a grinding halt. In more serious cases they may even result in practitioners taking an evil path. In particular, certain supernormal abilities might be used by people with inferior xinxing to do bad things. There have been cases in which a person's unreliable xinxing has resulted in supernormal abilities being used to commit bad deeds. Somewhere there was a male college student who developed the supernormal ability of mind control. With this he could use his own thoughts to manipulate the thoughts and conduct of others, and he used his ability to do bad things. Some people might witness visions appearing when they do the exercises. They always want to have a clear look and full understanding. This is also a form of attachment. A certain hobby might become an addiction for some, and they are unable to shake it. That, too, is a form of attachment. Because of differences in inborn quality and intentions, some people cultivate in order to reach the highest level while some cultivate just to gain certain things. The latter mentality surely limits the goal of one's cultivation. If a person doesn't eliminate this kind of attachment, his or her gong won't develop even through practicing. So practitioners should take all material gains lightly, pursue nothing, and let everything unfold naturally, thus avoiding the emergence of new attachments. Whether this can be done depends upon a practitioner's xinxing. One cannot succeed in cultivation if one's xinxing is not fundamentally changed or if any attachments remain.

6. Karma

(1) The Origin of Karma

Karma is a type of black substance that is the opposite of de. In Buddhism it is called "sinful karma," while here we call it "karma." So doing bad things is called "producing karma." Karma is produced by a person's doing wrong in this life or in past lives. For instance, killing, insulting others, infringing upon others' interests, gossiping about someone behind his or her back, being unfriendly to someone, and so on can all create karma. In addition, some karma is passed on from ancestors, family and relatives, or close friends. When one throws punches at someone else, one also throws one's white substance over to the other person, and the vacated area in one's body is then filled with the black substance. Killing is the worst evildoing—it is a wrongdoing and will generate very heavy karma. Karma is the primary factor causing sickness in people. Of course, it doesn't always manifest itself in the form of sickness—it can also manifest as encountering some difficulties and the like. All of these things are karma at work. So practitioners must not do anything bad. Any misconduct will produce negative influences that will seriously impact your cultivation. Some people encourage collecting the qi of plants. When they teach their exercises they also teach how to collect qi from plants; they discuss with intense interest which trees have better qi and the colors of different trees' qi. There were some people in a park in our northeastern region who practiced a kind of so-called qigong in which they would roll all over the ground. After they would get up, they would circle around the pine trees to collect their qi. Within half a year the grove of pine trees had withered and turned yellow. This was a karma-generating act! It was also killing! Collecting qi from plants is not right, whether it's viewed in light of our country's greening, the maintenance of ecological balance, or from a high-level perspective. The universe is vast and boundless, with qi available everywhere for you to collect. Knock yourself out and go collect it—why abuse these plants? If you are a practitioner, where is your heart of mercy and compassion?

Everything has intelligence. Modern science already recognizes that plants have not only life, but also intelligence, thoughts, feelings, and even super-sensory functions. When your Third Eye reaches the level of Fa Eyesight, you will discover that the world is a totally different place. When you go outside, rocks, walls, and even trees will talk to you. All objects have life. No sooner does an object form than does a life enter it. It is people living on Earth who categorize substances as organic and inorganic. People living in temples get upset when they break a bowl, for the moment it is destroyed, its living entity is released. It hasn't finished its life journey, so it will have nowhere to go. It will therefore have extreme hatred towards the person who ended its life. The angrier it gets, the more karma the person will accrue. Some "qigong masters" even go hunting. Where did their benevolence and compassion go? The Buddha and Dao Schools don't do things that violate heaven's principles for conduct. When one does these things, it is an act of killing.

Some people say that in the past they produced a lot of karma, such as by killing fish or chickens, by fishing, etc. Does this mean that they can no longer cultivate? No, it does not. Back then, you did it without knowing the consequences, so it wouldn't have created extra karma. Just don't do it anymore in the future, and that should be fine. If you do it again you will be knowingly violating the principles, and that is not permitted. Some of our practitioners have this kind of karma. Your attendance at our seminar means that you have a predestined relationship, and that you can cultivate upward. Shall we swat flies or mosquitoes when they come inside? As to your handling of this at your present level, it's not considered wrong if you swat and kill them. If you cannot drive them out, then killing them is no big deal. When the time has come for something to die, naturally it will die. Once, when Shakyamuni was still alive, he wanted to take a bath and asked his disciple to clean the bathtub. The disciple discovered many bugs in the bathtub, so he returned and asked what he should do. Shakyamuni said it again, "It is the bathtub that I want you to clean." The disciple understood, and he went back and cleaned the bathtub. You shouldn't take certain things too seriously. We don't intend to make you an overly cautious person. In a complicated environment it is not right, I think, if you are nervous at every moment and afraid of doing something wrong. It would be a form of attachment—fear itself is an attachment.

We should have a compassionate and merciful heart. When we handle things with a compassionate and merciful heart we are less likely to cause problems. Take self-interest lightly and be kindhearted, and your compassionate heart will keep you from doing wrong. Believe it or not, you will discover that if you always hold a spiteful attitude and always want to fight and contend, you will even turn good things into bad ones. I often see some people who, when right, won't let others go; when this type of person is right he has finally found some grounds for punishing others. Similarly, we shouldn't stir up conflict if we disagree with certain things. The things you dislike may at times not necessarily be wrong. When you continuously upgrade your level as a practitioner, every sentence you say will carry energy. You shouldn't speak as you please, since you will be able to restrain everyday people. It is particularly easy for you to commit wrongdoing and create karma when you aren't able to see the truth of problems and their karmic connections.

(2) Eliminating Karma

The principles in this world are the same as those in heaven: You must eventually pay what you owe others. Even everyday people must also pay what they owe others. All the hardships and problems you encounter throughout your life result from karma. You have to pay. The path of life for us genuine cultivators will be altered. A new path that suits your cultivation will be arranged. Some of your karma will be reduced by your master and what remains will be used to improve your xinxing. You exchange and pay for your karma through performing the exercises and through cultivating your xinxing. From now on, the problems you confront won't happen by chance. So please be mentally prepared. By enduring some tribulations, you will come to let go of all the things an everyday person can't release. You will run into many troubles. Problems will arise within the family, socially, and from other sources, or you may suddenly encounter disaster; it could even be that you will get blamed for what is actually someone else's fault, and so on and so forth. Practitioners aren't supposed to get sick, yet you may suddenly come down with a serious sickness. The sickness could come on with intense force, causing you to suffer to the point where you are no longer able to bear it. Even hospital exams might yield no diagnosis. Yet for an unknown reason the sickness might later disappear without any treatment. In fact, your debts are paid in this manner. Perhaps one day your spouse will lose his or her temper and start a fight with you for no reason at all; even very insignificant incidents may trigger big arguments. Afterwards, your spouse too will feel confused over his or her loss of temper. As you are a practitioner, you should be clear as to why this kind of incident takes place: it's because that "thing" came, and it was asking you to pay for your karma. To resolve such incidents, you have to keep yourself under control during those moments and watch your xinxing. Be appreciative and thankful that your spouse has helped you pay for your karma.

The legs will start to ache after one sits in meditation for a long while, and sometimes the pain is excruciating. People with a high-level Third Eye can see the following: When one is in great pain, there is a large chunk of the black substance—both inside and outside of the body—coming down and being eliminated. The pain one experiences while sitting in meditation is intermittent and excruciating. Some understand it and are determined not to unfold their legs. The black substance will then be eliminated and transformed into the white substance, and it will in turn be transformed into gong. Practitioners can't possibly pay for all of their karma through sitting in meditation and performing the exercises. They also need to improve their xinxing and enlightenment quality, and to undergo some tribulations. What is important is that we be compassionate. One's compassion emerges very quickly in our Falun Gong. Many people find that tears start to fall for no reason while they sit in meditation. Whatever they think of, they feel grief. Whomever they look at, they see suffering. This is actually the heart of great compassion that emerges. Your nature, your genuine self, will start to connect with the nature of the universe: Zhen-Shan-Ren. When your compassionate nature emerges, you will do things with much kindness. You will be very kind from the inside out. At that point no one will push you around anymore. If someone were to insult you then, your heart of great compassion would be at play and you wouldn't do the same to him in return. This is a type of power, a power that makes you different from everyday people.

When you encounter a tribulation, that great compassion will help you overcome it. At the same time, my Law Bodies will look after you and protect your life, but you will have to undergo the tribulation. For example, when I was lecturing in Taiyuan there was an older couple that came to attend my class. They were hurrying when they crossed the street, and upon reaching the middle of the road a car came speeding along. It instantly knocked the elderly woman down and dragged her along for more than ten meters before she finally fell in the middle of the street. The car couldn't stop for another twenty meters. The driver got out of the car and said some rude words, and the passengers sitting inside the car also uttered some negative things. At that moment the elderly woman remembered what I had said and didn't say anything. After she got up, she said, "Everything is all right, nothing is broken." She then went into the lecture hall with her husband. Had she said at that very moment, "Oh, it hurts here and it hurts there, too. You need to take me to the hospital," things would have turned out really badly. But she didn't. The elderly woman said to me, "Master, I know what that was all about. It was helping me pay for my karma! A great tribulation has been eliminated and a big chunk of karma has been removed." As you can imagine, she had very high xinxing and very good enlightenment quality. She was that elderly, the car was travelling that fast, and she was dragged that far before finally hitting the ground hard—yet she got up having a right mind. Sometimes a tribulation seems tremendous when it comes—so overwhelming that there looks to be no way out. Perhaps it stays around for quite a few days. Then a path suddenly appears and things start to take a huge turn. In fact, it's because we have improved our xinxing and the problem has disappeared naturally.

In order to improve your realm of mind, you must undergo all kinds of tests put forth by this world in the form of tribulations. If your xinxing has really improved and stabilized, karma will be eliminated during the process, the tribulation will pass, and your gong will develop. Don't be discouraged if during xinxing tests you fail to watch your xinxing and you conduct yourself improperly. Take the initiative to find what you learned from this lesson, to discover where you fell short, and to put effort into cultivating Zhen-Shan-Ren. The next problem that will test your xinxing might come shortly thereafter. As your gong potency develops, the next tribulation's test may come on even stronger and more suddenly. Your gong potency will grow a little bit higher with every problem you overcome. The development of your gong will come to a standstill if you are unable to overcome a problem. Small tests lead to small improvements; big tests lead to big improvements. I hope that every practitioner is prepared to endure great suffering and will have the determination and willpower to embrace hardships. You won't acquire real gong without expending effort. There is no principle in existence that will let you gain gong comfortably without any suffering or effort. You will never cultivate to become an Enlightened Being if your xinxing doesn't become fundamentally better and you still harbor personal attachments!

7. Demonic Interference

"Demonic interference" refers to the manifestations or visions that appear during the cultivation process and that interfere with a person's practice. Their goal is to prevent practitioners from cultivating to high levels. In other words, demons come to collect debts.

The issue of demonic interference will surely arise when a person is cultivating to high levels. It's impossible that one has not committed wrongdoing in one's lifetime, just as one's ancestors must have in their lives; this is called karma. Whether a person's inborn quality is good or not reflects how much karma this person carries with him or her. Even if he or she is a very good person it is still impossible to be free of karma. You can't sense it because you don't practice cultivation. Demons won't care if your practice is only for healing and improving health. But they will bother you constantly once you begin cultivating to high levels. They can disturb you using many different methods, the goal of which is to prevent you from cultivating to high levels and to make you fail in your practice. Demons manifest themselves in a variety of ways. Some manifest themselves as daily life happenings, while others take the form of phenomena from other dimensions. They command things to interfere with you every time you sit down to meditate, making it impossible for you to enter tranquility and, therefore, to cultivate to high levels. Sometimes the moment you sit down to meditate you will begin to doze off or will have all kinds of thoughts going through your mind, and you become unable to enter into a cultivation state. At other times, the moment you start to perform the exercises, your once-quiet surroundings will suddenly be filled with the noise of footsteps, doors slamming, cars honking, telephones ringing, and a variety of other forms of interference, making it impossible for you to become tranquil.

Another kind of demon is sexual lust. A beautiful woman or handsome man may appear in front of a practitioner during his or her meditation or dreams. That person will entice you and seduce you by making stimulating gestures that evoke your attachment to sexual lust. If you can't overcome this the first time, it will gradually escalate and continue to seduce you until you abandon the idea of cultivating to a high level. This is a difficult test to pass, and quite a few practitioners have failed because of this. I hope you are mentally prepared for it. If someone doesn't guard his or her xinxing well enough and fails the first time, he or she should truly learn a lesson from it. It will come again and interfere many times until you truly maintain your xinxing and completely abandon that attachment. This is a big hurdle that you must overcome, or you will be unable to attain the Dao and succeed in cultivation.

There is another kind of demon that also presents itself during one's performance of the exercises or in one's dreams. Some people suddenly see some horrifying faces that are ugly and real, or figures that are holding knives and threatening to kill. But they can only scare people. If they were to really stab, they wouldn't be able to touch the practitioner since Master has installed a protective shield around the practitioner's body to keep him or her unharmed. They try to scare the person off so that he or she will stop cultivating. These only appear at one level or during one period of time and will pass very quickly—in a few days, a week, or a few weeks. It all depends on how high your xinxing is and how you treat this matter.

8. Inborn Quality and Enlightenment Quality

"Inborn quality" refers to the white substance one brings with oneself at birth. In fact, it is de—a tangible substance. The more of this substance you bring with you, the better your inborn quality. People with good inborn quality more easily return to their true self and become enlightened, as their thinking is unimpeded. Once they hear about learning qigong or about things concerning cultivation, they immediately become interested and are willing to learn. They can connect with the universe. It is exactly as Lao Zi said: "When a wise man hears the Dao, he will practice it diligently. When an average man hears it, he will practice it on and off. When a foolish man hears it, he will laugh at it loudly. If he doesn't laugh loudly, it is not the Dao." Those people who can easily return to their true self and become enlightened are wise people. In contrast, a person with a lot of the black substance and an inferior inborn quality has a barrier formed outside of his body that makes it impossible for him to accept good things. The black substance will make him disbelieve good things when he encounters them. In fact, this is one role karma plays.

A discussion of inborn quality has to include the issue of enlightenment quality. When we talk about "enlightenment," some people think that being enlightened is the equivalent of being clever. The "clever" or "cunning" that everyday people refer to are indeed quite different from the cultivation practice we are discussing. These types of "clever" people usually can't attain Enlightenment easily. They are only concerned with the practical, material world so that they can avoid being taken advantage of and avoid giving up any benefit. Most notably, a few individuals out there who regard themselves as knowledgeable, educated, and smart, think that practicing cultivation is the stuff of fairy tales. Performing qigong exercises and cultivating xinxing are inconceivable to them. They consider practitioners foolish and superstitious. The "enlightenment" we speak of doesn't refer to being smart but to the return of human nature to its true nature, to being a good person, and to conforming to the universe's nature. One's inborn quality determines one's enlightenment quality. If one's inborn quality is good, one's enlightenment quality tends to be good as well.

Inborn quality determines enlightenment quality; however, enlightenment quality isn't entirely dictated by inborn quality. No matter how good your inborn quality is, your understanding or comprehension cannot be lacking. The inborn quality of some individuals isn't so good, yet they possess superb enlightenment quality and so can cultivate to a high level. Since we offer salvation to all sentient beings, we look at enlightenment quality, not inborn quality. As long as you are determined to ascend in cultivation, this thought of yours is a righteous one even though you bring with you many bad things. With this thought you only need to forgo a little more than others and you will eventually achieve Enlightenment.

The bodies of practitioners are purified. They won't contract illness after gong develops, because the presence of this high-energy substance in the body no longer permits the presence of the black substance. Yet some people just refuse to believe this and always think that they are sick. They complain, "Why am I so uncomfortable?" We say that what you have gained is gong. How can you not have discomfort when you've gained such a good thing? In cultivation one has to give things up in an exchange. In fact, all of the discomfort is on the surface and has no impact whatsoever on your body. It appears to be sickness but it's certainly not—it all depends on whether you can awaken to this. Practitioners not only need to be able to bear the worst suffering, but they also need to have good enlightenment quality. Some people don't even try to comprehend things when they are confronted with troubles. They still treat themselves as everyday people despite my teaching them at a high level and showing them how to measure themselves with higher criteria. They can't even bring themselves to practice cultivation as genuine practitioners. Neither can they believe that they will be at a high level.

The "enlightenment" discussed at high levels refers to becoming Enlightened, and it is categorized into Sudden Enlightenment and Gradual Enlightenment. "Sudden Enlightenment" refers to having the entire process of cultivation take place in a locked mode. At the last moment after you have completed the entire cultivation process and your xinxing has reached a high level, all of your supernormal abilities will be unlocked at once, your Third Eye will instantly open to its highest level, and your mind will be able to communicate with high-level beings in other dimensions. You will instantly be able to see the reality of the entire cosmos and its different dimensions and unitary paradises, and you will then be able to connect with them. You will also be able to use your great divine powers. The path of sudden Enlightenment is the most difficult one to take. Throughout history, only those people with superb inborn quality have been selected to become disciples; it has been passed on privately and individually. Average people would find it unbearable! The path I took was that of Sudden Enlightenment. The things I'm imparting to you belong to the path of Gradual Enlightenment. Supernormal abilities will develop in due time during your cultivation process. But the supernormal abilities that emerge will not necessarily be available for you to use, as it is easy for you to commit wrongdoing when you have not raised your xinxing to a certain level and are still unable to handle yourself properly. You won't be able to use these supernormal abilities for the time being, though they will eventually be made available to you. Through practicing cultivation you will gradually improve your level and come to understand the truth of this universe. Just as with Sudden Enlightenment, you will eventually reach Completion. The path of Gradual Enlightenment is a little easier and takes no risks. What's difficult about it is that you can see the entire cultivation process. So the demands you place upon yourself should be even more strict.

9. A Clear and Pure Mind

Some people can't achieve tranquility when they do qigong exercises, and so they search for a method. Some have asked me: "Master, why can't I become tranquil when I perform qigong exercises? Can you teach me a method or technique so that I can become tranquil when I sit in meditation?" I ask, how can you become tranquil?! You still couldn't become tranquil even if a deity were to come teach you a method. Why? The reason is that your own mind isn't clear and pure. Because you live amid this society, things such as various emotions and desires, self-interest, personal matters, and even the affairs of your friends and family come to occupy your mind too much and assume a high priority. How could you become tranquil when sitting in meditation? If you intentionally suppress something it will automatically come right back up.

Buddhism's cultivation teaches "precept, samadhi, and wisdom." Precepts are for letting go of the things that you are attached to. Some Buddhists adopt the approach of chanting Buddha's name, which requires concentrated chanting in order to achieve the state of "one thought replacing thousands of others." Yet it's not simply an approach, but a type of ability. You can try chanting if you don't believe it. I can promise you that other things will arise in your mind when you use your mouth to chant Buddha's name. It was Tibetan Tantrism that first taught people how to chant Buddha's name; one was required to chant Buddha's name hundreds of thousands of times each day for a week. They would chant until they got dizzy and then there would finally be nothing left in their minds. That one thought had replaced all others. That is a type of skill that you might not be able to perform. There are also some other methods that teach you how to focus your mind on your dantian, how to count, how to fixate your eyes on objects, and so on. In actuality, none of these methods can make you enter into complete tranquility. Practitioners have to attain a clear and pure mind, discard their preoccupation with self-interest, and let go of the greed in their heart.

Whether you can enter stillness and tranquility is in fact a reflection of your ability and level. Being able to enter tranquility the moment you sit down indicates a high level. It's all right if for the time being you can't become tranquil—you can slowly accomplish this through cultivation. Your xinxing improves gradually, as does gong. Your gong will never develop unless you attach little importance to self-interest and your own desires. Practitioners should hold themselves to higher standards at all times. Practitioners are continuously interfered with by all kinds of complicated social phenomena, many vulgar and unhealthy things, and various emotions and desires. The things that are encouraged on television, in the movies, and in literature teach you to become a stronger and more practical person among everyday people. If you can't go beyond these things you will be even further away from a cultivator's xinxing and state of mind, and you will acquire less gong. Practitioners should have little to no dealings with those vulgar and unhealthy things. They should turn a blind eye and a deaf ear to them, being unmoved by people and things. I often say that the minds of everyday people cannot move me. I won't become happy when someone praises me, and neither will I get upset when someone insults me. I remain unaffected no matter how serious the disruptions to xinxing among everyday people may be. Practitioners should take all personal gain very lightly and not even care about it. Only then can your intention to become Enlightened be considered mature. If you can be without strong pursuit of prestige and personal gain and even regard them as something inconsequential, you won't become frustrated or upset and your heart will always remain calm. Once you are able to let go of everything, you will naturally become clear and pure-minded.

I have taught you Dafa and all five sets of exercises. I have adjusted your bodies and installed Falun and energy mechanisms in them. My Law Bodies will protect you. All of what should be given to you has been given. During the class it's all up to me. From this point on, it's all up to you. "The master reveals the entrance, but it's the individual who cultivates." As long as you learn Dafa thoroughly, attentively experience and comprehend it, watch your xinxing at every moment, cultivate diligently, endure the worst sufferings of all, and forbear the hardships of all hardships, I believe you will surely succeed in your cultivation.

The path for cultivating gong lies in one's heart,

The boat to sail the boundless Dafa rides on hardships.

* * *

Additional Articles by Li Hongzhi

Cultivation Practice Is Not Political

Some practitioners are discontented with society and politics; they have learned our Dafa with this strong attachment that they do not release. They even attempt to take advantage of our Dafa to get involved in politics—an act born of a filthy mentality, showing their irreverence toward Buddha and the Fa. Without giving up this mentality, they absolutely will not complete cultivation.

In my lectures I have repeatedly stressed that the form of human society—no matter what type of society or political situation—is pre-destined and determined by heaven. A cultivator does not need to mind the affairs of the human world, let alone get involved in political struggles. As to how society treats us, isn't it to test a cultivator's heart? We should not get involved in politics.

Such is our Dafa's form of cultivation practice. We will not rely on any political powers at home or abroad. Those people of influence are not cultivators, so they certainly cannot hold any positions with responsibilities in our Dafa—either in name or in actuality.

My disciples, you must remember that we are practicing genuine cultivation! We should let go of the fame, profits, and sentimentality of everyday people. Do the conditions of a social system have anything to do with your cultivation practice? Only after you have abandoned all of your attachments and none remain can you complete cultivation. Other than doing a good job with his work, a cultivator will not be interested in politics or any political power; otherwise, he is absolutely not my disciple.

We are able to have cultivators obtain the Fa and achieve the Righteous Fruit, just as we are able to teach people's hearts to be good in society—this is good for the stability of human society. Dafa is not, however, taught for the sake of human society, but for you to complete cultivation practice.

Li Hongzhi
September 3, 1996

* * *

Wealth with Virtue

The ancients said, "Money is something external to this physical body." Everyone knows it, yet everyone pursues it. A young man seeks it to satisfy his desires; a young woman wants it for glamour and luxury; an elderly person goes after it to take care of himself in his old age; a learned person desires it for fame; a public official fulfills his duty for it, etc. Hence, everybody pursues it.

Some people even compete and fight for it; those who are aggressive take risks for it; hot-tempered people resort to violence for it; a jealous person might die for it in anger. It is the duty of the ruler and officials to bring wealth to the populace, yet promotion of money-worship is the worst policy one could adopt. Wealth without virtue will harm all sentient beings, while wealth with virtue is what all people hope for. Therefore, one cannot be affluent without promoting virtue.

Virtue is accrued from past lives. Becoming a king, an official, wealthy, or nobility all come from virtue. No virtue, no gain; the loss of virtue denotes the loss of everything. Thus, those who seek power and wealth must first accumulate virtue; by suffering hardships and doing good deeds, one can collect virtue among the masses. To achieve this, one must understand the principle of cause and effect. Knowing this can enable officials and the populace to exercise self-restraint, and prosperity and peace will thereby prevail under heaven.

Li Hongzhi
January 27, 1995

* * *

Realms

A wicked person is born of jealousy. Out of selfishness and anger he complains about unfairness towards himself.

A benevolent person always has a heart of compassion. With no discontent or hatred, he takes hardship as joy.

An enlightened being has no attachments at all. He quietly observes the everyday people blinded by delusion.

Li Hongzhi
September 25, 1995

* * *

What Is Mi Xin (Blind Belief, Superstition)?

Chinese people today really turn pale merely at the mentioning of the two characters "mi xin," because many people call everything that they do not believe "mi xin." In fact, these two characters, mi xin, were coated with an ultra "leftist" garb during the "Great Cultural Revolution," and they were used at that time as the most damaging term against the national culture. Being the most horrifying label, it has become the most irresponsible pet phrase of those simple-minded and stubborn people. Even those self-proclaimed, so-called "materialists" label everything beyond their knowledge or beyond the understanding of science as "mi xin." If things were to have been understood according to that theory, mankind would not have made any advancements; neither would science have developed further, because all of science's new progressions and discoveries have been beyond the understanding of its predecessors. Then aren't these people themselves practicing idealism? Once human beings believe in something, isn't that, itself infatuation? Isn't it true that some people's trust in modern science or modern medicine is also mi xin? Isn't it true that people's revering their idols is mi xin as well? Actually, the two characters, mi xin, form a very common term. Once people zealously believe in something—including the truth—it becomes mi xin; it does not denote any derogatory meaning. It is only that when those with ulterior motives launch their attacks on others that they coat "mi xin" with the connotation of feudalism, and thus it has become a very misleading and combative term that can further incite simple-minded people to echo it.

As a matter of fact, the two characters, mi xin, themselves should not be used this way, neither should the imposed connotation exist. What the two characters, mi xin, imply is not anything negative. Without mi xin in discipline, soldiers would not have combative capabilities; without mi xin in their schools and teachers, students would not acquire knowledge; without mi xin in their parents, children would not be brought up well-mannered; without mi xin in their careers, people would not do a good job in their work; without beliefs, human beings would have no moral standards, the human mind would not have good thoughts, and it would be overcome by evil thoughts. At such a time, human moral values would decline rapidly. Possessed by evil thoughts, everyone would become enemies of one another and would stop at nothing to satisfy their selfish desires. Although those bad people who have imposed negative connotations on the two characters of "mi xin" have achieved their objectives, they have very likely ruined mankind in terms of its original nature.

Li Hongzhi
January 22, 1996
Revised on August 29, 1996

* * *

Further Comments on Superstition (Mi Xin)

Initially, "superstition" was just an ordinary term. Some people in political circles in China hyped it into a term with deadly power. Actually, superstition as publicized by those in political circles is not superstition, but a political label and a political slogan; it is a political term used specifically when attacking others. Once something is slapped with this label, it is made antithetical to science and can thus be blatantly attacked.

In fact, those who have gone through different kinds of political movements possess very strong analytical abilities. In the past, they had beliefs, disappointments, and blind worship, and they learned their lessons from these experiences. In particular, they endured an unforgettable blow to their souls during the Cultural Revolution. How can it be possible for these people to casually believe in anything? People today are the most capable of distinguishing clearly whether something is the truth or so-called "superstition" cooked up by political people.

Whether something is science or superstition is not to be decided by people involved in politics. Instead, it should be appraised by scientists. Yet the so-called "scientists" being used by political purposes are actually political figures as well. It is impossible for these kinds of people to genuinely draw a fair and scientific conclusion from an objective, scientific standpoint. This being the case, they cannot be called scientists whatsoever. At most, they can only serve as a club held in the hands of politicians and be used to strike at people.

The understanding of the truth of the cosmos by students of Dafa cultivation is their elevation through reason and application. It is futile for man, regardless of what perspective he takes, to negate the Fa and principles of the universe that are beyond all theories of human society. Especially when the morality of human society is on the verge of total collapse, it is the mighty universe that has once again shown great compassion and given mankind this final chance. This is the hope that mankind should treasure and cherish above all. Out of selfish desires, however, man is undermining this last hope the universe has granted him, thereby incurring the wrath of heaven and earth. Nevertheless, ignorant people take various catastrophes as natural phenomena. The universe does not exist for mankind. Man is only one form of expression of the lives existing at the lowest level. If mankind has lost the standard for existence at this level of the universe, it can only be eliminated by the universe's history.

Mankind! Wake up! The vows of Gods throughout history are being fulfilled. Dafa is evaluating all lives. The path of life is under one's own feet. A single thought of his own will also decide his own future.

Treasure and cherish it. The Fa and the principles of the universe are right in front of you.

Li Hongzhi
July 13, 1999

CHAPTER 19
INTERNET RESOURCE GUIDE

Here is a list of websites with extensive information about Falun Gong and the Chinese government crackdown. Most of these sites have a variety of links to other related sites.

FALUN GONG WEBSITES

www.falundafa.org
"Official" Falun Gong website. Information on Falun Gong teachings, the crackdown, and their struggle for international recognition. Includes an offshoot site: www.worldfalundafaday.org. Links to many other Falun Gong sites in the US and around the world.

http://www.falundafa.org/world.htm
Comprehensive listing of Falun Gong websites around the world, including Australia, Austria, Belgium, Canada, China, Czech Republic, Denmark, Europe (general), Finland, Germany, Ireland, Israel, Japan, Korea, Malaysia, New Zealand, Norway, Russia, Singapore, Slovak Republic, Sweden, Switzerland, United Kingdom, United States (separate websites for more than forty states).

www.faluninfo.net
Falun Dafa Info Center. Contains recent Falun Gong–related news and events, as well as writings by practitioners from around the world. Includes writings and photos by Li Hongzhi.

CHINESE GOVERNMENT AND MEDIA WEBSITES

www.china.org.cn
www.chinaguide.org
Official Chinese government website. Contains many articles from the Communist Party press. Highly critical and extensive reporting on Falun Gong. Text in both Chinese and English.

mingjing.org.cn/ppflg/e-falun/index.htm
"Truth on 'Falun Gong'" website. Index of articles attacking Falun Gong.

www.sinopolis.com
Sinopolis. Daily China news and information in English.

www.Xinhua.org
Xinhua News Agency (state news agency of PRC). Very extensive section attacking Falun Gong.

www.peopledaily.com.cn
People's Daily. Chinese newspaper. Access to many anti–Falun Gong articles.

HUMAN RIGHTS WEBSITES

www.hrichina.org
Human Rights in China

www.hrw.org
Human Rights Watch

www.amnesty-usa.org/asa/china
Amnesty International

www.svdc.org
Silicon Valley for Democracy in China. Grassroots organization dedicated to the promotion of democracy and human rights in China. Includes recent news articles.

www.laogai.org
Laogai Research Foundation. Researches conditions in forced labor camps in China.

GENERAL CHINA-RELATED WEBSITES

www.voicesofchinese.org/falun
Voices of Chinese website. Michigan-based volunteer organization "committed to making the voices of Chinese people heard for a better future of China."

www.insidechina.com
Inside China Today (owned and operated by the European Internet Network). Daily stream of news, analysis, commentary, and culture from various worldwide sources.

www.qis.net/chinalaw
China Law Web. Information about Chinese law and translated versions of Chinese legislation.

www.cnd.org
China News Digest. Volunteer organization providing "balanced news coverage" on China and China-related affairs. "Strives to be impartial on the news it reports."

www.asiasource.org/news
Asia Source. Run by the Asia Society, "an institution dedicated to fostering understanding of Asia and communication between Americans and the peoples of Asia and the pacific." Features news updates, special reports on pressing topics of the day, country profiles, and more.

US GOVERNMENT WEBSITES

www.usinfo.state.gov/regional/ea/uschina/
Official US government site for US-China relations. Contains official speeches, reports, etc.

www.state.gov
Official US State Department website. Related material can be found by searching the site with keywords "Falun Gong."

ACADEMIC WEBSITES

www.let.leidenuniv.nl/bth/falun.htm
Website of Leiden University in the Netherlands with extensive section on Falun Gong.

www.cesnur.org/testi/falun_updates.htm
Center for Studies on New Religions. List of Falun Gong articles from worldwide sources. English and Italian.

www.humboldt.edu/~mhk1/falungong.html
Humboldt State University website (Arcata, CA). Connected to Hsu's Religious Studies Virtual Reading Room. Lists news articles (pro– and anti–Falun Gong) and has links to Falun Gong websites.

www.louisville.edu/library/ekstrom/govpubs/
international/china/falungong.html
Maintained by University of Louisville's Ekstrom Library of Government Publications. Links to BBC news stories on Falun Gong and other related information and websites.

www.religiousmovement.org
University of Virginia's Religious Movements Homepage. Detailed profiles of more than 250 non-traditional religious and spiritual groups, including Falun Gong.

MEDIA WEBSITES

www.scmp.com
South China Morning Post (Hong Kong).

www.mediachannel.org
Non-profit "eye on global media" site. Has carried reports on coverage of Falun Gong, including a first-person account by a journalist fired by her news company for her human rights coverage, and expelled from China.

news.bbc.co.uk
British Broadcasting Corporation (BBC). Extensive coverage of the Falun Gong crisis.

www.nytimes.com
New York Times

www.wsj.com
Wall Street Journal

www.washingtonpost.com
Washington Post

INDEX

Veteran journalist and Emmy Award-winning broadcaster Danny Schechter has been reporting on and producing programming about human rights issues, including Chinese affairs, for years. He has written about China for *Newsday* and *Z Magazine,* and visited the country in 1997 to speak at an international symposium sponsored by Beijing TV. He recently reported and directed Globalvision's hard-hitting documentary, *Falun Gong's Challenge to China,* which was selected for the Ready for PBS Film Festival, and has won both Missouri University's Unity Award for Investigative Reporting and the Sigma Delta Chi Award for Television Documentary from the Society of Professional Journalists.

Schechter is the author of *The More You Watch, The Less You Know* (Seven Stories) and *News Dissector: Passions, Pieces, and Polemics 1960-2000* (Akashic Books). He co-edited (with Roland Schatz) *Mediaocracy: How the Media "Stole" the US Presidential Election 2000* (Innovatio Verlag and Electronpress.com). He is the executive producer of Globalvision and executive editor of the Media Channel, a global media watchdog website (www.mediachannel.org).